law of desire

Contemporary Issues in the Middle East

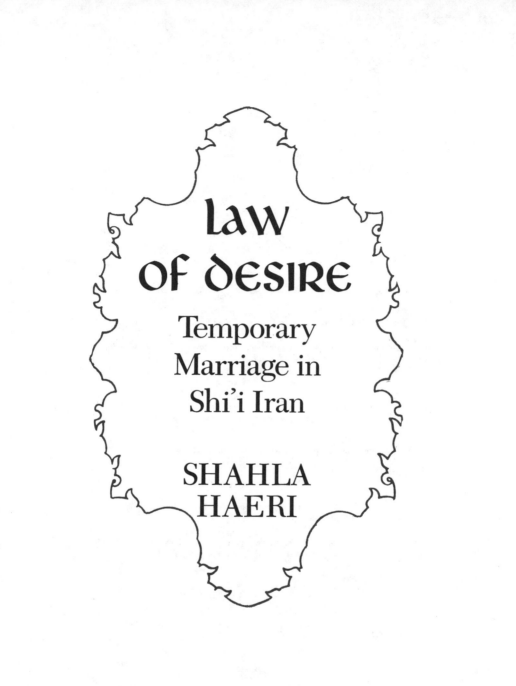

law
of desire

Temporary
Marriage in
Shi'i Iran

SHAHLA
HAERI

SYRACUSE UNIVERSITY PRESS

The publication of this book was assisted by a generous grant from the MEH Foundation.

Portions of this book were previously published in a different form in: "Ambivalence Toward Women in Islamic Law and Ideology," *The Middle East Annual*, vol. V. Copyright 1985 and reprinted with the permission of G. K. Hall & Co., Boston. "Power of Ambiguity: Cultural Improvisations on the Theme of Temporary Marriage," *Iranian Studies*, vol. XIX, no. 2.

The paper used in this publication meets the minimum requirements of American National Standard for Information Sciences — Permanence of Paper for Printed Library Materials, ANSI Z39.48-1984. ∞™

Library of Congress Cataloging-in-Publication Data

Haeri, Shahla.
    Law of desire: temporary marriage in Shi'i Iran / Shahla Haeri. —
— 1st ed.
       p.   cm. — (Contemporary issues in the Middle East)
    Bibliography: p.
    Includes index.
    ISBN 0-8156-2465-4 (alk. paper)   ISBN 0-8156-2483-2 (pbk.)
    1. Marriage — Iran. 2. Sex customs — Iran. 3. Muta. I. Title.
II. Series.
HQ666.4.H34   1989
306.8'1'0955 — dc19   89-4343
                                            CIP

Manufactured in the United States of America

hargiz namirad ankih dilash zindih shud bih `ishq

A heart touched by love will never die

For my parents
JAMAL and BIHJAT

Shahla Haeri received her Ph.D. in cultural anthropology from the University of California at Los Angeles. She was a postdoctoral fellow at the Pembroke Center for Teaching and Research on Women at Brown University in 1986–87, and is now a Research Associate at the Center for Middle Eastern Studies, Harvard University.

CONTENTS

TABLES

FIGURE

PREFACE

THIS BOOK IS A STUDY of the institution of temporary marriage, *mut'a*, and its practice, popularly known as *sigheh*, in contemporary Iran. It is not just about women, though women's worldviews, welfare, and status are a major preoccupation herein. My focus is on the perception of the institution by some Iranian men and women whose lives have been tied together by a contract of temporary marriage. This book is also about law and custom, religion and morality, public and private contracts, eroticism and desire. An important chapter is devoted to Shi'i legal interpretation, exploring its underlying logic and assumptions concerning women, men, marriage, and sexuality. Although Islamic law has gotten the lion's share of the Orientalists' attention, the Shi'i school of law and its specifics, outside of the Shi'ites' own contribution, has not received the careful and exhaustive discussion given to the Sunni legal system — at least not until recently, when the Islamic revolution of 1979 attracted interest in Shi'i Islam. Still fewer studies have been devoted to analyzing the Shi'i view on marital law, contracts of permanent and temporary marriage, sexuality, and marital relations.

To understand a Muslim society, it is argued, we must decode the way that society perceives women (Sabbah 1983). Concurring with this view, I suggest that the institution of marriage, with its focal value in society, presents a suitable framework for disentangling the complex and elusive life of Muslim women. A culturally specific signifier, marriage constitutes its own "language," the knowledge of which enables one to appreciate a particular form of social organization, its structure, and the meaning of gender relations within it. Accordingly, I wish to bring to light the underlying logic of marriage and its associated doctrinal assumptions, conceptualizations, and images of women, men, and their relationships in Shi'i Islamic law of marriage and sexuality.

A Shi'i marriage is defined as a "contract of exchange" that involves "a sort of ownership." This is to say, in return for granting the right of sexual union, a woman is entitled to receive a certain amount of money or valuables (Hilli SI, 517). Much has been written on the form and procedures of Islamic contracts. Little, if any, however, has been written on the underlying logic of a marriage contract. Discovering this logic and its implications for gender relations in society is the central focus of the present study. The questions I am therefore asking are, What does it mean to conceive of marriage in terms of a contract of exchange? What does such conceptualization reveal about the legal assumptions concerning women, men, and their relationship? What are some of the ramifications of superimposing a contractual commercial metaphor onto marital relations? How does the logic of this "language," this symbolic order, influence the gender's sense of self and the other? I hope to bring to light the fact that contracts are not simply a dominant feature of interpersonal obligations and commercial transactions in a Muslim society; they are also *models for* (Geertz 1973) male-female interpersonal relationships in society, forming the gender's dialectical worldview toward the self and the other.

Outside of the religious establishment and the ongoing disputes between Shi'i and Sunni scholars, the attitude toward temporary marriage has been primarily one of ambivalence and disdain. Before the revolution of 1979, the secular Iranian middle classes dismissed temporary marriage as a form of prostitution that had been legitimized by the religious establishment, who, to use a popular Persian expression, "put a religious hat on it." The religious hierarchy, on the other hand, becoming increasingly vocal and critical of the decadence of the Pahlavi regime, particularly its tolerance of women's autonomy, advocated temporary marriage as God's mercy on humanity, necessary for the individual's health as well as for maintaining social order.

Both points of view, I contend, are simplifications of a complex and dynamic social institution. The ambiguities inherent in this form of marriage have sustained it through its long history and allowed it to be intimately interconnected with other aspects of social life in Iran. Sometimes the institution has been dismissed by the state as archaic, a remnant of backwardness no longer suitable for a modern state poised on the brink of development and progress. At other times, it is advanced by the religious establishment as one of the "brilliant laws of Islam" (Mutahhari 1981, 52), devised for the welfare of human beings and their society. Sometimes it is used by women as a means of asserting autonomy and exerting some degree of control over their lives; at other times they are abused by the same set of laws. Often men abuse the law, but other times they are manipulated by women into submission and obedience of their wants and desires. Sometimes, temporary marriage is used to reinforce the structure of sex segregation, at other times as a means of subverting it.

Categorical condemnation or exoneration of the institution, there-fore, I have not attempted here. Nor do I believe such attitudes—not uncom-mon among some Iranians—would help us to unveil the enigma of the en-durance of the custom of temporary marriage in Iran.

Likewise, the bipolar, oppositional, and lifeless debate over whether Muslim women's status is "high" or "low" is not pursued here, for both views are static and simplistic, bordering sometimes on dogmatism. Rather, I have approached Muslim women's status developmentally, at-tempting to demonstrate that their legal status fluctuates as they go through successive stages of their life cycle (virginity, marriage, and widowhood or divorce), each stage having its own set of legal rights and its own status. Un-derstanding the turns and twists in Muslim women's legal status and corre-sponding social changes would in turn help us to appreciate the bewildering and conflicting data on Muslim women that are emerging from the Middle East.

Finally, aspects of Shi'i Muslim's worldview concerning men and women, their respective statuses in society, and their relationships no doubt find echoes in part in other societies and in other world religions. I have not attempted to compare one religion's worldview with another or pointed out the weaknesses of one and the strengths of another. I am, for now, interested in a specific branch of a particular religion, a specific institution within a particular legal system, and a specific group of people within a particular society.

A dissertation grant from the Social Science Research Council and the American Council of Learned Societies enabled me to go to Iran in 1981 –82. The Department of Anthropology at UCLA provided the initial travel grant in the summer of 1978. Their support I gratefully acknowledge.

Many colleagues and friends have been supportive all along, and I am certain that without their intellectual insights and encouragement this book would have been a lot leaner. Particularly, I would like to thank Profes-sors John G. Kennedy, my dissertation chairman at UCLA; Sally F. Moore, Lewis L. Langness, Amin Banani, George Sabbagh, and Nancy Levine. Many thanks are also due to Kaveh Safa-Isfahani, Dale F. Eickelman, Eliz-abeth Weed, Farzaneh Milani, Victoria Joralemon, Mary E. Hegland, Ra-fique Kashavjee, Mary H. Hebert, Emily W. Gianfortoni, and Jean Barstow, who read various drafts of this manuscript and provided invaluable critical comments. I wish to thank John Emerson for his meticulous proofreading of the glossary and bibliography.

It would be hard to imagine how this book could have been finished without the love and support of my family. My deepest appreciation goes particularly to my husband, Walter (Rusty) Crump, who remained composed and cool as I fretted about getting the logistics of this book in order; to my youngest sister, Niloofar Haeri, who competently edited and proofread this manuscript; and to my brother Mohammad-Reza Haeri, who provided library access to the National University of Iran.

Had it not been for the graciousness of my host Kubra Khanum and the humorous spirit of her mother, the indomitable Bibi M'sumih, my life in Qom would have been a dull one. Finally, I wish to thank Mr. Mas`ud `Attarha in Kashan, Dr. Hussain Adibi in Tehran, Mr. and Mrs. `Aba`i in Mashhad, and most of all my informants for their willingness to share with me intimate details of their lives at a time when Iranian society was undergoing dramatic political and social changes.

Boston, Massachusetts   SHAHLA HAERI
October 1988

SYSTEM OF TRANSLITERATION, CITATION, AND DATES

No SYSTEM OF TRANSLITERATION is without its problems, often leaving much to be desired. I have used the system of transliteration adopted by the Library of Congress but with some modifications. As a rule I have followed the Persian pronunciation of the Arabic loan words and names, for example, Maybudi rather than al-Maybudi, Ja'far-i Sadiq rather than Ja'far al-Sadiq. For words ending in the unpronounced "h" I have opted to substitute "ih" rather than "ah," which is closer to Persian pronunciation. For words that have become common in English I have used the established form rather than follow the Library of Congress system, words such as alim and ulama, ayatollah, Shi'i and Shi'ites, mulla, shaikh, and the like. Except for such Anglicized words, all other foreign words have been italicized. Diacritical marks are used only in the glossary, where Persian terms that are used in the text are defined. When a Persian term first appears in the text, a brief definition is given. When definitions are repeated, I have intended to draw the reader's attention to the shifting nuances of meaning that many of these terms have, depending on context and situation.

Several frequently cited sources have been abbreviated in references to them in the text: For Hilli, who is cited for two sources, the following system has been adopted: SI, for *Sharay' al-Islam*, and MN, for *Mukhtasar-i Nafi'*. Unless otherwise indicated, all references to *Luma'ih* are from volume 2 of its Persian translation.

For the sake of simplicity, all dates in the text are recorded according to the Gregorian calendar, with the indigenous dates appearing only in the bibliography.

law of desire

INTRODUCTION

tHIS STUDY ATTEMPTS A CULTURAL AND CRITICAL UNDERSTANDING of the institution and practice of temporary marriage, *mut'a*. Temporary marriage is a complex Shi'i religious institution with which much cultural and moral ambivalence has been associated historically. Yet, in Iran since the revolution of 1979 it has become more commonplace.[1] *Mut'a*, meaning marriage of pleasure, is a pre-Islamic tradition of Arabia still retaining legitimacy among the Twelver Shi'ites, who live predominantly, though not exclusively, in Iran. *Mut'a* marriage is a contract, *'aqd*, in which a man and an unmarried woman decide how long they want to stay married to each other, and how much money is to be given to the temporary wife. The custom of *mut'a* of women, as it has been called, was outlawed by the second caliph, 'Umar, in the seventh century A.D.,[2] but the Shi'ites continue to consider his command as legally nonbinding and religiously ineffective. In response, they argue that *mut'a* marriage is sanctioned in the Qur'an 4:24, and that it has been permitted by the Prophet Muhammad himself. Despite the early prohibition of the institution, the custom of *mut'a* marriage did not completely die out among the Sunni Muslims, either.[3] Nor was it left unchallenged by some secular leaders. In the ninth century the Caliph Ma'mun proclaimed *mut'a* marriage legal once again, but faced with stiff opposition and the threat of denunciation from the Sunni ulama (religious scholars), he was forced to withdraw his edict (Levy 1957, 132; 1931, 1:166; "Mut'a" 1927; Snouck Hurgronje 1931, 12–13).

A point of chronic disagreement, passionate dispute, and at times animosity between the Sunnis and Shi'ites, the social history and actual practices of *mut'a* marriage in Iran or elsewhere has eluded the detailed documentation that has been devoted to its legal procedures.[4]

Primarily an urban phenomenon in contemporary Iran, temporary marriage has been associated with pilgrimage and long-distance trade. It occurs more frequently around the shrines of religious figures, but because of

1

the supportive policies of the Islamic regime, this pattern may be changing now. Temporary marriage is a contract between a man and an unmarried woman, be she a virgin, divorced, or widowed, in which both the period that the marriage shall last and the amount of money to be exchanged must be specified. In a contract of *mut'a* marriage witnesses are not required, and the marriage need not be registered, although in practice both conditions have been subject to variations and local requirements. The life expectancy of a temporary marriage is as long — or as short — as the partners wish it to be: from one hour to ninety-nine years. At the end of the specified period the temporary spouses part company without any divorce ceremony. Ideologically, Shi'i doctrine distinguishes temporary marriage, *mut'a*, from permanent marriage, *nikah*, in that the objective of *mut'a* is sexual enjoyment, *istimta'*, while that of *nikah* is procreation, *tulid-i nasl* (Tusi 1964, 497–502; Hilli SI, 524; Khomeini 1977, P#2421–32;[5] Mutahhari 1974, 38).

A Shi'i Muslim man is permitted to contract simultaneously as many temporary marriages as he desires. This is in addition to the four wives legally allowed to all Muslim men. Imam Ja'far-i Sadiq, the founder of Shi'i law (Nasr 1977, 14), was asked, "Is a *mut'a* wife one of four [legally permitted wives in Islam]?" The imam is said to have responded, "Marry from among them one thousand, for they are wage earners, *ajir*" (Hilli SI, 487).[6] That men can have more than four temporary wives simultaneously, or that married men can — or should — contract temporary marriages, however, has been disputed by some of the contemporary ulamas (Mutahhari 1974, 50; Khomeini 1982a, 89).

A Shi'i Muslim woman, be she a virgin or divorced, is permitted to marry temporarily with only one man at a time, provided that after the dissolution of each temporary union, no matter how short, she undergoes a period of sexual abstinence. This is to identify a child's legitimate father in case she is pregnant. The children born as a result of temporary unions are considered legitimate and theoretically have equal status with their siblings born of permanent marriages.[7] Here lies the legal uniqueness of *mut'a*, that which distinguishes it ideologically from prostitution, despite their striking resemblance.[8]

Although an apparent legal safeguard for mother and child is provided, the law almost negates its own spirit by supporting the father should he deny his child's legitimacy.[9] Whereas he would be put through the awesome procedure of taking the oath of damnation, *li'an*, in a case involving a permanent marriage, he is not put through the same kind of legal and moral testing in the case of a *mut'a* marriage.[10] Nonetheless, it would be a mistake to dismiss *mut'a* as merely another variation of prostitution, or to discuss it primarily from that perspective. The problem is more complex than the apparent similarities might suggest. In addition to this legal distinction between the two types of sexual unions, further conceptual and ideological distinctions exist, which I shall discuss.

The inherent ambiguities built into the form and structure of the institution of temporary marriage challenge the view of law as an unchanging set of institutional parameters, the concept that social structure should "fit" ideology (cf. Moore 1978), and the stance that laws are independent of other sociological phenomena (cf. Nader 1965). The actual practices of *mut'a* marriage defy the tendencies to view the rules of sex segregation as a given in Muslim societies, to reify Muslim law, and to view it as immutable and determinate. The ambiguities in this form of marriage and the multiplicity of its meanings lend themselves to a wide range of alternative interpretations, manipulations, and negotiations of the institution, not only by those who interpret the law but also by those seeking erotic pleasure or wishing to find moral guidelines for their action: to establish interpersonal relationships, to communicate with members of the opposite sex, and to cross the boundaries of sexual segregation.

Mut'a marriage is an institution in which the relationships between the sexes, marriage, sexuality, morality, religious rules, secular laws, and cultural practices converge. At the same time it is the kind of custom that puts religion and popular culture at odds. Whereas religiously there is no restriction for virgin women to contract a temporary marriage, popular culture demands that a woman be a virgin for her first permanent marriage. The institution of temporary marriage brings into focus theoretical issues concerning relationships between systems of rules, values, and meaning, on the one hand, and systems of action and decision making, on the other. The obliviousness of many Iranians toward *mut'a*, or their derisive attitude toward the institution, mask its pervasive though submerged influence in almost all aspects of social life.[11] One of my objectives is to bring to light the ambiguities in the law of temporary marriage, despite the claims of the contemporary ulama to the contrary, by looking at its variations in practice.

Both forms of marriage, temporary and permanent, are categorized as contract, but to which category of contracts they actually belong has often been left vague in the Shi'i literature on the subject, more so in the works of the contemporary Shi'i ulama. Trying to minimize the profound legal and conceptual differences between the two forms of marriage in Iran, the contemporary Shi'i ulama have consistently overlooked the differences between the two forms of sexual unions, stressing that they are both marriages that differ only in that one has a time limit and the other does not. This, as we will learn, is a misrepresentation of the institution of temporary marriage, leading many women who use the custom into erroneous expectations of marital obligations and relations. I argue that the two forms, temporary and permanent marriage, fall into separate categories of contracts, namely, those of the contracts of lease and sale, respectively. More specifically, part one, Law as Imposed, discusses the significance of the concept of contract and its ubiquity in Iranian society. To understand each form of marriage contract in relation to the other, I describe and discuss the legal structures of permanent and temporary marriage. Part two, Law as Local Knowledge, examines improvisations on the theme of temporary marriage, bringing to light the diversity of interpretations and manipulations of the institution by many resourceful Iranians. With the legal limits and contextual boundaries of temporary marriage having thus been established, part three, Law as Perceived, presents the life stories and perceptions of individual Iranian men and women who have actually made use of the contract of temporary marriage. The conclusion looks at themes recurrent in the life stories of my informants, discussing them within the context of the logic of contracts.

ISLAMIC APPROACHES TO LAW AND SEXUALITY

The genealogy of Islamic law begins with the Holy Qur'an as revealed to the Prophet Muhammad in the seventh century A.D. For Muslims, the Qur'an is the miracle that contains the supreme truth. It is the word of God, and so is believed to be divine, perfect, and timeless. The legislations in the Qur'an cover a relatively limited area of social life, leaving other spheres of the increasingly more complex Islamic society open to improvisation and individual interpretation. To accommodate these divine legislations and to contain the diversity of legal opinions, the sayings of the Prophet Muhammad, the Traditions, were collected and used as the second source of divinely inspired legal guidelines for settling disputes in juridical matters. Despite sharing these two primary sources of Islamic law, the Shi'ites and Sunnis have emerged with different, though overlapping, corpuses of "authenticated" traditions, the *hadiths*. Likewise, despite attempts to limit the boundaries of Islamic jurisprudence, Islamic law clearly bears the intellectual mark of the personalities who gathered and systematized it, be they Shi'i or Sunni. The existence of five officially recognized schools of Islamic law is evidence of this. Nonetheless, all the schools of Islamic law maintain the scripture to be divine and unchanging, superseding all other human legislations and interpretations.

The Shi'i Muslim belief in the finality of Islamic law is paralleled only by a similar belief in another set of presumably immutable laws, namely, the law of nature, which determines the makeup of a man and a woman and what their relationship ought to be. Thus nature imprints men and women fundamentally, differently, and inescapably. Just as law is believed to be absolute because it is rooted in the Qur'an and inspired by the Prophet's deed and action, sexuality is perceived to be absolute because it is anchored in nature, it is instinctual, unchanging, and inescapable.[12] This double strand of the divine and nature that encodes and informs the Shi'ites' beliefs and worldviews form the backbone of the ulama's arguments on the sexes, their "nature," and their relationships, and of their justifications for these arguments.

Islamic ideology on marriage and sexuality is celebrated by the Shi'i ulama as being positive, self-affirming, and cognizant of human needs. Marriage is a tradition of the Prophet and has been emphasized as an act of piety. Celibacy, on the other hand, is considered evil and unnatural. Islam, according to the majority of Shi'i ulama, is a divine religion anchored in human nature, *fitrat*. Its objective is to minimize human suffering and to satisfy not just the yearnings of the spirit but also the burnings of the flesh (Tabataba'i et al. 1985). Acknowledging the pleasures of the flesh, the Shi'i ulama simultaneously view it as dangerous and disturbing to the social order; it must be legally contained and morally guided. In Iran, as in many other Muslim countries, the social structure is construed on the principle of sex segregation, implying that before the forces of the nature (e.g., sexual instinct), moral scruples implode. Therefore, not only must strict rules and mores of gender avoidance be devised but external forces must be brought to bear upon the behavior of the sexes, to keep them segregated and hence to control them.

The coexistence of the institution of temporary marriage and the paradigm of sex segregation may seem paradoxical at first. Yet they are in fact complementary aspects of the same worldview, a view that celebrates sexuality yet tries to contain it within religiously sanctioned boundaries, a view that on one level denies the association of genders yet on another level provides alternative legal frameworks for making such associations easily attainable.

Some of the specific contextual questions I explore are, How is an institutionalized yet vaguely prescribed form of marriage actually translated into practice? How does the ideology of sex-is-good-but genders-must-be-kept-separate function in everyday life? How do the broader cultural and institutional conceptualizations affect the lives of individuals, their self-perceptions and motivations? Or conversely, how do individuals choose, adopt, or manipulate their given sets of structural constraints? On a more concrete level, who practices *mut'a*? What motivates them? What do men and women consider to be proper behavior and the inviolable boundaries of *mut'a* marriage? What are the negotiable edges that can be manipulated irrespective of the legal framework, or in the light of legal reference?

While tacitly—and sometimes explicitly—acknowledging the similarities between prostitution and temporary marriage, the Shi'i ulama distinguish the former from the latter on the basis of their implications for individual well-being and for the social order. Ideologically, in an authoritarian, patriarchal, and apparently sex-segregated society like Iran, prostitutes are perceived to be antisocial and disobedient women. Prostitution is a negation of social order and a challenge to the sanctioned and established rules; it is fornication that is explicitly condemned in the Qur'an; it is indulgence in sinful and unlawful sexual activities. It is viewed as detrimental to the society's general health and welfare, and it goes against its stated ethics and ethos. On the contrary, the ulama maintain that temporary marriage, while performing a similar sexual function for the individual, symbolizes social control, that it finds its harmonious niche within the social order. Those who practice the custom, therefore, are considered to follow a divinely recommended way in order to satisfy some "natural" needs. Not only is temporary marriage not considered immoral from a religious and legal point of view, it actually is perceived to combat corruption and immorality (Tabataba'i et al. ca. 1985).

At the cultural level, however, the distinctions between *mut'a* and prostitution are not so neatly clear. On the spectrum from permissible to forbidden sexuality in Iran, popular perceptions of *mut'a* marriage fluctuate dramatically between the two poles of permanent marriage and prostitution, between purity and pollution, corruption and legitimacy. Despite its legal sanctity and religious legitimacy, the custom of *mut'a* marriage has never gained overwhelming popular support—not, at least, up to the revolution of 1979. Outside of religious circles, temporary marriage has had a somewhat stigmatized, ambiguous, and marginal status. While the more educated urban Iranian middle class perceive *mut'a* as legalized prostitution, the more religiously inclined Iranians view it as a divinely rewarded activity, preferable to the "decadent" Western style of "free" male-female associations.[13] The manifested social acceptability of temporary marriage and its popularity, however, seem to rise and fall according to the prevailing policies and attitudes of the ruling regime, and its relationship with the religious hierarchy. Whereas the attitude of the Pahlavi regime (1925–79) was one of disdain and its policy was one of benign neglect, the present Islamic regime has publicly endorsed temporary marriage, advocating it as evidence of Islamic understanding and foresight on matters of human sexuality.

Despite frequent negative valuations, or perhaps in defense, a whole body of sayings and beliefs has developed around the practice of temporary marriage. These sayings place great emphasis on its religious merit, arguing that it incurs God's reward, *savab*,[14] that it is approved by the Prophet, and that it was practiced by many of his companions and other revered Shi'i leaders (Amini 1952, 5–6: 220–38). One frequently cited saying is attributed to the Imam Ja'far-i Sadiq: "Every drop of the ablution water [ablutions are required after sexual intercourse] transforms into seventy angels who will then testify on the Day of Judgment on behalf of he who has practiced *mut'a*" (Ardistani n.d., 236; Muhammad ca. 1985, 144–47; and personal communication with mullas). Another saying, also attributed to the Imam Sadiq, is: "I never dissimulate, *taqiyyih*, on the subject of *mut'a*" (Qa'imi 1974, 297).

An equally frequently cited story, attributed to both the Imam Ja'far-i Sadiq and his father, Imam Muhammad-i Baqir, is about a man who asked the imam whether temporary marriage has *savab*. The imam is said to respond: "He who contracts *mut'a* with a woman only to please God, or to follow the teachings of religion and the tradition of the Prophet, or to disobey the command of him who has banned *mut'a* [a reference to 'Umar], for every word he exchanges with that woman, the Merciful God writes him a *savab*. When he stretches his hand toward that woman, God writes him a *savab*. As soon as he consummates the marriage, the Almighty God forgives his sins. And when he performs his ablution, God's mercy and forgiveness will be bestowed on him for the number of each hair that is drenched by the ablution water" (cited in Ardistani n.d., 236; Muhammad ca. 1985, 144). Further, temporary marriage is said to gain God's reward because it directly challenges the Second Caliph's ban on its practice in the mid-seventh century; a ban pointedly viewed as worthless by the Shi'ites, which will be discussed later.

The establishment of the Islamic regime in 1979 marks a significant turning point in the state policies, which are aimed at bringing about a positive change in the public perception of temporary marriage. Before 1979 the public's knowledge of *mut'a* was vague and its attitude was ambivalent, at best. Those who practiced it learned its specifics primarily from a mulla (a general term for a religious official), a friend, or a neighbor. Under the Pahlavi regime, though *mut'a* marriage was not categorically outlawed, it was restricted, and men and women who made contracts of temporary marriage tended to keep a low profile or keep their contracts secret altogether. On the other hand, the Islamic regime has made an orchestrated effort to educate the public of the specifics of the institution, its divine roots, its contemporary relevance, emphasizing its positive effects for the individual and social moral health.[15] In high schools, in the mosques, at religious gatherings, on radio and television, and in newspapers, the Islamic regime is advocating the blessings of temporary marriage, encouraging familiarity with and use of the institution. The public drive to encourage temporary marriage has become particularly intense because of the deaths of hundreds of thousands of men in the Iran-Iraq war (Rafsanjani ca. 1985, 13).

Presently, the Islamic regime is conducting an intensive campaign to revitalize temporary marriage, reinterpreting it as a "brilliant law of Islam" and reintroducing it to the society as the appropriate Islamic response to resolving human (read "men's") needs for multiple sexual partners (Tabataba'i et al. ca. 1985, 39). Drawing attention to its legal and moral framework, the ulama view this form of marriage as an Islamic substitute for the "decadent" Western style of "free" gender relations. Above all, they argue that temporary marriage, unlike permanent marriage, is easily contracted and involves little reciprocal responsibility. It is thus, so goes their argument, a very timely and modern means for satisfying youth's sexual needs without preventing them from pursuing their educational and professional objectives (Tabataba'i et al. ca. 1985). Drawing parallels between the time of the Prophet and the recent war between Iran and Iraq, the Ayatollah Khomeini has instructed men to marry the widows of martyrs of the war either permanently or temporarily. He has also advised the martyrs' widows not to be too fussy and to marry soldiers of this war (*Ittila'at*, March 15, 1982, 1–2). Many mullas and religious preachers have followed suit in encouraging men and women to marry widows and soldiers of the war. Mrs. Maryam Bihruzi, a woman representative in the parliament, lectures Iranian women on the advantages of *mut'a* while admonishing them to put aside their selfish feelings: to be more understanding of, and attentive to, their husbands' "natural" needs if they wish to *sigheh* other women.[16]

By educating the masses publicly and formally and encouraging the practice of *mut'a* marriage, the Islamic regime has raised the public consciousness of the affordability and attainability of sexuality (euphemistically called "marriage"), suggesting, as we shall soon learn, realms of activities that were perhaps previously all too foggy.

METHOD

Perhaps the most difficult methodological issue was to identify people who contract temporary marriage in the pilgrimage centers of Qom, Mashhad, and other cities, and then to select a sample that would be representative. Feeling ambivalent toward the custom, many practicing Iranians keep their temporary marriages secret or, at most, share that information with only a chosen few. Even after 1979, and despite the Islamic regime's positive attitude toward *mut'a*, most people are still reluctant to discuss their experiences with strangers and to put one in contact with those who have been temporarily married. This is in spite of the fact that many would go to great lengths to emphasize the religious merit of *mut'a* marriage and its conttributions to public health, physically and psychologically.

No accurate statistics of the number of *mut'a* marriages are available. This is partly because no separate entry is made in the census for distinguishing a temporary marriage from a permanent one, partly because no requirements for its registration exist,[17] and partly because of the secrecy surrounding its practice. During my preliminary fieldwork in 1978, I found that many people in Tehran assumed that *mut'a* marriage was obsolete. Others in Qom and Mashhad firmly believed that the reports of the demise of the custom were greatly exaggerated. The claims of the latter were borne out, for by 1981 virtually everyone with whom I talked believed that *mut'a* marriage was making a rapid comeback, not only in the pilgrimage centers but in other cities as well.

Before describing my method in the field, I wish to describe briefly the atmosphere and ambience of the shrines in the pilgrimage centers, where reportedly most contracts for temporary marriage take place. It is common knowledge in Iran that if one wants to marry temporarily, one should go to either Qom or Mashhad, the two most important and popular pilgrimage centers in Iran. These shrines are walled-in architectural monuments comprising several intricately related buildings, always packed with a multitude of believers and worshipers. Women in these pilgrimage centers are required to veil, and they adhere closely to the rules of modesty. A unique feature of the holy places is the spatial relationship of the sexes in the inner sanctum of these mausoleums. So long as men and women are immobile, sitting or praying in one of the shrine's labyrinthine corridors or lofts, they tend to gather in segregated quarters. Should they, however, be moving, or wishing to get closer to the decorated steel and silver latticed tombs, they do in fact come to very close physical proximity of each other. This particular congregation of male and female worshipers is such that it communicates conflicting nonverbal messages about gender association and avoidance. The mere physical closeness of the flesh in the shrine enclosure, the body heat, scent, and energy that are thereby generated, coupled with the constant circumambulation of the pilgrims around the holy tombs, communicate a strong sense of sensuality. This does not negate the simultaneous presence of spirituality that may be genuinely generated among thousands of worshiping pilgrims. The point is that while the sexes are required to strictly observe veiling and avoidance, they can at the same time break through this physical boundary by moving very close to the inner shrine and thus to each other.

Evidently, this sensuality, and subversion of the system of veiling, has not been lost on the Islamic regime, either. As soon as it consolidated its power, the regime erected a glass wall separating the male and female quarters of worship around the tombs. No longer are the pilgrims allowed to circumambulate the inner sanctum together. Presently, a little more than half of the space inside the shrine is devoted to men, with the other part reserved for women.[18] Such official policies aimed at keeping men and women segregated, however, do in fact make each gender highly conscious of the presence of the other.

   The ever-present and ever-changing crowd in the shrines and the continual influx of pilgrims to these pilgrimage centers are conducive to making direct or indirect contact with members of the opposite sex, facilitating arrangements for making contracts of temporary marriage by interested pilgrims. Having lived in Qom and Mashhad for some time, I began to realize that two of the most outstanding — though not readily noticeable — characteristics of these magnificent shrines are the *novelty* of the place, the experience, and the people, and the *anonymity* of the environment. Pilgrims who travel to these holy shrines leave behind their known and mundane social worlds, and they are momentarily separated from their daily routines. During their sojourn, the pilgrims come in contact with many people who are from cities, villages, or communities other than their own. Being in a "transitional" state, the pilgrims are thus in an ideal position to draw upon this vast human resource to make a short-term contract of temporary marriage and yet to remain anonymous. Liminality is thus the hallmark of the pilgrims, who in Turner's words are "standing aside not only from [their] own position but from all social positions" and are "formulating a potentially unlimited series of alternative social arrangements" (1974, 14). The prevailing mood of communitas and liminality in the shrines need not involve just the pilgrims; it engulfs the entire shrine space and marks its ambience (Turner 1974, 166). By crossing the threshold of these crowded sanctuaries, the pilgrims may transcend their structured and routinized lives and reap the advantages of the ambiguities afforded them as a result of their transitionality.

   Just exactly how potential *sigheh* women are identified and distinguished from all other women present, or, conversely, how women target men, requires some personal ingenuity on the part of both men and women, and familiarity with the folklore. Contrary to my expectations, I learned from my informants of the variety of ways women may take the initiative and communicate their desire for a temporary union. A woman, for instance, may wear her veil, *chadur*, inside out to signal her interest and availability.[19] Or she may use a facial veil, *pushiyih*, to convey the same message. The way women carry themselves may also indicate their intention. Women who seem to be walking aimlessly, or those who look around all too frequently, are assumed to be signaling their availability and interest. Paradoxically, however, it seems that the more covered a woman is, the more veiled she is, the more transparent her intention seems to be. A direct approach is, of course, always appreciated. Amin Aqa, a religious preacher in Mashhad, put it succinctly: "He who seeks, shall find!" (see his interview, chapter 6).

I spent most of my time in the cities of Qom and Mashhad, where the major Shi'i shrines are located. Qom is an unattractive, oppressive city on the border of the Salt Desert. It is 135 kilometers south of Tehran. Qom hosts the shrine of Ma'sumih, the sister of the Shi'ites' eighth imam Riza. Before the revolution of 1979 it was the only major urban center in Iran where women were compelled to be totally veiled. Like a veiled woman, Qom is massive and formless, defying any attempt at recognition of its real identity. Qom is one of the two most prestigious centers for religious training and teaching in Iran. Much to the displeasure of the religious establishment, it is known as a *sigheh* city.

Mashhad, on the other hand, is less homogeneous and more diverse politically, religiously, and culturally. It is one of the greatest Shi'i pilgrimage centers, located in the northeast province of Khorasan. Mashhad is among the most populous and prosperous cities in the country. The magnificent tomb of Imam Riza, the Eighth Imam, is the center of attraction there.

Inside the intricately designed shrines and their labyrinthine structures are specific areas identified with activities regarding temporary marriage. Men and women who want to meet prospective temporary spouses gather in these popularly known places. Certain corners of the mosque — a lamp post, a specific door gate, windows, and the like — are some such known spots. One such strategic — and also controversial — location is around the so-called Steel Latticed Window, *panjirih-i fulad*. This is a huge floor-length latticed window that overlooks Imam Riza's tomb from the shrine yard. It is rumored that women who engage in temporary marriage frequently — known as *sigheh-ru* — linger in this area. They convey their intentions to interested pilgrims through some mutually understood codes or receive clues from prospective men. Consequently, the allusion "under the Steel Latticed Window,"[20] *zir-i panjirih-i fulad*, has become idiomatic in Persian vernacular, implying some kind of questionable sexual activity.

The Shi'ites' holy city of Najaf in Iraq is another significant religious center, enjoying the same reputation as Mashhad and Qom. Prior to the sociopolitical changes in Iraq in the late 1950s, Najaf reportedly superseded the other two cities in popularity for *mut'a* marriage.

Outside of these important religious centers, major urban areas of Iran have their share of association with *sigheh* marriages, though one may never know the exact number of temporary marriages that take place in any one of these centers. Several locations in Tehran, the capital city, make it stand out from other cities. Particularly famous is the shrine of the Shah 'Abdul 'Azim in the ancient city of Ray in south Tehran. Moreover, temporary marriages occasionally occur in the United States and Europe.[21]

The data for this book were collected during two field trips in the summer of 1978 and in the second half of 1981. Within this short period Iranian society underwent a tremendous transformation. The whole nation was pulled through an ideological metamorphosis: from a society with a vision of pre-Islamic grandeur and glory, to be captured with the aid of Western technology and science under the shah (1941 – 79), to one with a vision of return to the Islamic golden age, to be achieved with a total rejection of the West, its technology, and philosophy. The only overt features that these two world-views share is their adherence to a vision of the past: one to pre-Islamic Zoroastrianism and the other to Islam.

During the summer of 1978 I lived with a family in Qom who were acquaintances of my grandparents. Being an Iranian, a woman, and a grand-daughter of a well-known ayatollah, I was easily accepted in the community and was able to establish relationships with the residents in our neighborhood. I had informal and formal talks with many men and women from all walks of life and age groups. I participated in women's religious gatherings that were becoming increasingly popular at that time, interviewed several women preachers, and talked to women collectively and individually. I frequented the shrine of Ma'sumih in Qom and the crowded courtyard of the Ayatollah Shari'atmadari's residence. My father, himself the son of an ayatollah, arranged my audiences with the then two highest-ranking ayatollahs in Qom, namely, the Ayatollah Najafi Mar'ashi and the Ayatollah Shari'atmadari.[22] Initially, he traveled to Qom with me and was crucial in facilitating my meetings with several mullas and arranging interviews with others. His presence in some of my interviews and his intermittent visits to Qom, helping me gain respect in the eyes of the mullas and the community where I was living, lent credibility and legitimacy to my research endeavors.

During the summer of 1978 I spent many days in the shrines and talked to as many women and men as I could. Like many other pilgrims, I would sit in different parts of the shrine and start a conversation with those who happened to be sitting next to me. The mood in the shrine is gregarious, and many who go to these pilgrimage centers are strangers from outside the city. They look forward to finding companions, however temporary.

My criteria for choosing these "sitting sites" were the constitution of the crowd: the relative age of those congregated in a particular place and the homogeneity of gender. For instance, I would choose a corner where at least one mulla was "stationed."[23] Women usually gather around a mulla asking questions and discussing issues of importance to them. I found some of these discussions challenging my preconceived notions of propriety, modesty, and male-female association. Often these conversations involved a frank dialogue between the mulla and the women on a variety of subjects, including child rearing, relationships with their husbands or their cowives, and, on a more general level, the correct ways of performing their religious duties and rituals. In this way I could join in the conversation and ask questions from either the mullas or the women without looking conspicuous. However, if I wanted to talk to a mulla, I would approach one that did not have many followers, for otherwise it would be difficult to pursue a conversation. As a rule I sought out middle-aged or older women, for the chances that younger women had been temporarily married or would know of one were more limited. Because of the significance of virginity in Iran at the time of the first marriage, young virgin women, it is believed, do not practice *mut'a*, even though the law does not forbid them to. The five young Qomi women who befriended me, though claiming to approve of *mut'a* in principle, maintained a dislike for the custom personally. Their rationale was that a *mut'a* marriage would jeopardize their reputations and minimize their chances to a suitable permanent marriage.[24]

Many men and women pilgrims were quite friendly and willing to talk with me. After some initial conversation, I would tell them that I was writing a book about the different forms of marriage in Islam, and that I was interested in interviewing those who had married temporarily and to hear their life histories, *sarguzasht*, personally. Not all turned out to be temporarily married at the time—at least not admitting it to me—but most knew of cases firsthand, which they described to me.

I let the shrine workers, the *khadamih*, know about my research and also about my intention to interview the pilgrims. They did not express much enthusiasm about my research but did not object to it either, particularly once they had learned that I was a granddaughter of an ayatollah and had interviewed such important religious leaders as the ayatollahs Najafi Mar'ashi and Shari'atmadari.

I went back to Qom in 1981, but the situation had changed profoundly. My host's husband had died the year before, and being a relatively young widow, she was constantly worried about "what others might say" or think of her. Her anxiety reached a critical level when one of my informants, Mulla Ifshagar, came to visit me at her house one afternoon. Fearing her neighbors' gossip, she left her house without telling me, leaving me alone with the mulla. Later, I learned that her action placed me and the mulla in a potentially dangerous situation vis-à-vis the revolutionary guards. Therefore, I had to be very careful about the people with whom I associated or those whom I invited for a visit.

Politically, the Islamic regime had consolidated its power, the hostage crisis (1979–81) had just come to an end, and the rhetoric of belligerence and animosity toward the American government and those associated with the United States had reached a new peak; the air was thick with suspicion. An unfounded accusation of spying was enough to send one to jail for many months, if not years. Consequently, many were simply too apprehensive to disclose their private lives to me, at least not in a public place such as a shrine. I, too, was nervous about being misunderstood or accused of wrong-doing. I had to be more mindful of the shrine workers, who were ever-vigilant about people's "proper" Islamic behavior. Consequently, I was much more hesitant about initiating a conversation and, if I did, was inhibited from being open about it. Although I eventually managed to talk about temporary marriage to quite a number of mullas and some women in the shrines, our conversations tended to be abstract and formal rather than personal and substantive.

Faced with such logistical problems, I relied more on a network of friends and relatives and less on my technique of open-ended interviewing in the shrines in the pilgrimage centers. I let everyone know that I was interested in meeting and interviewing men and women who had contracted *mut'a* marriage. Much to my delight, it turned out that many people did indeed know of at least one person who, at one point or another, had been married temporarily. Not surprisingly, however, some shied away from approaching their friends or acquaintances directly, asking them to talk with me, and some flatly refused to be interviewed. Many others, however, showed a willingness to meet with me. In addition to these interviews, I asked virtually everyone I met to tell me stories and cases of *mut'a* marriage of which they knew personally.

The sensitivity of the subject and people's ambivalence toward it, the uncertain political situation in Iran, and the changing travel laws that affected the length of my fieldwork in Iran, all made the process of gathering intensive data on a larger sample virtually impossible. While I was in Iran, the Islamic regime passed a law that made it illegal for Iranians who were holding permanent residency in foreign countries to stay in Iran beyond a six-month limit. Further, the law stipulated that an entry would be granted only once a year. Therefore, much to my regret, I had to leave Iran once my six months' limit was up. Confronted with the restrictions of access and the residency permit, I oriented my research toward an intensive analysis of sixteen case histories and a collection of interviews associated with them.

The significance of the custom of *mut'a* marriage, however, cannot be measured by its statistical frequency alone. According to the Iranian census bureau, from 1962 through 1971 the total number of the first-time temporary marriages given for both men and women is 1,146 and 1,105, respectively (*Salnamih-i Amari* 1971, 43). Women who have cared to register their second temporary marriage outnumber men three to one, 198 to 60, for the same time period. Given that historically this form of marriage — and even until recently permanent marriage — has not required witnesses or registration, the data provided in the Iranian census are neither reliable nor representative. The statistical infrequency of temporary marriage, however, has contributed to maintaining the submerged status of the institution of temporary marriage, keeping it thus unclear and enigmatic to many Iranians, including even those who have used it. Much of the significance of temporary marriage, rather, lies in its sheer existence: the fact that it is legitimate, that it is religiously encouraged, and that it is easily contracted in this apparently puritanical society; that despite all the walls and veils, the very same structure that forbids association between the sexes allows them to come together unceremoniously by simply uttering the *mut'a* marriage formula privately.

Given the nature of my subject, the time-honored anthropological method of participant observation offered a poor prospect. There is no such thing as a community of temporarily married people in which one could pitch one's tent and observe interactions between husbands and wives. Second, most temporary spouses do not set up separate households. They often live away from each other and in separate family units, as we shall see. Consequently, I directed my efforts toward collecting biographies and life histories, focusing on what people say and how they perceive themselves and others, on the perspectives adopted by them, and on their gender-differentiated narrative styles.

I kept an extensive list of contextual questions with me and interviewed my informants in a style the Iranians call *dard-i dil*, stories of the heart. The phrase refers to an intimate, informal, and open-ended dialogue. The vital contextual information I collected included variables such as socioeconomic and religious background, education, profession, age, marital status, attitude toward *mut'a*, legal knowledge, awareness of the role and function of *mut'a*, and the like. However, before proceeding with any systematic questioning, I let my informants tell me about their life in the manner that made them feel comfortable.

This approach suited the women. They usually began by describing some critical events in their life cycles. In retelling their stories, however, I have used a more chronological approach, while remaining faithful to the style of my informants' narratives. As the conversation gained spirit and became more intimate, I would participate more actively by asking pertinent questions, or by redirecting the conversation if I felt we were moving too far away from the subject. I interviewed some of my informants a few times and had extensive interviews with others. For some, I was able to gather additional information from mutual acquaintances.

I talked to more than forty women of different ages and backgrounds, and I collected extensive interviews with thirteen of them. Of these women, eight had been involved in one or more temporary marriages, and the other five had temporary cowives. Because of the focus of this book, I have not included the latter's case histories, but some of their opinions and views have been incorporated into the main body of the study. Likewise, the sample of male informants presented here includes the nine most extensive and informative interviews I had with men, eight of whom are mullas of different ranks. Except for the ayatollahs Najafi Mar'ashi and Shari'atmadari, the names of the rest of the informants are fictitious.

My being an Iranian Muslim woman, my intimate familiarity with Persian language (my mother tongue), and my knowledge of the culture were invaluable assets in establishing trust and rapport with my informants. I escaped the usual anthropological headaches of orientation, adjustment, acceptance, and overcoming language barriers. Because of this, I was able, for the most part, to offset the time restrictions imposed on my research by the Islamic regime and to gather data that under similar circumstances would have been very difficult for anyone but a native to collect. On the other hand, my being a native Iranian and a woman had its own constraints. I had to strictly observe certain restrictions regarding the traditional expectations of modesty, sexual segregation, and feminine propriety, restrictions that perhaps would have been spared an outsider.

The uniqueness of my enterprise, and the fact that I was both an Iranian yet not actually living among Iranians, afforded me and my informants the "familiar distance" (Crapanzano 1980, 12) that encouraged my informants to open up and share with me some intimate aspects of their lives. I was delighted, and surprised, to find many of them eager to listen to my questions, to reflect on them carefully, and to tell me the stories of their lives. For many women, it was as if they had been waiting all their lives for such an opportune moment to pour out their hearts to someone who was willing to listen to them.

Most of my male informants were mullas of differing rank and status. I met some of them in the shrines of Qom and Mashhad, and some were introduced to me by other mullas I interviewed. When I asked to be introduced to men who were temporarily married, I was often directed to mullas because it is widely believed, even by many mullas themselves, that the religious figures, *ruhaniyun*, are more prone than others to making contracts of *mut'a* marriage. Perhaps because of their religious knowledge, stature, and public role, mullas are generally more agreeable and willing to talk about such topics than other men are. Also, because I had read the primary Shi'i sources on the subject, I was able to engage them in discussions on their own level. This, I believe, not only gained their respect but their willingness to talk. Although making up the majority, mullas are not the only ones who engage in temporary marriage. Other men, as will become clear from the life stories of my female informants, also make use of temporary marriage.

Mullas are agents of religious teaching and training who perform a variety of religious ceremonies and rituals for people in the shrines, in mosques, and at their homes. As a result, they establish alliances with families and individuals, and they come to know extended networks of men, women, and their families. This places them in a powerful position, and perhaps because of the prestige associated with their status, role, and function, many believing men try to emulate them, and many women — particularly those who are divorced or widowed — seek them out as a source of solace, guidance, and religious confirmation.

As were the women informants, these men proved to be very cooperative and forthright in their opinions. Unlike the women, however, they usually avoided talking about their individual experiences. They were more interested in making generalizations and abstractions about the institution of *mut'a* marriage, the society, and the individual; they tended to emphasize the public aspects of *mut'a* marriage. Perhaps the fact that the majority of them were mullas — or that their interviewer was a woman — partly explains such responses. Frequently they emphasized what *ought to be* at the expense of reflecting on what *is*. Some of them were very inquisitive about my intentions to study *mut'a;* they did not see much merit in interviewing many people, least of all women, particularly after they had expressed their own opinions. They argued that I should devote my time to studying Islamic law instead. In their view, that would be sufficient for understanding the institution. Many of them had a pedagogical approach and turned out to be, not surprisingly, good preachers.

The ethnographic data presented in this book confirm the view that because of the structure of sex segregation and the particular position men and women have in the social structure, each has come to have different though overlapping perceptions of "reality" (see Rosen 1978, 562). On the other hand, the data challenge the view that tends to reify the structure of sex segregation in Iran, believing it to be static, given, and immutable (see Vieille 1978). The images of the genders, their relations and interactions, that emerge in this study are different not only from those perceived by some outside observers but from that advanced by the official Shi'i view. The diversity of women's experiences with temporary marriage and their articulation of their motivations challenge the official myth that the woman's motive in seeking a *mut'a* marriage is transparently financial and the underlying presumption that all women are "naturally" passive and have the same objective in their marital and sexual relations. My findings bring out the divergence of perceptions not only between women and the lawmakers, but among the women themselves. As a corollary, I try to unburden the belief that assumes an ever-active role for men in initiating marital and erotic relations.

The paucity of data on the social history and actual practices of the institution of *mut'a* marriage hampers the delineation of the custom in its many sociocultural aspects. Although rumors and stereotypes abound, substantive information on the actual practices and social conditions of *mut'a* is wanting. To reconstruct aspects of the social history of temporary marriage in Iran, I have relied on the following sources.

From the memoirs of the Western diplomats, travelers, and missionaries of the past two centuries who passed through Iran under one profession or another, we may catch glimpses of the practice of *mut'a* marriage in Iran (Morier 1855; Sheil 1856; Binning 1857; Willes 1866; Curzon 1892; Browne 1893; Wishard 1908; Sykes 1910; Wilson 1941). We learn virtually nothing, however, about the age range of the participants, nor do we get a picture of their socioeconomic, professional, or educational backgrounds. Fascinated, and at times appalled, by the eroticism implied in temporary marriage, these observers either gave free rein to their ethnocentric biases or relied on stereotypes, hearsay, value judgments, and clichés. For example, De Lorey states: "It is the women of the lower class, called *Sighehs* or more exactly, *Mouti*, who devote themselves to it" (De Lorey and Sladen 1907, 130). Or the city of Mashhad, where *mut'a* has been common, is referred to as "probably the most immoral city in Asia" (Curzon 1892, 165).

In his book *Queer Things about Persia,* De Lorey attempts to link temporary marriage with a pre-Islamic Iranian custom: "The temporary marriage is a time-honored Persian Institution, if one can judge by legend, which says that Restum, the Hercules of Persia, contracted such a union during a hunting excursion with Tamineh, the daughter of the King of Samangam, of which a son, the celebrated Zohrab, was born" (1907, 129).

Some twenty years earlier, Benjamin (1887) described the same legend but with a more accurate spelling of the Persian names. He too seems to have confused the brief length of the visit between the legendary husband and wife with the temporariness of this form of marriage. On the basis of the fact that Shi'i Muslims are permitted to make contracts of temporary marriage with the "Magians," Benjamin declares, "this is conclusive evidence of the Zoroastrian origin of this form of marriage" (451).

The rather intricate and symbolic plural marriages that existed among the pre-Islamic Zoroastrians do indeed share some basic characteristics with the pre-Islamic forms of marriage prevalent in Arabia. A discussion of these similarities, however, is beyond the scope of this work. Suffice it to say that although apparently a form of temporary marriage (no known indigenous term was found) did exist in pre-Islamic Iran, it was not the same as the institution of *mut'a* marriage. In its Zoroastrian version, the husband, or the head of the family, had a right to "hand over his wife [or his daughter] — by a formal procedure and in response to a formal request — to another man belonging to his community, as [his] temporary wife for a definite period" (Perikhanian 1983, 650; Parsa et al. 1967, 123–31; cf. Surushian 1973, 183–84). In this case, the wife remained permanently married to her first husband at the same time that she entered a temporary marriage with one of his countrymen. Any children born during this temporary union belonged to the wife's permanent husband, or to her father, as the case might be (Perikhanian 1983, 650).[25]

Unlike the curious Westerners, until recently the Iranian literati paid little attention to describing, documenting, dramatizing, or analyzing the implications of temporary marriage for the genders or the society.[26] The Constitutional Revolution of 1906 generated much intellectual fervor and excitement among the intellectuals, prompting them to take direct stands on issues such as veiling, child marriage, and lack of educational opportunities for women.[27] However, hardly any direct or well-articulated commentaries were made on the subject of temporary marriage or on its implications for men and women in Iran or elsewhere.

The theme was eventually picked up by a few Iranian novelists, who with increasing sophistication dramatized different dimensions of the custom of temporary marriage, particularly dwelling on its negative implications for women. In his novel *Tehran-i Makhuf* (Horrid Tehran), Mushfiq-i Kazimi (1961), as a subtheme, depicts the wretched life of a temporary wife, an unwilling victim of the social system. Chubak (1967) focuses his long story of *Sang-i Sabur* (The patient stone) on the life and death of a temporary wife, but he assigns no voice to the woman to articulate her own thoughts and feelings; she is murdered early on in the story.

Al-i Ahmad (1969) in his short story entitled "Jashn-i Farkhundih" (The auspicious celebration) brings to light manipulation of the custom by a religious leader in 1936 who is ordered to attend a government-sponsored woman's "emancipation" party.[28] Rebellious of the government's newly enacted unveiling law, yet not wishing to disobey the royal command, the high-ranking mulla arranges a temporary marriage with the daughter of a friend for two hours. He attends the ceremony with his unveiled temporary wife of two hours, at the same time subverting the state's unveiling law by keeping his own wife secluded at home.

Gulistan (1967) in "Safar-i 'Ismat" ('Ismat's journey) skillfully sketches the structural parallelism between prostitution and temporary marriage by dramatizing the transition of a young repentant whore from prostitution to temporary marriage. Her guide in this endeavor is a young handsome mulla. Finally, Jamalzadih (1954) in *Ma'sumih Shirazi* (Ma'sumih from Shiraz) contrasts the beauty of the spirit of an ill-reputed *sigheh* woman with the meanness of spirit and lechery of a high-ranking mulla.

In the last two decades of the Pahlavi regime, the topic of temporary marriage came under attack from several quarters, including such women's journals as *Zan-i Ruz* (see also Manuchihrian 1978). These critical comments, however, prompted quick and sharp responses from some of the religious leaders, most notably the late Ayatollah Mutahhari.[29]

In sharp contrast to the paucity of sociological studies stands the abundance of the religious and legal documents on the subject.[30] The numerous books and articles written on women, marriage, and family in Islam all have stressed the legal and moral aspects of the law, emphasizing what ought to be. Often religiolegal documents are accompanied by a defense of the institution in the face of charges of "fornication" leveled by the Sunni Muslims. Faced with new adversaries from the West, however, as well as some educated Iranian women and men, the Shi'i official interpretation of *mut'a* has shifted, from defending it as a form of marriage to justifying it in terms of its relevance to a contemporary society.

What is noteworthy about all these published sources of data on the issues of temporary marriage, gender relations, women, men, sexuality, prostitution, and the like is that they are all written by men. Whether they express a derisive attitude or a sympathetic, critical, or supportive one toward the subject, these works communicate an essentially male perspective. Women's own thoughts and perceptions on the subject seem to have been considered irrelevant and traditionally have gone unnoticed.

Part One

law as imposed

1

MARRIAGE AS CONTRACT

Exchange, as a total phenomenon, is from the first a total
exchange, comprising food, manufactured objects, and
that most precious category of goods, women. . . .
It should not be surprising then to find women
included among reciprocal prestations; this they
are in the highest degree, but at the same time as
other goods, material and spiritual.
—LEVI-STRAUSS, *The Elementary Structures of Kinship*

SLAMIC MARRIAGE IS A CONTRACT of exchange that involves a sort of ownership. In exchange for some money or valuables the men pay women,
they gain an exclusive right of sexual union. All schools of Islamic law consider marriage to be a contract, an *'aqd*. This contractual exchange that lies
at the heart of a Muslim marriage legitimizes it in the eyes of law and
religion.

Little analysis has been made of the concept of marriage contract
and what it means to conceive of marital relations in terms of a contract of
exchange. Likewise, little has been done on what such a conceptualization
reveals about the lawmakers' assumptions about and images of men, women,
and their relationships, or on what the rationale is behind it. This part con-
centrates on the concept of marriage contract, describing and discussing its
Shi'i variations in some detail. I bring to light the ubiquity of the logic of contract, and its structural and functional implications for each gender's perception of the self and the other.

My aim in decoding the concept of contract in Shi'i Islam is twofold:
First, to focus on the concept of contract in order to demonstrate that Islamic
ideology has a more complex as well as ambivalent view of women and female
sexuality than the prevalent (and almost classic) polar arguments of "exaltation" and "objectification" have maintained. Second, to look at women's sta-

tus developmentally, offering a long-term perspective on losses and gains, continuity and change, conflict and compromise in Shi'i Muslim women's fluctuating legal status as they live through childhood (the age of virginity) to adulthood (the age of marriage and sexuality) to divorce and widowhood (the age of liminality and marginality). Each of these stages has its own associated legal and social injunctions.

THE STATUS OF WOMEN

A dramatic surge has occurred in ethnographic information regarding the status and position of Muslim women in the Middle East during the past two decades. Enhanced as our knowledge has become of the area, however, the diversity of opinions expressed concerning the status of Muslim women has rendered the phenomenon steadily more enigmatic, raising fundamental methodological and theoretical questions. This diversity leads both to problems associated with particular perspectives and to problems of conceptualization of women's status and worldviews. We can see this in the two dominant, and apparently opposing, perspectives taken on the position of women in the Middle East.

The first view is formulated by ideologically committed contemporary Muslim commentators—primarily men—who have been prompted to defend Islam in response to a pervasive Western perception of the status of Muslim women as inferior. The point of departure for these scholars is the Qur'an and the tradition of the Prophet, the two divine sources of Islamic law. Consequently, their rationales and justifications are much the same. They argue that not only has Islam "elevated" the status and position of women in society, in comparison with the women of *jahiliyah* (the age of "ignorance," i.e., before Islam), but that Islam has been far more progressive toward women than have other world religions. They point out that Islam banned infanticide, limited polygamy, accorded women a share in their parents' inheritance, and gave them the right to enter into contracts and dispose of their possessions according to their own will (Abdul-Rauf 1972; Aminuddin 1938; Badawi 1972; Elwan 1974; Bihishti ca. 1980; Gazder 1973; Mutahhari 1974; Qutb 1967; Saleh 1977; Khomeini 1982; Fahim Kirmani 1975; Siddiqi 1959; Fayzee 1974; Tabataba'i 1975; Kashif al-Ghita' 1968; Nuri 1968; Sani'i 1967).

The second perspective takes a more historical view of the impact of Islam on the role and status of women and is offered by mostly modernized, educated Muslim women—and some men. In contrast to the first view, this one is less homogeneous, attributing the unfavorable position of Muslim women to a host of variables: the continuity of the pre-Islamic tradition, the economic mode of production, the veiling and seclusion of women, the segregation of the sexes, the lack of educational training, and the like. Scholars of this persuasion, too, attribute primary importance to the Qur'anic precepts. They are, however, usually cautious not to single out religion as the sole factor responsible for the inferior position of women in the Muslim countries. Nonetheless, they view the overall effect of Islamic religion as inimical to women's self-realization and progress. They point out that women's share of inheritance is half as much as men's, that they are barred from becoming judges or leaders, and that they cannot participate in wars. Further, they argue, a woman's activities as a wife are restricted and controlled by her husband. In short, Islam, they say, has assigned an inferior status to women, contributing to their "objectification" in society[1] (Berque 1964; Bullough 1973; Khan 1972; Mernissi 1975; Mikhail 1975; Mohsen 1974; Phillips 1968; Keddie and Beck 1978; Youssef 1978; Mahdavi 1985).

     The particular school of Islamic law under study here is that of Shi'i Islam regarding women, men, sexuality, and marriage in Iran. My argument, however, is also relevant to Sunni law and Muslim women in general. This is partly because, with the exception of inheritance, few fundamental conceptual and legal differences exist among various schools of Islamic law concerning the basic rights of women (e.g., financial maintenance, brideprice). This unity of legal conception owes its historical uniqueness to the particular Islamic worldview that perceives the Qur'an to be the divine word of God, as revealed to the Prophet, and is therefore perceived to be immutable. Islam, argues Makdisi, "is, first and foremost, a nomocracy. The highest expression of its genius is to be found in its law; and its law is the source of legitimacy for other expressions of its genius" (1979, 6). Since the legal structure for marriage and divorce (constituting the bulk of laws related to women) is laid down in the Qur'an (see particularly suras 2:221–41; 4:3–35; 65:1–7), they, too, are believed to be atemporal and unchanging. For the same reason, Islamic societies have historically resisted changes in the structure of the family law, more than in other spheres. It is therefore very important and of direct contemporary relevance in the face of fundamentalist Islamic revivalism to reexamine and reinterpret legal and theological Islamic texts. In doing so I am not of course presuming that there is a perfect fit between articulated Islamic precepts and everyday social and cultural practices. For the sake of clarity, I wish to keep the levels of analysis, that of law and practice, separate.

     Whether law is imposed or generated from within has been debated frequently (see Burman and Harrell-Bond 1979; Kidder 1979), and I do not intend to involve myself in this debate. But I wish to posit that since Islamic law is believed to be the word of God, it may be argued to be an imposed law

in both the general and specific senses of the term. By "imposed law" I do
not mean a set of rules and commandments that once issued, or imposed, are
either universally enforceable or taken to heart by a specific community. By
arguing that Islamic law is imposed, I mean to focus attention on its ideological aspect, in the sense that it was revealed to the Prophet Muhammad and
thus has been maintained by the Muslim to be supreme and unchanging. I
wish to illustrate that Islamic law, though imposed in this sense, is constantly
being negotiated, interacting with particular historical currents.

The imposition of Islamic law may be inferred on two grounds. The
first is the degree of "social distance" between the lawmakers and the gov-
erned. Islamic law was revealed to the Prophet, and through him it was communicated to the believers. The community of the believers, however, was
not lacking hierarchy, either in terms of rank and status or in terms of gender.
Muslim men, most specifically the entire religious hierarchy, played the role
of intermediaries in passing God's words to women. The Qur'an itself is addressed to men; women are referred to. Further, Islamic law, *shari'a*, has
been interpreted and elaborated by male theologians and legal scholars exclusively. Patriarchal Islamic law, like that of other great religions, has steadfastly maintained an outsider's perspective on women, their nature, needs,
and wants.

Second is the unequal distribution of "resources," or ideological approaches toward the genders, differences between them, their relations, and
sexuality. Despite the Shi'i rejection of the role of analogy, *qias*, in theolog-
ical reasoning, the Shi'i ulama have consistently used a fundamental and
paradigmatic analogy in referring to male, female, and their relationship,
namely, that of "the law of nature," *ain-i fitrat* (Mutahhari 1974:211; Mustafavi 1972, 159–60; Nuri 1968, 15–37). In their view, sexual differences between men and women are rooted in their nature and so are analogous to that
of other "animal pairs." Maintaining sexuality as "instinctive," *gharizi*, the
Shi'i ulama acknowledge male sexuality. They have a clear idea of a man's
wants and needs and present them as unavoidable and undeniable. Male sexuality is accommodated by permanent and temporary marriages, concubi-
nage with one's own slave girls, and the unilateral right to divorce. Female
sexuality, by contrast, has escaped representation in the legal discourse. It
is, rather, perceived to be a bundle of ambiguities and uncertainties. It has
been consistently misunderstood or alluded to only in relation to male sexual
needs and caprice. This does not mean that the Shi'i Islamic law does not
have an idea of female sexuality; rather, it means that it is ambivalent and
derived from a masculine understanding of what female sexuality ought to
be, not in and of itself but always in relation to male sexuality.

In the realm of status and legal capacities, let us pause and discuss
in some detail concepts of legal adulthood and legal capacity for both men

and women. Islam is, of course, diverse both religiously and culturally, covering vast geographical areas of the globe (see al-Zein 1977). Here I wish to concentrate on the legal concept of personhood, ignoring for the moment its sociocultural dimensions.

The rights, duties, and capacities of Muslim men and women, ideologically, are derived from the two paradigms of immutable divine law, on the one hand, and the instinctual nature of human sexuality, on the other.[2] This is most evident in the ulamas' interpretation of the institution of temporary marriage and their justification for its sexual and moral benefits for the individual and society (Rafsanjani 1985; Bahunar 1981; Mahmudi 1980; Bihishti ca. 1980; Mutahhari 1974, 27–28, 173–90; 1981, 52–56; ca. 1979–80; Kashif al-Ghita' 1968, 251–81; Makarim-i Shirazi 1968, 372–90; Fahim Kirmani 1975, 300–306).

Against the background of these two overarching paradigms, Islamic law does accord certain rights and capacities to men and women both. Those of women, however, are considered inferior to those of men. A Muslim's legal capacity, *ahliyyat*, begins at birth and ends with death (Imami 1971, 4:47, 151–59; Schacht 1964, 124). His legal responsibilities are subsumed under his legal capacity and are distinguished as a "capacity of execution" and a "capacity of obligations." Writes Schacht: "Capacity of execution is the capacity to contract, to dispose, and therefore also validly to fulfill one's obligations; it can be full or restricted, and is harmonized with [capacity of obligations] by considering the 'qualification' [*hukm*], the essential character of the obligation" (1964, 124–27).[3] The highest degree of legal capacity is that of the free Muslim man who is sane and of age. Second in line is the free Muslim woman, who, though given certain rights, from the point of view of the law is generally counted as half a man.

The difference in men's and women's legal capacities become particularly noticeable once they reach adulthood and engage in matrimony. An adult, from the Islamic point of view, is a "legally and morally responsible person, one who has reached physical maturity, is of sound mind, may enter into contracts, dispose of property, and be subject to criminal law. Above all, he is responsible for the religious commands and obligations of Islam" (Lapidus 1976, 93). This could be interpreted to mean to apply to both men and women. In fact, however, a woman's right to dispose of her own property, for instance, is in conflict with the requirement that she remain obedient to her husband (see Imami 1971, 4:450–52). A wife's obligation to secure her husband's permission for her outside activities effectively deprives her of the exercise of her right to negotiate a contract, for instance, and of much of the autonomy and independence usually associated with adulthood. To this theme I shall return later.

Upon reaching maturity, a Muslim man is considered a full-fledged citizen, enjoying legal responsibility and autonomy. Whether he is seventeen or seventy, married or unmarried, divorced or widowed does not significantly change his legal rights, responsibilities, or capacity of execution, either in relation to other individuals or in society at large. Stability and autonomy mark a Muslim man's legal status. Unless he becomes insane, his legal status remains unchanged throughout the stages of his adult life cycle —although his social status, like that of women, may be enhanced by a strategically well-placed marriage.

The legal identity of a Muslim woman, too, begins at birth, but with this difference: by the time she reaches the end of her life cycle, her legal capacity and status have undergone several shifts and changes. A Muslim woman's de facto membership in her society is often problematic, for her coming of age and physical maturity do not necessarily coincide with her legal autonomy and independence. She is a ward of her father as a child and restricted as a decision-making adult. Depending on her stage of development, her legal persona and social status are marred by ambiguities and uncertainties. The determining factor is *not* whether her share of inheritance is half that of her brother's. It is, rather, the state of her sexuality—whether she is a virgin, married, divorced, or widowed. I am not assuming here that the concept of femaleness in Muslim cultures is uniform (Waines 1982, 653; Thaiss 1978, 8) or that congruency exists between the dominant ideological images of women and women's own self-images. Significant though these concepts are, their discussion falls outside our scope. (For an excellent discussion on the Iranian female-centered worldviews, see Safa-Isfahani 1980.) What I wish to emphasize here is, rather, the crucial distinction between the stability of men's legal status as opposed to the instability of women's, and as a corollary, the difference of perception between the "fullness" of a man's persona as opposed to the "mutilatory" character of a woman's.[4]

THE CONTRACT

In the seventh century the Prophet Muhammad called upon the Arabs to denounce the multitude of their gods and idols, and instead to worship one invisible almighty Allah. He also tried to unify the multiplicity of pre-Islamic modes of sexual unions by outlawing all but one form of marriage, namely, marriage by contract. Fundamental to this rearrangement of the existing social structure was the realignment of the roles of husband and wife into those of the principal transacting parties. As opposed to pre-Islamic form of "marriage of dominion," Islamic law recognized the wife—not her father—to be the recipient of brideprice (sura of Woman, 4; Nuri 1968, 118; Robertson

Smith 1903, 96; Levy 1957, 95). That is to say, Islamic law "transfer[red] the wife from the position of sale-object to that of contracting party who, in return for her granting the right of sexual union with herself, is entitled to receive the due consideration of the dower. She is now endowed with a legal competence she did not possess before" (Coulson 1964, 14). Implicit in this act of realignment of gender relations is an assumption of a degree of women's autonomy, individuality, and volition.

This shift in the conceptualization of marital relations and in brideprice destination, I suggest, is the key to understanding the precarious legal position of women and the ambivalence toward them in Muslim societies. As a party to the contract, the woman herself has to give her consent—however nominally—for the contract to be valid. And it is the woman herself, not her father (custom aside), who is to receive the full amount of brideprice, be it immediate or deferred. In other words, an Islamic marriage is essentially a commercial mode of transaction superimposed onto the interpersonal marital relation. In a Shi'i Muslim marriage, then, a woman is given some legal autonomy in order to bargain over her own destiny. She is now faced with the unenviable task of having to trade her autonomy and identity for social prestige and status, associated with marriage.

An Islamic marriage contract is of course more than a mere exchange of material goods. As with other forms of social exchange, a contract of marriage is at once a legal, religious, economic, and symbolic transaction (see Mauss 1967, 76). Mauss and other social scientists have cogently argued that exchange and reciprocity form the very foundations of human society. Contracts are but one specific form of social exchange and reciprocity. The concept of contract is deeply embedded in the Perso-Islamic culture, providing the grid for social order as well as giving meaning to social relations. The continuous exchange of gifts, prestations, and counterprestations that characterize different forms of marriage in Iran create complex and crosscutting networks of kinship and alliances. They touch the lives of individuals at every stage of their life cycles. In the context of Iranian society, the all-prevailing concept of contract functions as a "root paradigm" (Turner 1974, 64), informing people's consciousness and orienting their behavior in their daily interactions and transactions.

A most noteworthy illustration of the embeddedness of the concept of contract in the Iranian belief is that between God and the believers. Allah, in whose name people are to "fulfill their contracts" (Wolf 1951, 339), in the Qur'an Sura of *Taghabun*, "Mutual disillusion" (4:15–17), promises the believers: "If ye lend unto Allah a goodly loan, He will double it for you and will forgive you, for Allah is Responsive, Clement" (see also Mauss 1967, 75). Almost all religious and charitable acts are undertaken with the specific objective of pleasing God, who in turn reciprocates these deeds with religious merit, or *savab*. It is as if one enters a "commercial relation" with God (Betteridge 1980, 145), in addition to a spiritual one. A more compelling and currently applicable example of this concept is martyrdom. For martyrs of the Iran-Iraq war, the reward is paradise and eternal pleasure. In a contract of marriage, legal principles, economic transactions, and sociocultural meanings converge.

SHI'I MARRIAGE: THE CONTRACTUAL MODEL

According to the Qur'an, sura of Woman:24 and 25, the Shi'i jurisprudence classifies three types of marriage as legitimate: permanent marriage, *nikah;* temporary marriage, *mut'a;* and slave marriage, *nikah ul-ima'* (Tusi 1964, 457; Kulaini 1958, 5:364; Hilli SI, 428). The Sunnis accept the two forms of permanent and slave marriage as legitimate but reject *mut'a* as fornication, and thus forbidden. Although slavery was modified by Islam, it was not categorically outlawed. Sexual intercourse with one's own slave girl, therefore, continued to be legitimate until recently in most Islamic societies.[5] Slave ownership should not be confused with slave marriage. Slave marriage involves marriage of a slave with another person, be it another slave or a free born, granted that the permission of the slave master is secured. A slave marriage could be of the permanent or temporary kind. In the case of slave ownership, however, marriage is not necessary between a male slave owner and his female slaves. His ownership entitles him to a right of intercourse, a right denied a female slave owner. My concern here is only with the two institutions of permanent and temporary marriages.

An Islamic marriage is defined as "that type of contract, *'aqd,* which gives ownership, *tamlik,* over intercourse, *vaty,* not like buying a slave girl whose ownership entitles her master a right to intercourse" (Hilli SI, 428). Scholars of Islamic law classify marriage, *nikah,* as a contract but shy away from specifying the type of contract to which it actually belongs. This is particularly true in the works of contemporary ulama, who have become increasingly aware of the implications of the assumptions of ownership and purchase in the marriage contract for male-female relationships. Noel Coulson is among a few scholars who have drawn attention to similarities between a contract of marriage and a contract of sale, *bay'.* In his view, "if *nikah* is classified, however artificially, by Muslim jurisprudence as a type of sale, *bay',* which results in the transfer of an absolute proprietary, *mut'a* falls under the head of hire or lease, *ijarih,* as being the transfer of the uses only for a limited period" (1964, 111). With this view I concur. Having made this analogy, however, Coulson does not pursue the argument further, but I believe the legal, economic, and social implications of conceptualizing the marital relationship in this way are far-reaching and profound.

Little analysis has been made of the logic of marriage contract from the point of view of Islamic jurisprudence. Schacht argues that since there is no general term for obligation in Islamic legal terminology, the most common ground for an obligation is the contract, *'aqd,* which is the field of "pecuniary transactions" (1964, 194–95). *'Aqd* is an Arabic term meaning literally "to coagulate" or "to knot." Unlike the concept of contract in the West (see Kressel and Gilmore 1970), "Islamic law does not recognize the liberty of contract, but it provides an appreciable measure of freedom within fixed types. Liberty of contract would be incompatible with the ethical control of legal transactions" (Schacht 1964, 144). Freedom within fixed types of contracts means inserting mutually agreeable clauses in the contract, legally known as "conditions decided at the time of the contract" (Sadiqi Guldar 1986, 707).

Shi'i jurisprudence defines a contract of sale as "the exchange of valuables for the ownership, *tamlik,* of a specific object" (Jabiri-Arablu 1983, 62–63; Langarudi 1976, 118; Imami 1974, 1:416–17). Meaning to purchase, *bay'* is an irrevocable, *lazim,*[6] contract that legally constitutes the core of Islamic law of obligations and is the most comprehensive form of contracts in Islam (Schacht 1964, 151–52; Imami 1974, 1:416; "Bay' " 1953, 47). In a contract of sale one distinguishes the object of sale, *mabi',* from its price, *saman,* each being the exchange value, *'avaz,* of the other. The structure of a contract of marriage, *nikah,* as will become gradually clear, closely replicates the essential elements of a contract of *bay'*.

A contract of lease, *'ijarih,* on the other hand, is defined as "the exchange of the *usufruct* of a specific object for a specific *sum*" (emphasis added). Like a contract of sale, a contract of lease is an "exchange contract," with the difference that in the case of sale what is exchanged is the good itself, whereas in the case of lease it is its usufruct (Hilli MN, 196; *Luma'ih,* 5; Langarudi 1976, 7; Imami 1973, 2:1; see also Schacht 1964, 154–55). In a contract of lease, the object of lease, *musta'jirih,* is to be distinguished from its wage, *ajr,* each being the exchange value of the other. A contract of *mut'a* marriage belongs to this category of contracts.

Contracts of sale and lease differ in that the assumption is that ownership is permanent in the former but is temporary in the latter. Further, the object of lease can be either the usufruct of objects, as in the rental of a house, or of animals, as in the rental of a horse for transportation, or of the fruits of labor of a human being, as in the hiring of a person to perform a task. A contract of *mut'a* marriage is closest to the last category. The object of lease ought to be clearly spelled out. If, for instance, one hires a person as a cook, one cannot demand housecleaning as well, unless otherwise agreed upon (for details see Hilli MN, 196–98; *Luma'ih*, 2–19; Imami 1973, 2:1–65; Schacht 1964, 154–55; see also the section on nonsexual *sigheh*, chapter 4).

The analogy between a contract of temporary marriage and a contract of lease is not really new. Many of the classic ulama, religious and legal scholars, and even some of the contemporary legal experts have explicitly or implicitly alluded to the similarities between the two, referring, unreflexively, to the woman as the object of lease, *musta'jirih* (Hilli SI, 509–10; Tusi 1964, 497–502; Imami 1973, 2:1–65; Langarudi[7] 1976, 118–23; Katuzian 1978, 149–52). The present work aims to decode such formulation, to shed light on the underlying conceptual assumptions, and to explore the implications of this analogy for the genders and their relationship. This analogy, however, has been vehemently contested by some of the contemporary ulama, who are more cognizant of the image of woman as projected in a contract of temporary marriage. They have espoused different interpretations of the institution of temporary marriage, which I shall discuss later (see Khomeini 1982a, 38–40; Mutahhari 1981, 54; Makarim-i Shirazi 1968, 376; Kashif al-Ghita' 1968, 254–81).

As for categorizing a contract of permanent marriage, the ulama have been more ambivalent as well as ambiguous. All agree that *nikah* is a form of commutative contract, an *'aqd,* or a "sort of ownership," in Hilli's words (SI, 517; see also Kashif al-Ghita' 1968, 253). Most, however, seem to "misrecognize" (Bordieu 1977, 5–6) the structural similarities between the two, though acknowledging it implicitly in their works.

2

PERMANENT MARRIAGE: *NIKAH*

RECOMMENDING MARRIAGE HIGHLY, the Prophet Muhammad condemned celibacy. "Marriage is my tradition," he is said to have stated. "He who rejects my tradition is not my follower." Not only does marriage bestow social prestige and status on men and women, particularly on women, it also incurs religious merit, *savab*, on its practitioners. It involves elaborate public rituals and ceremonies and is one of the most socially crucial rites of passage in Iranian society. Traditionally, marriages have been arranged by the parents and are the culmination of involved and often lengthy negotiations between the families of bride and groom. A permanent marriage is of particular importance, and, if a couple's first marriage, it is publicly announced and celebrated lavishly. The institution of permanent marriage constitutes the core of Islamic law of marriage and divorce. A temporary marriage, by contrast, is often a man or a woman's second marriage, usually negotiated by the couple independently. It is performed individually, unceremoniously, and often even secretively.

Throughout the centuries, virtually unchanging language is used to define the Shi'i institution of marriage. Hilli (SI, 428), the thirteenth-century scholar, defines a contract of marriage as "that type of contract which ensures dominion over vagina, *buz'*, without ownership, *milkiyyat*," as in the case of a slave girl.[1] Hilli's ambivalence regarding similarities between a contract of sale and of marriage is underscored by yet another of his definitions of *nikah*. On the one hand, he suggests that "marriage is a kind of ownership" (517), but on the other, he argues "an *'aqd* [marriage] and ownership, *milkiyyat*, do not mix" (446), meaning that a man may have intercourse with his own slave girl but he may not marry her — unless he first sets her free.[2] He can, however, marry another man's slave girl. Note that Hilli's distinction is not between the existence or lack of ownership, but between what I call a "complete ownership," as in the case of owning a slave girl, and a "partial ownership," as in the case of a contract of marriage. Although legally this in-

junction makes it unlawful for a man to own his wife completely, it allows him
to own part of his wife's body and, consequently, the right to control her activities. In the tradition of his predecessors, Jabiri-Arablu, a contemporary
scholar, after giving several interpretations of the term *nikah*, concludes that
"*nikah* is a contract for the ownership, *tamlik*, of the use of [the] vagina"
(1983, 175).

Despite such a clear assumption of ownership and purchase, the
ulama have consistently avoided discussing the implications of this analogy
for the marital relationship, or what it means to conceive of marital relations
in terms of contract of exchange. Hilli provides an example again; though on
the one hand he writes that *nikah* is a "sort of ownership" and that it is
"similar to a [contract of] sale," on the other hand he emphasizes that "the
purpose of the exchange of vagina, *mu'avizih-i buz'*, is reproduction *and*
recreation, and not just financial exchange" (SI, 509–510, 450; see also Jabiri-
Arablu 1983, 175). Distinguishing a contract of permanent marriage from
that of a contract of sale, and in the spirit of the commandments in sura
2:236–37, the ulama have opined that the amount and the nature of brideprice may be left unspecified at the time of drawing up a contract (Hilli SI,
444; *Luma'ih*, 137; Mazandarani Haeri 1985, 29; Khomeini 1977, P#2419).
In this act of delay lies the lawmakers' "institutionalized misrecognition"
(Bourdieu 1977, 171) of the commercial symbolism inherent in a contract of
permanent marriage: that the structure of marriage is one in which a woman's sexual organ — and by extension herself — is "bought," or that she is
"owned" by her husband.[3] As the most important structural element in a
marriage contract, however, brideprice can never be eliminated. It is understood that one way or another, some sort of exchange will have to take place.

The ambivalence regarding classification of the contract of marriage
is underscored by the confusion surrounding the definition of the term *nikah*
itself. Emphasizing its literal meaning, some have interpreted it as intercourse, *vaty*.[4] Others, stressing its contractual and obligational aspects, have
referred to it as an *'aqd*, a contract. Citing Sahib-i Javahir, Murata writes:
"For the Sunnis *nikah* means intercourse, and since marriage implies intercourse, then the word *nikah* has been used in the contract" (1974, 2). In contrast, Murata continues, Raghib maintains, "Intercourse is not the meaning
of *nikah* because of its shamefulness, *qubh*, but that it is used as an analogy
for that [intercourse]. Therefore, the real meaning of *nikah* is *'aqd*, contract" (see also Jabiri-Arablu 1983, 174–75; Farah 1984, 14; "Nikah" 1927,
912).

Noting the diversity of opinions, Langarudi, a contemporary Iranian Shi'i scholar, argues, "*Nikah* cannot be defined as an agreement for the
establishment of family or household between a man and a woman, because
that does not include *mut'a* marriage" (1976, 3), i.e., the objective of *mut'a*

TABLE 1
Shi'i Marriage

Type of marriage	Sexual	Affinal	Legitimacy of children
Permanent, *nikah*	+	+	+
Temporary, *mut'a*	+	±	±
Nonsexual *sigheh*	−	+	−

NOTE: A plus sign (+) denotes legitimacy; a minus sign (−) denotes an implicit legal prohibition; both together (±) indicate cultural ambivalence.

is sexual pleasure. "Nor can it be defined," he continues, "as an agreement for sexual relations, for in the case of nonsexual *sigheh* [discussed in chapter 4, below] intercourse is not the objective of the agreement." Dismissing nonsexual *sigheh* as invalid, however, on the basis of the ulama's consensus, Langarudi argues, "intercourse is the raison d'être of marriage" (5).

Likewise, Imami defines *nikah* as a "legal relationship, created between a man and a woman as a result of a contract that permits them to enjoy each other sexually" (1971, 4:268). He concludes: "Therefore, the general definition of marriage as being for the purpose of establishment of family, *khanivadih*, is incorrect in the Iranian case because it does not include temporary marriage" (268),[5] that is to say, temporary marriage is contracted not for the purpose of procreation.

One is left in want of a legal definition of marriage that is structurally and functionally meaningful, as well as inclusive of permanent marriage, temporary marriage, and its variations of nonsexual *sigheh*. We may, however, summarize the essential forms and functions of Shi'i marriages (see table 1). With the aid of table 1, one can define the institution of Shi'i marriage as a contract that (1) establishes ownership and control of the husband over his wife's sexual organ, *buz'*, whether actually or symbolically, as in the case of nonsexual *sigheh*, and (2) creates bonds of affinal kinship, whether factually or fictitiously. In other words, the essential components of a Shi'i marriage are the legitimation of sexuality and the creation of affinity. The issue of legitimacy of children is therefore not at the core of a marriage contract, though it is a probable natural consequence of it (cf. Gough 1959, 68; Levine and Sangree 1980, 388). A Shi'i marriage, in its broadest meaning, takes place not to legitimate children, but to legitimate a relationship between a man and a woman, either as sexual partners or as affinal kin—a relationship that may or may not lead to the begetting of children.

THE STRUCTURAL ELEMENTS OF
PERMANENT MARRIAGE: *ARKAN*

A valid permanent marriage has three basic components: the legal form of
contract, *aqd;* the limitations on interfaith marriages, *mahal;* and the submission of brideprice, *mahr.*[6]

The Contract: *'Aqd*

An Islamic marriage is a contract and, like all forms of Islamic contracts, requires an act of offer and acceptance made in the same session.[7] An
act of "offer" involves uttering a ritualistic formula by the woman, and "acceptance" involves a similar formulaic reply by the husband. The marriage
contract ritual may be performed by a couple's representatives. The basic
rights of the spouses, such as plural wives for the husband and brideprice for
the wife, are preordained, unchanging, and inalienable. Marriage is thus a
form of contract in which "laws regarding the rights of husband and wife cannot be modified by the parties at the drawing up of the contract" ("Nikah"
1927, 914). And because of its sociological dimension, "freedom of will does
not play an important part at the time of making the contract" (Imami 1971,
4:276).

Limitations on Interfaith Marriage: *Mahal*

Islamic law places limitations on interfaith marriages. Despite the
controversy surrounding the marriage of Muslim men to non-Muslim
women, many of the Shi'i ulama view intermarriage between Muslim men
and the women of the Book—Christians and Jews—as not objectionable.
Some have included Zoroastrian women, but such inclusion or permission
has been debated among the ulama. Without any hesitation, however, intermarriage between Muslim women and non-Muslim men has been ruled out
(Tusi 1964, 463; Hilli SI, 491; *Luma'ih*, 96, 119; Khomeini 1977, P#2397;
Langarudi 1976, 93).

Brideprice: *Mahr*

The most essential component of a marriage contract is the submission—in fact or theory—of brideprice, *mahr,* to the bride herself (sura 4:4).[8]
In exchange, the husband gains a legitimate ownership right over the object

of sale, which in this case is his wife's sexual and reproductive organ. Essentially an economic transaction, brideprice payment in an Islamic marriage is also symbolically meaningful. It signifies a woman's and her family's status and prestige in the community, as well as the groom's and his family's esteem for the woman. Such symbolic meanings, however, are not uniformly shared by Iranians. In contemporary Iran, many urban educated women and men have objected to brideprice payments, viewing them as demeaning to women (see *Zan-i Ruz*, issues from 1966 to 1968).

Etymologically meaning "price" or "ransom," *mahr* is the money, or other valuables, paid or promised to be paid to the bride by the groom or his family. It is this exchange, immediate or deferred, symbolic or actual, that legitimizes a contract of marriage. The exchange of this money is so essential for the effectiveness of the contract that the wife can demand the full payment of her brideprice before agreeing to consummate the marriage, a right structurally similar to that of a vendor's refusing to submit the object of sale unless it is paid for. In fact, many of the ulama argue that paying something to the wife, no matter how small, is religiously meritorious, for "it legitimizes the intercourse" (Tusi 1964, 477). Should the wife, however, agree to consummate the marriage before actually being paid, she can no longer renege and withhold her consent in exchange for on-the-spot receipt of her brideprice. Now her action is considered disobedience, *nushuz*, and thus an infringement on the right of the husband, to whom obedience is legally due (*Luma'ih*, 143–44; Tusi 1964, 483; Hilli MN, 242; Langarudi 1976, 132–33; Imami 1974, 1:459). Nonetheless, her ownership rights over the brideprice remain intact. Usually, brideprice becomes payable when a marriage ends in divorce. So long as a wife remains obedient to her husband during the course of the contract, she is legally entitled to financial support, *nafaqih*. The legal requirement for a wife's obedience toward her husband, I suggest, rests on this element of exchange in the marital transaction.

Because marriage is a contract, from an Islamic point of view the phenomenon of intercourse, *vaty*, is inevitably intertwined with monetary exchanges. The Islamic maxims "Sexual relations invoke either payment or punishment"[9] and "Intercourse is respected," *vaty muhtaram ast*, are repeatedly invoked to indicate legitimacy — or its lack — of a sexual relation (*Luma'ih*, 2:130; Hilli SI, 450; Razi 1963, 362; Tusi 1964, 477; see also Murata 1974, 51). The exchange of this money is so indispensable that even in the case of an "intercourse on the account of a misunderstanding," *vaty-i bih shubhih*, some money in the form of brideprice must be given to the woman in order to ensure legal and moral propriety[10] (Tusi 1964, 477; Hilli SI, 520; Langarudi 1976, 28, 84; Imami 1971, 4:426–27; see also Shafa 1983, 710–11).

On the basis of the logic of a contract of sale and from the perspective of Shi'i law and ideological assumptions concerning the nature of male and female sexuality, marriage exchange involves goods of a different kind. Intercourse is not, presumably, a relational matter in which pleasure may be reciprocated in kind. It is instead perceived to be transferred in one direction only. In exchange for the sexual pleasures men receive, women ought to be compensated financially. In other words, legally, the female sexual organ and brideprice are exchanged as each other's exchange value, *'avaz*.

THE LEGAL CONSEQUENCES OF PERMANENT MARRIAGE: *AHKAM*

The Contract: *'Aqd*

Because marriage is a contract, a couple may agree on a variety of provisions as long as they do not transgress the Qur'anic boundaries. For example, a woman may insert a clause in her marriage contract requiring that she not be taken out of her place of residence. On the other hand, a woman cannot legally demand that her husband refrain from marrying a second wife while still married to her. This condition, the ulama claim, is against the explicit Qur'anic text that allows a man to make contracts of permanent marriage with four women simultaneously; it is his divinely ordained right. All agree, however, that she can use this condition as a ground for divorce (Tusi 1964, 481–82; Hilli MN, 242; Khomeini 1977, P#2451).

Permission of the Guardian: The *Vali*

The legal issue most relevant to a virgin woman's first marriage is that of her father's matrimonial guardianship, *vilayat*, the extent of his authority in controlling her choice, and his right to arrange a marriage contract for her (Hilli SI, 447). Stern (1939, 37) argues that the institution of *vali* is an Islamic creation that gives jural authority and power to the father over his daughter's activities. Howard (1975), likewise, says, "The fact that many girls were married while still children — 'Ayasha [the Prophet's wife] is the outstanding example — makes it altogether unlikely that in the days of the Prophet a virgin daughter could normally contract a marriage without the consent of her father" (83). Schacht, however, argues that the maxim "there is no valid marriage without a *vali*" was not originally self-evident in Islamic law, but that it gradually gained recognition, was adopted, and eventually projected back to the time of the Prophet (1950, 182 – 83). Schacht's view makes sense, given the fact that the wife herself was appointed by the Prophet to give her consent and to receive the brideprice.

Consequently, the vagueness in the legal boundaries of the role and function of matrimonial guardianship has led to frequent debates and disputes among Muslim legal scholars throughout the ages (for a detailed discussion of the role and function of *vali*, see Hilli SI, 447–56). Although al-Shafi'i and Malik, for instance, maintain the father's ultimate authority, *jabr*, in arranging a marriage contract for his daughter, there are traditions of the Prophet abrogating the marriage of a virgin whose father had not asked her permission (Howard 1975, 84).

For the Shi'ites, however, the extent of legal authority of a *vali* and of his right over his daughter has been particularly fraught with ambiguity. As Shi'i law developed, notes Howard, the function and role of the *vali* became intertwined with two other phenomena, namely, the necessity of witnesses for marriage and the custom of *mut'a*. The Shi'ites, he argues, opposed the abolition of *mut'a* and the requirement that a guardian's permission be necessary for a divorced woman to remarry. But faced with stiff opposition from the Sunnis, they partially accepted the advisability, not the necessity, of witnesses for a permanent marriage (1975, 85–87), but not without much dispute.

The ideological ambivalence regarding the requirement for a guardian's permission (control of women), on the one hand, and the custom of temporary marriage (male sexuality), on the other, is reflected in the interpretations of different Shi-'i scholars. Whereas Kulaini (*Al Furu' Min al-Kafi*, vol. 5) seems to uphold a view similar to the mainstream Sunnis, Tusi (1964, 472, 499) and Hilli (SI, 523) have favored the view that a mature woman—nine years and older—does not need the permission of her father to arrange a marriage contract for herself, though both concede that having his permission would be preferable. This ambivalence has persisted. Summarizing the diversity of opinions among the Shi'i ulama, Imami argues that a *vali* has the right to arrange a marriage for his minor son or daughter (1971, 4:283–88). However, on the issue of marriage of an adult virgin, *rashidih-i bakirih*, the ulama are most divided. Some believe that an adult virgin cannot marry without her *vali*'s permission, but that she does not need her father's consent to marry if she is not a virgin. In the latter case she can marry whomever she wants. Others argue that an adult virgin, like an adult man, does not need her father's permission at all. Some make a distinction between a permanent and a temporary marriage, maintaining that a father's permission is required for an adult virgin's permanent marriage, but that it is not necessary for a temporary marriage. Still others argue that, on the contrary, an adult virgin may arrange her own permanent marriage but must obtain her father's permission for a temporary marriage (Imami 1971, 4:283–88; see also Hilli SI, 443; Langarudi 1976, 23–28; cf. Katuzian 1978, 69).

Before the revolution of 1979, the Iranian civil law slightly modified
the classic Shi'i interpretation by according an adult virgin Shi'i woman,
eighteen or older, some degree of autonomy. Under certain circumstances
she could arrange her own marriage, provided that the legislators were assured of the unreasonableness of her father or paternal grandfather in their
objection to her marriage (Article 1043, cited in Langarudi 1976, 24; Katuzian 1978, 70). After the revolution, however, the Ayatollah Khomeini issued
a legal opinion, *fatwa*, asserting the necessity of the father's permission for
a virgin's first marriage, be it permanent or temporary, but without addressing the issues of age and adulthood directly (n.d., 342, 376; cf. Mutahhari
1974, 55–56).

The ambiguity in the law of matrimonial guardianship is further
compounded by the conflicting traditions attributed to the Prophet himself,
whose deeds and words constitute one of the major sources of Islamic law.
Although he sought his daughter's consent at the time of her marriage to 'Ali,
the Prophet himself married 'Ayasha, a child of six or seven, with the consent
and authority of her father. In other words, the fact that Islam requires wom-
en's consent in marriage is effectively nullified by another Islamic injunction
that permits child marriage, thereby giving fathers (or *valis*) the right to arrange marriages on behalf of their virgin daughters. A woman as a child obviously is too young to understand the magnitude of the demands on her and
is unable to make independent decisions.

Divorced and widowed women have greater legal autonomy and can
negotiate on their own behalf (Tusi 1964, 474; Hilli MN, 221; Levy 1957, 111).
In practice, however, this depends on a woman's socioeconomic background
and is subject to local variations.

Coitus Interruptus: *'Azl*

Coitus interruptus, *'azl* (lit., discharge), is perhaps the only form of
birth control permitted in Shi'i Islam, and its practice is a prerogative of the
husband.[11] Its degree of exclusivity, however, depends on whether it is exercised within the confines of a permanent or temporary marriage, or on
whether the wife is a free woman or a bondmaid. Likewise, whether the
wife's sentiment should be considered and her permission obtained has been
debated by the ulama. Whereas Tusi regards coitus interruptus not forbidden for a free woman (1964, 491), Hilli, though he considers it reprehensible,
makruh, is of the opinion that unless otherwise agreed upon *'azl* is forbidden. Should a man do so, however, he ought to pay the "blood money for em-
bryo," *diyih-i nutfih* (SI, 437).[12]

Although coitus interruptus may seem irrelevant at first, viewed within the contractual form of Shi'i marriage its discussion here makes sense. Because a man has paid the brideprice, logically, he is in "charge" of, or the "owner" of, his wife's sexual and reproductive organ. Only he can decide when and how he wants to have a sexual relation (Qur'an 2:223).

Inheritance: *Irs*

"Unto the men (of a family) belongeth a share of that which parents and near kindred leave, and unto the women a share of that which parents and near kindred leave, whether it be little or much — a legal share"[13] (Qur'an 4:7). One of the significant actions taken by Islamic law toward improving women's status was to grant them a share in their family's inheritance. Implicit in this legal provision is a recognition of a degree of woman's volition, autonomy, and independence, despite the fact that in all categories a man is to receive "the equivalent of the share of two females" (4:10 – 12, 177; see also Levy 1957, 97). In a permanent marriage, the husband's share of his wife's legacy is one-half if there are no children, and one-fourth if they have surviving children. The wife, however, is to take one-fourth and one-eighth, respectively, under the same circumstances.

The Shi'i and Sunni legal scholars, however, differ significantly in their interpretations of the principles underlying the Qur'anic injunctions in general, and the categories of agnatic and cognatic women to whom a share can be rightfully allocated. A discussion of the differences between the Sunnis and Shi'ites and the dispute between them, however, is beyond the scope of this chapter (for a full discussion, see Fayzee 1974, 387 – 467; Langarudi 1978, 2 vols.).

The Dissolution of the Marriage

Being a contract, an Islamic marriage has inevitably its own demise built into its structure. A marriage contract may be dissolved in one of at least three ways besides the death of either partner, the most important one of which is divorce, *talaq*. Other means for cutting the tie of marriage are mutual consent and annulment, *faskh*, by either the husband or the wife.

"When ye (men) put away women, put them away for their (legal) period and reckon the period, and keep your duty to Allah, your Lord. Expel them not from their houses nor let them go forth unless they commit open immorality" (sura 65:1). "Of all things permissible, divorce, *talaq*, is the most reprehensible" (Prophet Muhammad). The institution of divorce brings to light not only the profound legal differences that exist between permanent and temporary marriages but also the fundamental differences in conceptualizing the genders' needs, social statuses, roles, and relationship.

Although socially disapproved of and religiously frowned upon, divorce is a divine right of the husband (Qur'an 2:226–37 and sura of Divorce) that cannot be infringed upon. The perception of its reprehensibility is merely that, a perception, a moral injunction; it does not affect its legal permissibility.[14] He who repudiates his wife or wives must be of sound mind, mature, and willing. Further, he should recite the divorce formula in the presence of two "just" men and in clear terms, but not necessarily in the presence of his wife. Women are not permitted to stand as witnesses for a case of divorce regardless of their number (in other cases, the testimony of two women is considered equal to that of one man). A written divorce is considered invalid unless accompanied by its verbal pronouncement (Tusi 1964, 519 – 31; Hilli SI, 751 – 859; Khomeini 1977, P#2498 – 516; Imami 1974, 1:185).

Etymologically meaning to untie a knot or to let go, *talaq* legally belongs to the category of unilateral acts, *iqa'at* (sing., *iqa'*). This is to say, whereas marriage is a form of contract based on mutual consent, divorce is a unilateral decision made by the husband. We may ask here: if marriage is a contract requiring mutual consent, then how could its dissolution preempt the right of one of the parties? Here lies the most important distinction between a contract of marriage and a contract of sale. A contract of sale establishes a legal relationship between any two individuals (or groups). An irrevocable contract, if entered into under lawful conditions, it can be canceled by either party in case of fraud, deception, or defect. But a contract of marriage is both irrevocable and revocable simultaneously! This is to say, as far as the husband is concerned, a contract of marriage is both permissible, *ja'yiz*, and revocable; he can divorce his wife any time he wants. The same contract, however, becomes irrevocable, *lazim*, as far as the wife is concerned. She cannot cancel the contract unilaterally; that right is reserved for her husband. In addition to establishing a legal relation, a contract of marriage legitimizes a *sexual* relation between a man and a woman. Acting as an intermediary between God and his wife, a husband is empowered to act individually.[15] Just as a divine command supersedes human laws, a husband's wishes take precedence over those of his wife. It follows that, although marriage is essentially a contract of sale in form and procedure, its termination does not necessarily require mutual consent.

At the time of divorce certain conditions must be met by the wife before it can be finalized. First, she must be a permanent wife, *zaujih*, and not a temporary wife, *sigheh*, for no divorce exists in the case of the latter.

Second, the wife ought not be in her menstrual period and ought to be cleared of impurities associated with childbirth, that is to say, she must have had at least one menstrual cycle since the delivery. Finally, in case a man has more than one wife, the wife to be divorced ought to be named in person. Should the situation not meet any of these conditions, the law requires that the divorce be postponed.

On the other hand, five categories of women may be divorced at *any time*. These include women "who are obviously pregnant"; "who have not been penetrated after signing the marriage contract"; "whose husbands have been absent for a long time," that is, no possibility of sexual intercourse exists; "who have not begun their menses yet," that is, are below the age of nine;[16] and those "whose monthly cycles have ceased," that is, are past menopause (ibid.).

These provisions are all essentially based on two premises: (1) whether or not the act of intercourse has taken place, that is to say, the object of sale has been used; and if so, (2) whether or not the woman is pregnant, to determine paternity. The underlying assumption is that since a contract of marriage establishes ownership of the wife's sexual and reproductive organs, any products of this relationship also belong to the father.

It is within this context that brideprice payment must be understood. Brideprice usually becomes payable upon divorce. The actual payment, however, depends upon the accomplishment of "penetration," *dukhul*.[17] Further, depending on whether the brideprice has been specified in the marriage contract at the time of drawing up the contract, two possibilities may exist. First, if the wife is divorced before penetration, the majority of the ulama maintain that she is entitled to half of her brideprice. If, however, she is divorced after penetration, she is to receive the full amount. Second, where the brideprice is left unspecified in the contract, if the wife is divorced before consummation, she is entitled to a sum or other valuables given to her according to her husband's wishes; but if she is divorced after the consummation of marriage, the husband must give her a sum befitting her status and family pedigree (Hilli MN, 241; Tusi 1964, 477–78; *Luma'ih*, 128).

According to Shi'i Islamic law, a divorce may take several forms, the most common form of which is that of returnable divorce. A returnable, *rij'i*, divorce is a semifinal divorce in which bonds of marriage are not completely severed. Although the husband and wife are separated from each other, the wife cannot marry within the next three months following the divorce, and the husband has the right of returning to his wife during this period (discussed below) and to resume his marital duties. A husband's right to return is unilateral, meaning that legally the wife's consent is not sought. Just as he has the right of return, however, she has the right to maintenance (Khomeini

1977, P#2525; Langarudi 1976, 245–48; Katuzian 1978, 382). Before Islam, a husband could apparently return to his wife indefinitely and could thus keep her in a suspended state. The Prophet Muhammad tried to put an end to this practice by limiting the number of times a husband could have the right to repudiate his wife and then take her back again (Qur'an 2:231; Maybudi 1952–61, 1:617; Langarudi 1976, 92). Islamic law stipulates that a man may divorce his wife twice and then return to her during her waiting period. But after the third time the divorce is no longer returnable but is, rather, irrevocable. Unlike the Sunni law that permits the pronouncement of a triple "I divorce thee" at once, Shi'i law prohibits such an act, viewing it unbinding.

An irrevocable divorce, *ba'in*, occurs when the dissolution of marriage is final from the moment of its pronouncement. In this form of divorce the husband's right to return and the wife's right to maintenance are both curtailed. The wife, however, has to abstain from sexual intercourse by observing her allotted three-month waiting period. Divorce of a woman past her menopause, a girl who has not reached the age of menstruation,[18] or a woman who has been divorced twice under the returnable kind is irrevocable. In the former two cases, however, the wife is also not bound to maintain abstinence after divorce.

Despite a general perception otherwise, Islamic law does have provisions whereby a woman can initiate divorce proceedings. Her right to apply for dissolution of marriage, however, is different from that of the man's: she cannot implement her decision unilaterally; it has to be litigated upon. The dissolution of marriage initiated by women may take two forms. A woman may initiate divorce and buy back, as it were, her freedom. The Qur'an puts it this way: "And it is not lawful for you that ye take from women aught of that which ye have given them; . . . And if ye fear that they may not be able to keep the limits of Allah, in that case it is no sin for either of them if the woman ransom herself" (2:229). Apparently, fearing the inevitable transgression of God's limit, Islamic law has adopted the second part of this rather ambivalent injunction in the form of divorce of the *khul'* kind.

In metaphorical language the Qur'an refers to man and wife as each other's "raiment" that clothe and cover one another (2:187). Properly speaking, *khul'* means to take off, for instance, one's clothes. A divorce of the *khul'* kind is initiated by a woman who feels strong reluctance toward her husband and is no longer willing to "wear" him, as it were. Because marriage is a contract, and because some money in the form of brideprice has been exchanged, actually or symbolically, the wife therefore may obtain her freedom *in exchange* for some money equal to, more, or less than her brideprice (Hilli MN, 257; Khomeini 1977, P#2528; Langarudi 1976, 252; Robertson Smith 1903, 92; Levy 1957, 122).

Significantly, *khul'* is not a unilateral privilege of women, the same way divorce, *talaq*, is for men. Rather, it is considered as a contract of exchange in which mutual agreement and acceptance play fundamental roles. Legally speaking, therefore, *khul'* is not the equivalent of divorce, *talaq*, though it serves the same purpose. This is why the term *khul'* and not *talaq* is used. Although local custom may greatly influence the custom of *khul'*, in the Muslim tradition "*khul'* can never be enforced unilaterally by the wife herself" (Coulson 1959, 19). This means that the husband must agree to it, for *khul'* is a contract and so requires the mutual consent of husband and wife. A divorce of the *khul'* kind is irrevocable: the husband and wife both forgo their rights of return and maintenance during the wife's three-month waiting period.

Meaning separation, *mubarat* is another variation on the theme of divorce, with this difference: here the feeling of dislike is mutual. Like repudiation of the *khul'* kind, *mubarat* is an irrevocable divorce, meaning that no provisions are envisioned for the spouses during the wife's waiting period. Here, too, she has to ransom herself by paying something equal to or less than her brideprice to her husband in return for her freedom. It ought not be more than her brideprice, because in this situation neither one is happy with the marriage.

The existence or lack of certain conditions in a marriage contract gives *both* the husband and wife an option to annul the marriage contract (Imami 1971, 4:363; Schacht 1964, 148).[19] Because of the greater sociological dimension of marriage, argues Imami, the option to annul a marriage contract is limited to three of the several other variations of cancellation specified for a contract of sale (1971, 4:363). Although in the case of both annulment and divorce the marital relation is severed, annulment is not legally equivalent to divorce (Hilli MN, 238; Imami 1971, 4:476).

Divorce and annulment are antitheses, for they reflect the divine and the secular dimensions of a marriage contract, respectively. Whereas divorce cuts across the law of Muslim contract of sale by being the exclusive right of the husband, the annulment of marriage follows directly the procedures and format of a contract of sale: it is a mutual privilege. The husband and wife both have the right to annul a marriage contract.

As for temporary marriage, however, the consensus of the ulama is that the temporary wife has no right to annul the contract, for she is the object of lease.

The Waiting Period: '*Idda*

'*Idda* is the prescribed period of sexual abstinence for a woman, starting immediately after a divorce or the husband's death. During this period she cannot remarry and must wait a divinely specified number of months. The *'idda* of divorce is three menstrual cycles for women who menstruate regularly (Qur'an 2:228), or three months for women who are at an age where they normally ought to menstruate but for some physiological reason are unable to. Women past their menopause are exempt from sexual abstinence. The waiting period of a divorced pregnant woman lasts until the delivery of the child. The death of a husband, however, confines his wife to a period of four months and ten days of sexual abstinence, regardless of whether she is pregnant, past her menopause, or below the age of puberty (Qur'an 2:234).

The purpose of observing *'idda* is twofold: First, to make sure the woman is not pregnant by the man who has divorced her, and second, to "purify her womb," *tathir-i rahim*, for the next man who might be marrying her. Paternity, according to Islamic patriarchal ideology, must be known in order to establish legitimacy and to prevent the so-called confusion of parentage, *khilt-i nasab*.

No comparable provision for sexual abstinence is deemed necessary for men. They are, however, obliged to pay *nafaqih*, financial support, to their wives during this waiting period. This obligation is mandatory only if the divorce is of the returnable kind, *rij'i*. Despite a wife's obligation to observe an even longer period of abstinence in the case of her husband's death, she is not entitled to a comparable right to financial maintenance during the same period.[20]

The obligation to keep *'idda*, like the payment of brideprice, depends on the accomplishment of penetration. Keeping *'idda* is not required where marriage has not been consummated. Nor is abstinence necessary for women past menopause, *ya'isih* (from the verb to despair, i.e., of pregnancy). Those under the age of nine likewise are exempt from abstinence, regardless of whether or not consummation has taken place. In all these categories the assumption is that a possibility of pregnancy is remote, and therefore a mixing of parentage is prevented. Legally, such women can make another contract of marriage immediately after a divorce (Khomeini 1977, P#2510; Khu'i 1977, P#2510; Imami 1973, 5:75, 128). Purity of womb—or its pollution—is religiously meaningful insofar as the separation of potential paternal genes is concerned. A woman past menopause, therefore, does not pose a threat to men by getting their seeds mixed up.

THE RECIPROCAL RIGHTS AND OBLIGATIONS OF THE SPOUSES

The reciprocal marital rights and obligations emanating from the contractual form of marriage are essentially laid out in the Qur'an and are believed to be divine, fundamental, and unchanging. In exchange for the legitimate and exclusive right to his wife's sexuality, the husband is obliged to support her financially. Hijazi puts it parsimoniously: "sexual pleasure, *tamattu'* is the inalienable right of a husband, and maintenance, *nafaqih* is that of the wife" (1966, 155). The prompt payment of a wife's maintenance is, however, tied in with her obedience, *tamkin*, and good behavior toward her husband. The importance of obedience—which is legally binding on married women—is repeatedly underscored in the Qur'an, resonating in the literature of the religious elite as well as in popular culture throughout the centuries. The Holy Book instructs men to treat their disobedient wives accordingly: "As for those of whom ye fear rebellion, admonish [banish] them to beds apart, and scourge them. Then if they obey you, seek not a way against them. Lo! Allah is ever High, Exalted, Great" (2:34; see also Maybudi for an interpretation of the sura of Women, 1952–61, 2:401–792).

The Ayatollah Khomeini's comments are indicative of the continuity of his predecessor's rationale. "A permanent wife," he writes, "must not leave the house without her husband's permission, and must submit, *taslim*, herself for whatever pleasure he wants. . . . In this case her maintenance is incumbent upon her husband. If she does not obey him, she is a sinner, *gunahkar*, and has no right of clothing, housing, or sleeping" (1977, P#2412–13, and 1983, 115; see also Hilli SI, 715–32; Tusi 1964, 483; Khu'i 1977, P#2412; Imami 1971, 4:47; Langarudi 1976, 173; Ardistani n.d., 239; Schacht 1964, 166). Majlisi, the most prominent seventeenth-century Shi'i scholar, relates the following sayings from the Prophet: "Any time a husband wants to have intercourse with his wife she should not deny him, not even if she is riding a camel" (n.d., 76). This is to say, even if she is all but ready to go on a trip, she should cancel her own plans and obey her husband.

Given the logic of a contract of sale, a wife's right to sexual pleasure and intimacy is more limited than her husband's, and apparently it involves completely different categories of logic and thought. Legally, men are required to spend every fourth night with one of their wives. This is known as the right of sleeping arrangement, *haqq-i hamkhabigi*—though Ayatollah Khomeini does not see this as necessary—and its purpose is that a man fulfill the quota of justice and fairness to all of his wives. Should he have one wife, he can of course spend as many nights with her as he wishes. But the minimum number of nights allocated to any particular wife is once every fourth night (Khomeini 1977, P#2417–18; Imami 1971, 4:445). Even though by law a man is obliged to spend certain evenings with one of his wives, he is *not* required to have intercourse with her.

Islamic law, however, is not totally oblivious to female sexuality. Muslim women are entitled to a right of intercourse, *haqq-i vatye*, which obliges the husband to be intimate with his wife no less than once every fourth month. The assumption here is that, biologically, men and women have fundamentally different sexual makeups and needs. Whereas a man cannot—and should not—sexually restrain himself and must be satisfied on demand, a woman can and must wait her turn. The underlying assumption is twofold. First, as "purchasers" in a contract of marriage, men are "in charge" of their wives because they pay for them (sura 4:34), and naturally they ought to be able to *control* their wives' activities. Second, women are required to submit that for which they have been paid—or have been promised payment. It follows that women ought to be *obedient* to their husbands.

The legal term for both a wife's disobedience and a husband's refusal of support is *nushuz*, meaning disobedience of one's marital duties (Langarudi 1967, 173; Imami 1971, 4:453). However, a wife who refuses to grant her husband's sexual wishes or who disobeys him altogether is popularly labeled *nashizih*, disobedient, or recalcitrant. Not only is the husband spared such a pejorative cultural categorization, but he can use his discretion in interpreting his wife's disobedience and execute his privileges accordingly. The ambiguity inherent in this injunction lends itself to caprice on the part of the husband, bringing his right directly under his own jurisdiction. He can exercise his privilege independently, individually, and immediately. Should he, for instance, have an eccentric taste in sexual matters that is not shared by his wife, he can stop providing for her should she refuse to concede (see Tuba's life history, chapter 5).[21]

In contrast, a wife's right is conditional and much more limited. If indeed she has been "disobedient," she has little if any legal recourse. However, if she believes that she has been unjustly deprived of her right, she can take her case to a judge and demand the resumption of her allowance. Upon hearing both sides, the judge will then make an appropriate decision. If the husband still refuses to support her, she can use this as grounds for divorce (Article 1129, civil law, cited by Langarudi 1976, 223; see also *Huquq-i Zan dar Dauran*, 1983:78–80). Unlike her husband's, a wife's right is conditional and passive: one that must be acted upon, not by the wife herself, but by some higher authority.

3

TEMPORARY MARRIAGE: *MUT'A*

I do not like a Muslim man who passes out from this world
without having practiced one of the Prophet's traditions.
One of these traditions is *mut'a* of women.
—IMAM JA'FAR-I SADIQ, as quoted by
Mulla Akhund-i Qazvini

KINSHIP AND MARRIAGE among the pre-Islamic Arabs has long been a
fascinating and controversial topic. The panorama of variations has tantalized many a writer's imagination and prompted a whole range of interpretations. Although there has never been an agreement as to how to interpret the status of the pre-Islamic woman, there seems to have been
relative unanimity on the diversity of conjugal unions and looseness of marital ties in pre-Islamic Arabia.

Contrary to what many Iranians, including some scholars, believe,
mut'a marriage is not an Islamic innovation created for the well-being of the
community of believers.[1] Rather, this form of sexual union was an ancient
pre-Islamic custom practiced by some Arabian tribes (Robertson Smith
1903, 35; Nuri 1968, 22–34; Fayzee 1974, 8; Patai 1976, 127).[2] In its pre-
Islamic form, *mut'a* was a "temporary alliance" between a woman and a
man, often a stranger who was seeking protection among her "tribe." He
would be given a "spear and a tent" as means of incorporating him into the
group politically and affinally. Since the woman lived among her own tribe,
Robertson Smith argues, she maintained close ties with her kin and continued to enjoy their support and protection. Children born during such temporary unions traced their descent through the mother's lineage and would
remain with her tribe, whether or not the father would take up a permanent
settlement among his wife's tribesmen (Robertson Smith 1903, 77, 82, 85;
Gibb 1953, 418; Patai 1976, 127–28).

49

This form of temporary alliance was common at the time of the Prophet Muhammad, and many of his early converts were children of *mut'a* unions: Adi, the son of Hatim and Maw'ya, is an example.[3] (See Amini 1924, 6:129, 198–240, for a list of the Prophet's companions who reportedly contracted temporary marriages; Tabataba'i 1975, 227; Robertson Smith 1903, 81.) The institution of temporary marriage was outlawed by the second caliph, 'Umar, who viewed it as fornication, a view perceived to be fallacious by Shi'i Muslims, who have continued to practice temporary marriage. The Shi'i and Sunni ulama never ceased to argue about the legitimacy of temporary marriage, a dispute I shall discuss after first describing and discussing the institution of temporary marriage in some detail.

Mut'a, an Arabic term, has been defined as: *(a)* "that which gives benefits, but for a short while"; *(b)* "enjoyment," "pleasure, i.e., to saturate"; and *(c)* "to have the usufruct of something" (Dihkhuda 1959, 318). It is from the same root word as *mata'*, meaning merchandise, goods, or commodity.[4] In the case of a marriage, "A man agrees to give a woman something for a specified period in return for her sexual favors, with the understanding that there would be no marriage (nikah) in the beginning nor a divorce at the end" (cited in Murata 1974, 37; Shafa'i 1973, 13–15). Ideologically, the Shi'i doctrine distinguishes temporary marriage, *mut'a*, from permanent marriage, *nikah*, in that the objective of *mut'a* is sexual enjoyment whereas that of *nikah* is procreation. This fundamental conceptual and legal distinction is embedded in Shi'i assumptions concerning the "natural" differences between men and women.

Whereas the Arabs make a linguistic and legal distinction between *nikah*, marriage, and *mut'a*, pleasure, the contemporary Iranian ulama collapse the two categories linguistically by referring to them as marriage: *iz-divaj-i da'im* and *izdivaj-i muvaqqat*, permanent and temporary marriage, respectively. One seldom hears a reference among the ulama to the term *mut'a*, sexual pleasure (still less to *sigheh*). Although the specified purpose of this form of marriage is sexual pleasure, the contemporary religious language that describes it places — or misplaces — the emphasis on its marital aspect, creating thereby the impression that *mut'a* is simply a form of marriage but with a built-in time limit. Such linguistic ambiguities, as we shall see, foster confusion and misunderstanding among many women and men who have made use of this form of marriage contract.

Outside of religious circles, everyday language has remained more faithful to the literal meaning of *mut'a*. Virtually everyone uses the term *sigheh*, which properly speaking means "form" or "type" of a contract, instead of *mut'a* or *izdivaj-i muvaqqat*. *Sigheh* is a pejorative term that has been colloquially applied to a woman who is temporarily married, but the term is not applied to a man. It is significant that there are different terms of address for "wife" used in the two forms of marriage. In a contract of permanent marriage a woman is referred to as wife, *zawjih*, but she is called a *sigheh* in a contract of temporary marriage. Further, Persians seldom if ever use the term *sigheh* marriage, *izdivaj-i sigheh*. Either they use the term *izdivaj-i muvaqqat*, "temporary marriage," or *sigheh*. A man does *sigheh*, whereas a woman, ambiguously enough, either becomes a *sigheh* or is a *sigheh*.

Because any clear Qur'anic prescriptions or prophetic instructions were lacking, *mut'a* marriage was gradually conceptualized and given legal boundaries that defined its relation to permanent marriage during the period of transition following the advent of Islam ("Nikah" 1927, 419). Rules and procedures regarding *mut'a* developed piecemeal and by analogical reasoning at a much later date.[5] This is to say, although *mut'a* is regarded as having a divine origin, its procedure has been reconstructed by the Shi'i religious leaders within the framework of a contract of lease, and in relation to permanent and slave forms of marriage. Its present form is the outcome of frequent dialogues and debates among the Shi'i scholars, the most prominent of whom is the sixth imam, Ja'far-i Sadiq.

THE STRUCTURAL ELEMENTS OF *MUT'A* MARRIAGE: *ARKAN*

A contract of *mut'a* marriage has four basic components essential for its conclusion: the legal form of contract, *sigheh;* the limitations on interfaith marriages, *mahal;* the duration of temporary marriage, *ajal;* and the consideration or payment, *ajr.*

The Legal Form of Contract: *Sigheh*

Mut'a is a contract, and like any other contract in Islam, it requires an act of offer, *ijab*, made by the woman, and acceptance, *gabul*, made by the man. Because *mut'a* is a contract, however, the act of offer and acceptance may be performed by either the man or the woman (Khomeini 1977, P#2363), and the ceremony may be performed by either the man and the woman themselves, or by a mulla. Usually, a couple negotiates the contract and executes the ceremony privately and alone. The *mut'a* marriage ceremony is very simple, becoming effective upon the utterance of the following formula. The woman says, "I, [name], marry [or *mut'a*] thee, for the amount of [money] and for such and such period," and the man says, "I accept." It may be performed privately and in any language as long as the partners know exactly what they are saying and what the terms of their agreement are. As distinct from the contemporary ulama, the classic Shi'i ulama have uniformly and consistently referred to *mut'a* woman as *musta'jirih*, the object of lease. Being more reflective on the implications of using such terminology, however, and mindful of the mounting objection to the images of women projected in this form of marriage, the contemporary ulama have vehemently objected to the use of this term (Mutahhari 1981, 54).

The Limitations on Interfaith Marriage: *Mahal*

A Muslim man is religiously permitted to enter upon a contract of *mut'a* marriage with women of the Book: Christians, Jews, and sometimes Zoroastrians. It is recommended that women be chosen from among the chaste ones and be asked whether or not they are in their waiting period, although it is reported that the Imam Ja'far-i Sadiq perceived such questioning as unnecessary (see also Hilli MN, 231; Khomeini 1977, P#2397; Shafa'i 1973, 177 – 78). Muslim women, on the other hand, are forbidden to marry anyone but Muslims.

The Duration of Temporary Marriage: *Ajal*

The time, *ajal*, that a *mut'a* marriage shall last must be made quantifiably clear (e.g., two hours or ninety-nine years). For that matter, one cannot designate one's lifetime as the length of a *mut'a* marriage because this timing is imprecise. Erroneously, however, many Iranian women are under the impression that a *sigheh* for life, known as *sigheh 'umri*, is not only legally correct but that it is a token of a man's esteem for them — presumably for its temporal resemblance to permanent marriage — and an indication of greater financial and emotional security. In addition, it is perceived to be more respectable. Many women, as we shall see, come to learn the facts in a hard way.

As in a contract of lease, the duration of a *mut'a* contract may be as long or as short as the partners want, provided that it is specified and that the partners are aware of it and agree to it. Drawing an analogy between a contract of lease and *mut'a* marriage, Katuzian writes: "The interpretation of a partner's agreement over the duration of marriage is that temporary marriage and lease, *ijarih*, are very similar" (1978, 441). On the issue of the clarity and specificity of the length of a contract of *mut'a* marriage, the Shi'i ulama have argued at length. Most are of the belief that specifying the number of occasions of intercourse, *jama'*, such as "once or twice," is not acceptable because the timing is indeterminate and imprecise (Hilli MN, 232; Shaikh-i Baha'i Amili 1911, 176; Imami 1973, 2:102). Should the partners, however, desire to be particular about their intercourse, they can do so by specifying the frequency within an unambiguous timetable in the contract. This, Hilli tells us, is not against the Qur'an or the Traditions (SI, 524). This condition, needless to say, is unique to *mut'a* marriage.

The Consideration or Payment: *Ajr*

Mut'a marriage payment, *ajr*,[6] must be of measurable quality and unambiguous; otherwise, the marriage contract is void. As I have said, brideprice, *mahr*, may be left unstated in a contract of permanent marriage. In a contract of temporary marriage, however, failure to specify the amount of consideration, *ajr*, renders the contract invalid, though this point has been challenged by a small minority of the ulama. "From a legal perspective," says Imami, "structurally a temporary marriage is exactly like the lease of people, *ijarih-i ashkhas*, and as with such contracts, in a contract of temporary marriage the length of the marriage and the money exchanged must be clear and unambiguous" (1973, 5:104). Legally, this is a major distinction between the two forms of marriage contract.

Despite, or perhaps because of, the structural similarities between a contract of *mut'a* marriage and a contract of lease, the law specifies that "no phrase or expression may be used in it [the contract] to imply that the woman is being given into the possession of the man for a valuable consideration, or a gift for hire" (Levy 1931, 1:166). Here the apparent linguistic clarity of prohibition masks the reality of exchange. As I have argued, a contract of marriage does indeed create some sort of ownership for the husband, not of the wife as a person but of her sexual and reproductive organ; whether a term to that effect can or cannot be uttered does not change the fact of the exchange and the meaning implied in it.

The payment of consideration, as in the case of a contract of permanent marriage, is directly dependent on the act of penetration, *dukhul*.[7] A contract of temporary marriage may either be dissolved at the end of the specified time or terminated unilaterally by the temporary husband. If the husband dismisses his temporary wife after the conclusion of the contract but before consummation, he is obliged to give her half of her consideration (Hilli SI, 519; Khomeini 1977, P#2431). On this issue the ulama are not

united. Some argue that she should not be given anything at all because she
has not performed the task for which she was hired.[8] If the marriage is consummated but he chooses to terminate the contract before its due time, he
is obliged to give her the full amount of her consideration (Hilli SI, 519; Imami 1973, 5:105, 121; Shafa'i 1973, 187–91). Should he, however, choose not
to have intercourse with his temporary wife yet not release her from her obligations, and assuming that she has been obedient, he is responsible for
compensating her fully: "It is as if someone rents a house but chooses not to
go there; he still has to pay" (Murata 1974, 47).

THE LEGAL CONSEQUENCES OF *MUT'A* MARRIAGE: *AHKAM*

The Legal Form of Contract: *Sigheh*

Being a contract of lease, a contract of *sigheh* must specify the precise nature
of the services rendered. Within the ordained boundaries of this form of contract, however, the partners are permitted to negotiate a variety of conditions, provided that they are not against the Qur'an and the Traditions of the
Prophet. A provision unique to *mut'a* marriage is the possibility of an agreement for nonsexual intimacy: the temporary spouses may agree to enjoy each
other's company as they see fit, except for having sexual intercourse[9] (Khomeini 1977, P#2421; Shafa'i 1973, 209). The inherent ambiguity in this condition has historically lent itself to ingenious interpretations and improvisations on the theme of temporary marriage, the subject of chapter 4.

Permission of the Guardian: The *Vali*

In their opposition to the Sunni questions about the legitimacy of
mut'a and objections to the nearly absolute power of a *vali*, the Shi'i ulama
sought to loosen the *vali*'s grip by granting autonomy to divorced or widowed
women. Accordingly, women in these categories have greater legal freedom
and personal autonomy to negotiate their own marriage contracts, be they
permanent or temporary. As for the degree of autonomy of virgin women in
negotiating their *mut'a* contracts, the ulama, as noted, are most divided.

Noting this controversy, Shafa'i relates the following *hadith* to the
Imam Ja'far-i Sadiq. "Qamat has related from Aba Abdullah who told the
Imam, 'this virgin, unbeknownst to her parents, has invited me to go to her
and expressed her interest in a *mut'a* marriage. Is it all right for me to *mut'a*
this girl?' The Imam said, 'Yes, but refrain from having intercourse with her,

for *mut'a* is shameful for virgins.' I asked, 'What if she is willing herself?' The Imam said, 'If she is willing, then it is not forbidden' " (1973:182, 226–29; see also Hilli SI, 518).

Coitus Interruptus: '*Azl*

According to Imam Ja'far-i Sadiq, "That sperm, *mani*, belongs to the man, and he can do with it whatever he pleases" (cited in Murata 1974, 54). Because the objective of *mut'a* marriage is sexual pleasure, the Shi'i scholars believe that the husband should not be burdened with the problem of unwanted children. Imam Ja'far-i Sadiq's reasoning, as represented in this quotation, was echoed repeatedly in conversations I had with mullas of different rank and stature. It is underscored frequently in the primary and secondary sources on Shi'i law and ethics. With rare unanimity, the Shi'i ulama have maintained that coitus interruptus is exclusively a man's right in a *mut'a* contract. The exclusivity of this right underlines the Shi'i conceptual ideal concerning the reciprocal role of the sexes in this form of marriage. By mutual consent, however, a wife may also practice coitus interruptus.

According to Ayatollah Mutahhari, "In fixed-term marriage the woman cannot refuse sexual intercourse with the man, but she has the option that, without causing interruption during coitus, which is harmful for the man, she may avoid pregnancy. The problems of contraception [then] have already been fully solved" (translation from source, 1981, 56). Let us consider the Ayatollah Mutahhari's comments. On the one hand, a wife cannot legally refuse her husband's sexual advances, but on the other hand, the burden of contraception is forced on her. She is the one responsible for making him feel good *and* also for preventing pregnancy. Shi'i Muslim women often find themselves in such legal and cultural double binds.

If, despite '*azl* (lit., "discharge"), a *mut'a* wife becomes pregnant, the child's legitimacy is legally secured on the basis of the Islamic maxim, "the child is of the bed." Since a contract of *mut'a* marriage requires no witnesses or registration, however, it is difficult to prove the validity of a claim. Further, should the father deny his paternity and the case is taken to court, his words are honored without the due process of *li'an*, "oath of damnation," which is required in the case of a permanent marriage.[10] Although his parental responsibilities are subsequently curtailed, depending on the circumstances and the judge's discretion, he may be reminded to be honest with himself and to fear God (Hilli SI, 525, 524; Tusi 1964, 535; Shafa'i 1973, 221; Langarudi 1976, 123). Culturally, too, children born of temporary unions often suffer stigmatized status and are usually regarded with moral ambivalence.

Inheritance: *Irs*

Temporary spouses are not legally assigned any share in each other's inheritance. Qa'imi provides the rationale: "The fundamental principle in this form of marriage is that the parties do not want to be burdened by moral, social, and economic obligations, otherwise they would marry permanently" (1974, 305). Because of the moral ambivalence associated with this form of relationship and the increasingly vociferous objections raised by the secular Iranian intelligentsia, however, the majority of contemporary Shi'i ulama have argued that because temporary marriage is a contract, the temporary spouses may negotiate such a condition in their contract. Given the form of the contract, the prevailing beliefs (such as that expressed by Qa'imi), the often extreme temporariness of the marriage contract, and women's precarious socioeconomic position at the time of making a contract of temporary marriage, it is highly unlikely that such a condition may be routinely negotiated by the partners. I did not come upon a single case in which a temporary wife had actually taken advantage of this option, or was considering it, or was even aware of it. .

The Dissolution of *Mut'a* Marriage

A contract of *mut'a* marriage dissolves *not* by a divorce decreed by the temporary husband, but simply by the expiration of the mutually agreed time. In this, *mut'a* and *nikah* are most dissimilar. The difference in the ways the two forms of Shi'i marriage are brought to an end, theoretically, is based on the broader legal categories of contracts to which they belong. On the basis of the Qur'anic right of a husband to divorce, however, the temporary husband is granted a similar right, euphemistically called "a gift of the remaining time," *bazl-i muddat*. The temporary husband has the right to summarily dismiss his *mut'a* wife by terminating the union at any time he wishes. The use of the word "gift," however, confuses the legal category of unilateral acts, *'iqa'at*, to which the husband's decision belongs.

Unlike *talaq*, however, terminating a contract of *mut'a* marriage need not be witnessed. Nor does it require the presence of certain conditions in the wife; for example, for *talaq* to be effective, the wife must not be in her monthly period. Further, a temporary husband has the right to cancel a *mut'a* marriage on the basis of all those legally perceived "imperfections" (e.g., blindness) of the wife that would give him the right to divorce in a contract of permanent marriage (Hilli SI, 762; Khomeini 1977, P#2509; Imami 1973, 5:119–20; Katuzian 1978, 443). Termination of a *mut'a* contract is always irrevocable, *ba'in*, whereas a divorce may be either of the returnable or irrevocable type.

A temporary wife, unlike a permanent wife, has no legal right to end the marriage should her husband be "defective," that is, without testicles, impotent, a eunuch. Theoretically, this should be no concern of hers, for *(a)* she is the object of lease, and *(b)* the purpose of a *mut'a* marriage is enjoyment, *not of both partners, but of the husband only*. Therefore, his physical imperfections — save that of his lunacy — are irrelevant to the efficacy of the *mut'a* contract (Imami 1973, 5:116; Shafa'i 1973, 224; Langarudi 1976, 199).

Should she, however, choose to leave him or refuse to be intimate with him, and granted that the condition of nonsexual relationship has not been specified in their contract, she must then compensate him accordingly. Here, the woman as the lessee is denying the man his right to the object of lease, her sexuality. It is presumed to be logical that she should forfeit part or all of her consideration. In such case, the temporary wife's consideration is computed on the basis of the husband's "use of the vagina," *istifadih-i buz'*. The underlying assumption is that as the object of lease, the *mut'a* woman must remain at her husband's discretion; only he can decide whether or not to be intimate with her or to dismiss her (Hilli SI, 519; Shafa'i 1973, 190; Imami 1973, 2:64, 5:106; Katuzian 1978, 443).

Some scholars have argued that "though the [*mut'a*] marriage may be terminated before the expiration of the stipulated period, it must end by mutual consent, and the husband has no power to divorce the wife without it" (Levy 1957, 117). That a husband cannot divorce his temporary wife is obvious, because there is no divorce in this form of marriage. Logically, however, though dissolving the contract should be based on mutual consent — excluding deception — such logic is not applied to a contract of temporary marriage. Were a temporary husband to be constrained from exercising his divine right to dissolve the marriage, then *mut'a* would lose any semblance of marriage altogether. Arguing that *mut'a is* marriage, Shi'i law bestows a right structurally similar to that afforded the permanent husband to the temporary husband, empowering him to cancel the temporary marriage contract before its due time. In other words, just as in the case of permanent marriage, a contract of temporary marriage is revocable by the husband but not by the wife.

The Waiting Period: *'Idda*

Regardless of the length of a *mut'a* marriage contract, women must keep a period of abstinence, *'idda*, after it ends. A feature of permanent marriages also, the *'idda* of *mut'a* is, however, shorter. The waiting period for *mut'a* marriage is two menstrual cycles for women who menstruate regularly, and forty-five days for women who are at an age where they normally ought to menstruate but for some physiological reason are unable to. As in a contract of permanent marriage, the *'idda* of pregnancy lasts until the delivery, and the *'idda* of death of the husband is four months and ten days (Tusi 1964, 548; Hilli SI, 527; Khomeini 1977, P#2515; Shafa'i 1973, 216; Imami 1973, 5:129).

The Shi'i ulama justify the *'idda* on the basis of the need to determine pregnancy and hence establish paternity. If this is the objective of the law, then the question is, Why should the *'idda* of *mut'a* be any shorter than that of *nikah?* I asked this question of many mullas and of the men and women I interviewed. As though the reason were self-evident, almost all said something to this effect: "Well, because one is marriage, *nikah*, and the other is *sigheh*," and that *nikah* is more respected. Finally, I had a chance to interview Muhsin Shafa'i, a contemporary authority on Shi'i law and the author of the book referred to above (Shafa'i 1973). He argued that in the case of divorce, there is always the possibility of return by the husband, assuming that the divorce was of the returnable kind. Therefore, the three-month waiting period is stipulated in case the husband changes his mind and decides to return to his wife. In deference to the husband and the marriage, the divorced woman must wait. In exchange, she is entitled to financial support, *nafaqih*, during this period. In a temporary marriage, on the other hand, the husband has no right of return, and by the same token, the *mut'a* wife has no right to financial support. Besides, Shafa'i argued, a temporary wife is a *musta'jirih*, the object of lease, and "should be freed to go on about her own business."

Renewal of the Temporary Marriage Contract

A *mut'a* marriage contract is renewable, but not until certain conditions are met. A temporary couple may wait for the term of the contract to expire and then renew their contract, or, just before the expiration of the ongoing contract, the husband may make a gift of the remaining time, however short, and release the wife from her obligations. They then may agree on a new contract, which could be for another temporary marriage or a permanent one. In these special cases the woman is not bound to keep *'idda*, since the marriage contract has been renewed at once with the same person[11] (Hilli MN, 232 and SI, 528; Khomeini 1977, P#2432; Imami 1973, 5:103; Shafa'i 1973, 219).

The Imam Ja'far-i Sadiq was asked whether it was lawful for a man to *mut'a* the same woman more than three times, the limit set for a permanent marriage. The imam is said to have responded: "Yes, as many times as he wants, for she is not like a free woman, *hurr*. She is an object of lease, *musta'jirih;* she [her status] is like [that of] a slave woman, *ama'* " (Kulaini 1958, 5:460).

THE RECIPROCAL RIGHTS AND OBLIGATIONS
OF TEMPORARY SPOUSES

Upon the conclusion of a contract of temporary marriage, the spouses assume a minimal number of reciprocal rights and obligations toward each other: the husband gains the right of the usufruct of the object of lease, here, of the woman's sexuality, and the temporary wife receives consideration, *ajr.* Unless it has otherwise been agreed upon, above and beyond the consideration, a *mut'a* wife is not legally entitled to financial support, not even if she is pregnant (Khomeini 1977, P#2424). "He who gets involved in a temporary marriage," Qa'imi rationalizes, "is like he who rents an inn or a hotel [i.e., a room] during his sojourn. There is no doubt that from the beginning he knows his residence is temporary" (1974, 304).

By the same rationale, although a temporary wife must obey her husband, the degree of her obedience is limited and is not as complete as that of a permanent wife; that is to say, her activities and movements do not completely fall under her husband's control. She has greater freedom and personal autonomy to establish relationships, maintain outside interests, leave the household without his permission, or even take a job.[12] He is to enjoy her company — that is, he has the right of usufruct but not of ownership. Consequently, a temporary wife's social and legal responsibilities toward her temporary husband are less restrictive than are those of a wife.

She may exercise her will as long as her activities do not interfere with her husband's rights, specifically, his right to sexual enjoyment; otherwise, her activities are forbidden (Khomeini 1977, P#2427; Katuzian 1978, 443). Part of the reason for the moral ambivalence associated with temporary marriage and *sigheh* women in Iran is to be found in the potential autonomy this form of marriage allows a woman.

In exchange, a temporary wife is not entitled either to *nafaqih* or to intercourse, which are provisioned for a permanent wife. The latter provision, however, has prompted disputes among the ulama. Hilli in his *Sharay'*, after specifying that a man should not abstain from intercourse with his wife for more than four months, adds, "this command is not limited to permanent marriage" (SI, 437), implying that the right of intercourse is extended to a temporary wife as well. In his *Mukhtasar*, however, he specifies this right in the section on permanent marriage only (MN, 220). Likewise, ayatollahs Khomeini (1977) and Khu'i (1977), although denying a *mut'a* wife's right to the every-fourth-night sleeping arrangement (1977, P#2425), assert that "a husband should not refrain from intimacy with his *mut'a* beyond a four-month period" (P#2422). Majlisi, on the other hand, while denying any right of sleeping arrangement or sexual intercourse for a temporary wife, cautions men to be aware of their wives' need for sexual satisfaction (n.d., 82). Shaikh-i Ansari and Sahab-i Javahir, on the other hand, flatly state that no

TABLE 2
A Comparison of Permanent and Temporary Marriage

Terms of contract	Permanent marriage, *nikah*	Temporary marriage, *mut'a*
Type of contract	Sale	Lease
Number of wives	Four	Unlimited
Number of husbands	One at a time	One at a time
Exchange of money	Brideprice, *mahr*	Consideration, *ajr*
Permission of *vali*	Needed	Not needed
Witnesses	Required	?
Registration	Required	?
Virginity	Required (for first marriage)	Not required
Inheritance	Spouses inherit	No inheritance
Dissolution	By divorce	By expiration of contract
Waiting period	3 months	45 days
Wife's financial support	Required	Not required
Children	Legitimate	Legitimate
Coitus interruptus	Wife's permission needed	Wife's permission not needed
Renewal of contract (marriage with the same person)	Limited	Unlimited
Denial of paternity	Oath of damnation, *li'an*, required	Oath of damnation, *li'an*, not required
Interfaith marriage	Not permitted for women	Not permitted for women
Right of sleeping arrangement	Applies	Does not apply
Right of intercourse	Applies	Does not apply

right of intercourse exists for a *mut'a* woman (cited in Murata 1974, 57), the assumption being that a temporary wife leaves the usufruct of her sexuality to the man's discretion. Technically, she has no claim over it as long as the contract is in force (see table 2).

DISPUTES BETWEEN SHI'ITES AND SUNNIS

Pinpointing *mut'a* as one of the most controversial and contentious issues in Islamic *shari'a*, Ibn-i 'Arabi (thirteenth century) succinctly summarizes the confusion surrounding the status of *mut'a* of women during the time of the Prophet (A.D. 621). According to him, *mut'a* was permissible, *mubah*, in the beginning of Islam but was forbidden after the *khaybar* war (A.D. 628), was once again permitted during the *utas* war (A.D. 629), only to be prohibited once more. In short, in Ibn-i Arabi's judgment, seven times *mut'a* was permitted and then forbidden (cited in Murata 1974, 85). Such a view, however, is vehemently disputed by the Shi'i ulama (*Luma'ih*, 126–27; Razi 1963–68, 358; Kashif al-Ghita' 1968, 256–63; Yusif Makki 1963, 13, 20, 29).

The ambivalence regarding the legitimacy of *mut'a* as marriage and its definitional attributes has persisted. The Sunni ulama generally agree with their Shi'i counterparts that *mut'a* existed at the time of the Prophet,[13] and that the Prophet even recommended it to his companions and soldiers (Fakhr-i Razi 1938, 38–53). The Shi'ites uphold the legitimacy of *mut'a* based on the sura of Woman, verse 24: "Beyond all that, is that you seek, using your wealth in wedlock and not in license. Such wives as you enjoy [*istamta'tum*] thereby, given their wages [*ujurahunna*] apportionate; it is no fault in your agreeing together, after the due apportionate. God is All-knowing, All-wise" (Qur'an 4:24).[14] Except for this rather controversial reference to *mut'a*, however, the Qur'an contains virtually no other references to this institution or to its form, procedure, and the reciprocal rights of the temporary spouses. Although the majority of the Sunni ulama agree with the Shi'ites that the reference is to *mut'a* of women—as it is often referred to by the ulama—they disagree on the following: (*a*) whether the reference in the Qur'an has been canceled, *naskh*, by subsequent Qur'anic commandments; (*b*) whether the Prophet himself took any unambiguous measures to ban it; and, (*c*) whether the second caliph, 'Umar, could legitimately outlaw *mut'a* marriage. A discussion of this chronic dispute between the Shi'ites and Sunnis sheds light on the differences in their respective worldviews of male sexuality, social control, and social order.

Anchoring their reasoning on the same sources, the Shi'i and Sunni ulama emerge with completely different interpretations and rationales for the Qur'anic commandments and the Prophet's Tradition. The Sunnis claim that the Qur'anic reference to *mut'a* was canceled by several subsequent verses in the Qur'an itself, namely, the suras of the Believers (23:5–6), Divorce (65:4), and Woman (4:3) (see also Razi 1963–68, 358–59; Shafa'i 1973, 90–92). Accordingly, the Sunnis argue that *mut'a* is not marriage because intercourse is lawful only within the confines of permanent marriage or slave ownership (Qur'an 4:3, 23:6). *Mut'a* of women, they say, is neither a form of marriage, *nikah*, nor slave ownership, *milk-i yamin*. Therefore, it is forbidden. No provisions, the Sunni argument continues, exist for inheritance for the *mut'a* spouses (4:12); that the *'idda* of *mut'a* is undetermined since its duration is not specified in the Qur'an, and that consequently the status of children in this form of sexual union is unclear. Moreover, the Sunni ulama maintain, since the number of *mut'a* wives a man can simultaneously marry is unlimited, and since there is no divorce in a *mut'a* union, therefore, the custom of *mut'a* of women has been canceled in the Qur'an itself (Fakhr-i Razi 1938, 48–51; see Shafa'i 1973, 89–96; Kashif al-Ghita' 1968, 256–61; Yusif Makki 1963, 54–57; Murata 1974, 71).

Rejecting all of these objections, the Shi'i ulama counter that *mut'a* is indeed a form of marriage and therefore legitimate. They argue that the sura of the Believers was revealed to the Prophet in Mecca before the Medinan sura of Woman in which the reference to *mut'a* is made. Logically, therefore, provisions made in the sura of Woman cannot be canceled by the sura of Believers, which precedes it. Inheritance, though a condition of permanent marriage, should not be disputed, and its absence in a *mut'a* contract need not render that union illegal. Since *mut'a is* a contract, the Shi'ites argue, the partners can thus negotiate individually and make inheritance a condition of the marriage contract.

The Sunni objection to the indeterminacy of *'idda* is also irrelevant, the Shi'ites maintain. Because *mut'a is* marriage, a waiting period is automatically envisioned for it. Acknowledging, however, that the objectives of *mut'a* and *nikah* are different, the Shi'ites have determined the waiting period assigned for *mut'a* to be two menstrual cycles, or forty-five days, just as in the case of slave marriage. As for the Sunni objection to the confusion of descent, the Shi'i ulama subscribe to the same rationale. Because *mut'a* is marriage, intercourse is therefore legitimate, and where the legitimacy of intercourse is upheld, the legitimacy of children is automatically maintained. In addition, women are required to abstain from sexual contact after the expiration of the contract. Therefore, not only are children born of such unions considered legitimate, but for the same reason the descent need not be confused at all.[15] That the Qur'anic injunction for a specific number of wives cancels out *mut'a* is also rejected on the grounds that this command precedes the reference to *mut'a* in the same sura of Woman, and therefore cannot logically cancel *mut'a* marriage. If *mut'a* had been canceled in the Qur'an, the Shi'ites submit, then the Prophet Muhammad would have had a better knowledge of its cancellation (Kashif al-Ghita' 1968, 260–61; Mazandarani Haeri 1985, 37–38; Shafa'i 1973, 95–96; Murata 1974, 66). Moreover, *mut'a* marriage was permitted and practiced during the reign of the first caliph, Abu Bakr, whose own daughter, Asima, contracted a temporary union.

The Sunnis maintain that *mut'a*, though a custom at the time of the

Prophet, is not marriage by virtue of 'Umar's interpretation of the Prophet's intention, but that its permission at one point in history is attributable to unusual conditions of hardship for individuals and society, that is, the long separations due to war. *Mut'a* was permitted to prevent chaos and social disorder by soothing individual discomfort. The Shi'i ulama do not dispute the fact that the Prophet might have indeed recommended *mut'a* to his soldiers, but they take issue with the Sunni position that it was meant to be restricted to that particular time in history.

The Shi'i ulama have maintained all along that Muhammad never outlawed *mut'a* and that the Sunni reasoning is, in fact, tantamount to blasphemy on the grounds that they attribute to the Prophet permission for fornication (explicitly forbidden in the Qur'an), lack of sound moral judgment, and indecisiveness (Kashif al-Ghita' 1968, 263–70; Tabataba'i 1975, 227; Yusif Makki 1963, 27). Not only did the Prophet not object to the custom of *mut'a* of women, the Shi'ites argue, he in fact acknowledged the urgency of sexual desire and approved of *mut'a* as a means to satisfy it. By making sexual satisfaction attainable within a legal framework, the Shi'i ulama assume that human libidinal desire then is contained and social order is thus maintained (see Bihishti ca. 1980, 333).

Undoubtedly, it was 'Umar and not the Prophet, the Shi'ites conclude, who equated *mut'a* with fornication and ordered the penalty of stoning for those who continued to practice it. The penalty imposed by 'Umar was so extreme that it effectively silenced even the most ardent supporter of *mut'a* (Murata 1974, 75–77; Shafa'i 1973, 39–41; Yusif Makki 1963, 42). Had the Prophet prohibited *mut'a* of women, then Muhammad's other companions would have been aware of it and would have refrained from practicing it. From the Shi'i point of view therefore, 'Umar's prohibition is neither legitimate nor binding because it goes against both the text of the Qur'an and the Prophet's Tradition. Rejecting 'Umar's commandment, the Shi'ites resort to the proverbial statement that "that which has been made lawful, *halal*, by Muhammad is *halal* till the Day of Resurrection, and that which has been forbidden, *haram*, is *haram* till the Day of Resurrection" (Hilli SI, 515; *Luma'ih*, 127; Razi 1963–68, 358; Kashif al-Ghita' 1968, 372–91; Nuri 1968, 179–96; Mutahhari 1974, 21–52).[16]

Some of the Shi'i Muslims have further charged that 'Umar was motivated by a racial prejudice against the non-Arabs, whom he perceived as a threat to the purity of Arab blood, and so tried to discourage sexual unions between the Arabs and non-Arabs (see *Nasikh at-Tavarikh* n.d. 4:365; Qa'imi 1974, 296).[17] The most striking Shi'i rebuttal to 'Umar, however, is one that alleges a purely personal motivation for his action against the custom of *mut'a* (Razi Qazvini 1952, 601–602; Shafa'i 1973, 119; Majlisi as cited by Donaldson 1936, 13:316–17; see also Amin Aqa's interview, chapter 6).[18]

The Shi'i ulama justify *mut'a* marriage on the basis of human nature. Acknowledging the nature of male sexual drive, often symbolically referred to as "volcanic," they seek to contain it by prescribing a morally acceptable means to satisfy it. This recognition of the nature of human sexuality, according to their reasoning, prevents chaos and corruption and maintains social order. The works of the Shi'i ulama, scholars, and laymen from the earliest times reflect their assumptions regarding male sexuality and the central importance it occupies in society. The law provides the framework for men to satisfy their needs, and the ideology and the belief system further reflect and reinforce the law.

The Ayatollah Tabataba'i, one of the greatest contemporary Shi'i scholars, states the Shi'i ideological position as follows: "Considering the fact that permanent marriage does not satisfy the instinctive sexual urges of certain men and that adultery and fornication are according to Islam among the most deadly poisons, destroying the order and purity of human life, Islam has legalized temporary marriage under special conditions" (1975, 229). Yusif Makki, in rebutting 'Umar's prohibition of *mut'a* marriage, argues, "Man's need for marriage [a euphemism for sex] is more than his need for eating and drinking" (1963, 69). Similarly, "When a man sees a beautiful woman but is unable to gratify his desire, he is stricken by all kinds of physiological and psychological illnesses" (Fahim Kirmani 1975, 199; see also Mutahhari 1974; Shafa'i 1973; Hakim 1971, 31–32).

The centrality of male sexuality and the clarity of Shi'i argument in favor of it stand in stark contrast to the ambivalence Shi'i scholars manifest toward female sexuality. Whereas they have debated at great length on the nature and form of different types of permissible human sexuality (for a summary, see Taqavi-Rad 1977), they have been conspicuously mute and unreflective on matters of female sexuality. Though sodomy between males is punishable by death, in a heterosexual relation it is viewed as a male prerogative. Although many of the ulama regard sodomy as reprehensible, *makruh*, only a few consider it to be forbidden, *haram* (Hilli SI, 437; Khomeini n.d., 450–53). Perhaps the root of the ambivalence lies in the following Qur'anic text, which has created numerous controversies: "Your women are a tilth for you (to cultivate), so go to your tilth as you will" (2:223; see also Dashti ca. 1975, 195–96).[19]

DISCUSSION

Lévi-Strauss points out that "the reciprocal bond basic to marriage is not set up between men and women, but between men and men by means of women, who are only the principal occasion for it" (quoted by Leacock 1981,

245). Commenting on the nature of exchange, Bourdieu writes: "the lapse of time separating the gift from the counter-gift is what authorizes the deliberate oversight, the collectively maintained and approved self-deception without which symbolic exchange, a fake circulation of fake coin, would not operate. If the system is to work, the agents must not be entirely unaware of the truth of their exchange . . . which at the same time they must refuse to know and above all to recognize," (1977, 6). Decoding the concepts of contract and marital exchange, I have sought to provide some insight into the ways the Shi'i ideology perceives social order in general and marital and sexual relationships in particular.

The concept of contract, as I have tried to demonstrate, is not simply a dominant feature of interpersonal obligations and commercial transactions in a Muslim society; it is also a *model for* the interpersonal male-female relationships in Iranian culture and thus is the backbone of marriage institutions. In this section I discuss some of the legal, economic, and social implications of such a model.

The Legal Dimension

I have argued that the two forms of marriage in Iran, temporary and permanent, are distinct phenomena, having little in common legally, conceptually, and culturally. They do seem to share certain similarities in the degree of marriage prohibition and incest. This is to say, the legal prescriptions for segregation and association of the sexes apply equally to both forms of marriage (see the section on the *mahram/namahram* paradigm, in chapter 4).

The most significant distinction between the two types of marriage contract, however, lies in brideprice specification and time stipulation at the time of drawing up the contract. A contract of permanent marriage may be concluded without any amount of brideprice stated. The payment is deferred but is payable at the time of divorce. On the other hand, because the objective of *mut'a* marriage is often immediate sexual gratification and because of "the stronger commercial aspect of temporary marriage" (Imami 1973, 5:104), nonspecification of brideprice renders the contract invalid. Although both types of Shi'i marriage involve the exchange of some form of valuables, in the case of a contract of permanent marriage the stress is on its symbolic exchange and long-term reciprocities, whereas temporary marriage rests on immediate exchange and the commercial aspects of the contract.

In comparing the two institutions of marriage, I wish to draw attention to the degree to which uncertainty and ambiguity exist in the legal forms themselves. Despite the aura of permanency that the term "permanent marriage" implies, an Islamic marriage has a built-in mechanism for its demise, namely, divorce. Although the laxity of the provision of divorce breathes a potentially inherent tension into the marital relation, which lends itself to the manipulation or abuse of women, nonetheless the contract is endowed with greater legal rigor and rigidity of form and fewer structural loopholes than is the case with *mut'a* marriage. The reciprocal rights and obligations of the spouses are more extensive and enduring. Further, no moral ambivalence exists regarding the propriety of the institution, or its focal value in society. Permanent marriage bestows social prestige on the spouses, particularly on women.

By contrast, the looseness of the form of temporary marriage and the ambiguities inherent in it provide margins for alternative interpretations of behavior, greater manipulation of the institution, and improvisations of its content (the subject of part two). By the same token, although the institution of temporary marriage theoretically confers greater autonomy and decision-making power on women, at the same time it leaves them vulnerable to stigmatization, personal ambivalence, and local gossip.

I have argued that the concept of contract is the key to understanding the underlying Shi'i doctrinal assumptions concerning men, women, sexuality, and marriage. My argument rests on the historical fact that the Prophet Muhammad granted women the right to enter into a contract of marriage personally. Theoretically, it is the Muslim bride who has to give her consent and agree to her own marriage contract. She does this, however, at her own peril; she surrenders her fragile legal autonomy in exchange for social prestige, economic security, and perhaps lifelong companionship.

Although it appears paradoxical at first, in an Islamic marriage the wife is not the object of exchange (cf. Levi-Strauss 1969, 60, 65; 1974).[20] Rather, she is perceived to be in possession of the object of exchange (her reproductive capacity and sexuality),[21] which in the eyes of the law she "voluntarily" exchanges for some valuables. Ironically, however, the same structure that gives a woman the right to exercise her decision-making power deprives her of it as soon as she uses it. Prior to signing the contract of marriage, an adult Shi'i Muslim woman is accorded a relatively independent legal autonomy, but after the conclusion of the contract she is legally associated with the object of exchange, and hence she comes under the jural authority of her husband. This *association of women with the object of exchange* is at the heart of the Islamic doctrinal double image of women (naïve/cunning; sexually insatiable/innocent) as well as at the root of the ideological ambivalence toward them.

This dichotomous (or multiple?) conceptualization of women has ramifications beyond the ideology and the law. It influences the nature of gender relationships and manifests itself in a variety of ways in Islamic culture. Within the context of this worldview, a man is legally empowered with a dual relationship toward his wife: one to her as a *person* and another to her sexual and reproductive functions as an *object*. The woman, too, assumes the dual characteristics of a person and an object—characteristics that, though often subjectively blurred, nonetheless color her self-perception. This duality of self-perception, ambivalent though it may be, as we shall see forms Shi'i Iranian women's sense of subjectivity, guiding (or misguiding?) them through the rough terrain of their shifting and precarious life course. Conceptually, therefore, the relationship between husband and wife is mediated through the object of exchange, an object, that though an inherent part of a woman's body is symbolically alienated from her and placed under the ownership and control of her husband, an object that has become a highly charged cultural symbol, a cultural cynosure—a gift that bestows power on the woman who has it and authority on the man who has legal control over it.

In its most culturally valued form, it is a woman's virginity, pure and untouched, that is viewed as the supreme gift. That in Iran a woman's virginity is symbolically referred to as her capital, *sarmayih*, is evidence of this. That divorced and widowed women, as will become clear from the life stories presented later, have a poor chance of remarriage in Iran is further evidence that their "gift" is perceived to be secondhand.

The Shi'i doctrinal images of men and women as conveyed through these two forms of marriage contract are determined on the basis of a set of preordained hierarchical divine commands and natural rights. Because of the inherent assumptions of ownership and purchase in an Islamic contract of marriage, although both men and women are assumed to be partners in the contract, only men are automatically and ideologically perceived to be complete, "full" individuals: biologically, legally, socially, and psychologically. They are considered to be independent, superior, and dominant.

The Shi'i perception of women, on the other hand, is ambivalent at best. The ambivalence may be traced to the multiple images of women alluded to in the Qur'an. Although an entire sura is devoted to women, they are not addressed directly. Women sometimes are referred to as *objects* to be treated kindly or harshly (compare suras 2:232–33 with 235–37, 3:14, and 4:34, for example) and at other times as *persons* created of a "single soul" with men (4:1). Sometimes they are considered to be adults capable of entering into contracts and negotiating on their own behalf, and at other times they are considered to be minors. At one point women are said to be a "tilth" of their husbands to be cultivated (2:223); elsewhere they are said to be on equal footing before Allah in piety. In one verse men are reminded that women have rights similar to theirs, but immediately following is a verse specifying that men have a rank above them (2:228, 4:34). Such ambivalence toward women has been reinforced historically through socialization, education, and enculturation, and legitimized by pervasive patriarchal ideologies and cultural beliefs.

Despite the contemporary Shi'i ulama's assertion that Islam has elevated the status of women, the Shi'i literature is saturated with the assumptions of "female deficiency," presumably rooted in their anatomy: women are biologically inferior to men (because they menstruate); they are sexually mutilated (because they lack a penis; on this issue, see Maybudi, 1:611, who is apparently a forerunner to Freud); they are legally subservient (because they inherit less than men); and they are socioeconomically dependent (because men pay for them — see Imam 'Ali 1949, 1 – 4:170 – 71; Razi 1963–68, 313; Majlisi n.d., 79–82). The prominence of the theme of inherent deficiency of women resonates historically, finding its rationalization in the following idiomatic expression in Iran: *zanha naqis al-'aqland*, "women are mentally deficient." (For contemporary interpretations, see the Islamic regime's *Layihih-i Qisas* ca. 1980; Tabataba'i 1959, 7–30; Mutahhari 1974; Fahim Kirmani 1975, 300–306).

Those who argue that Islam has elevated women's position and those who argue that it has objectified women are both partially correct: each looks at the problem from one perspective only. The theses of exaltation and objectification of women are two dimensions of the same phenomenon, however contradictory they might appear. The first point of view stresses the partial legal autonomy of women, choosing to ignore the complexities of real life and objectifications of women *after* marriage. The second view focuses on the shrunken legal status of women *within* the institution of marriage, generalizing it to other stages of their life cycle.

The perspective offered here allows for a more complex view, one that focuses on the doctrinal ambivalence toward women yet looks simultaneously at Muslim women's status from a developmental perspective. It considers women's status not as one-dimensional and static, but as a multifaceted, dynamic phenomenon that changes as they mature, establish families, and finally are divorced or widowed. That a Muslim woman inherits less than a man or that her testimony counts as half of a man's does not change during her entire lifetime and is not the subject of study here. As far as inheritance is concerned, a woman is always assumed to be inferior to a man. What I emphasize are the ways in which a Shi'i Muslim woman's capacity of execution and obligation may or may not converge. Her autonomy to execute her right —for example, to negotiate a contract—is restricted by her obligation of obedience to her husband. This obligation takes priority over her capacity of execution not only because of strictures in the Qur'an but also because of the contractual structure of marriage.[22] Although some of the woman's legal rights, such as that of inheritance, do not change, the capacity of execution and obligation undergo significant shifts, depending on the particular stage of her development. And most important, it changes in relational terms vis-à-vis her father or husband.

The Economic Dimension

Economically, the two forms of marriage highlight the contrasting values associated with ownership of an object as opposed to having the right of usufruct to it.

Permanent marriage is a contract of sale in which the ownership of the object of sale is complete and final: "It is like buying a house," as a mulla once explained to me. It usually involves greater monetary exchange both in terms of brideprice (particularly if it is for a virgin's first marriage) and the arrangement for the wife's proper daily maintenance. Where the ownership of the object of exchange is complete, as it is in a contract of permanent marriage, greater social value and prestige are bestowed on the transaction.

A contract of temporary marriage, by contrast, is like "renting a car," as one of my informants conceptualized it. Usually it does not entail a financial transaction of significant magnitude, nor does it involve greater personal, social, and moral responsibilities for the spouses. Beyond a minimal amount of consideration, the man is under no further financial obligation unless he agrees to it. Since the objective of temporary marriage is sexual satisfaction and not reproduction, and since the temporary husband has the right of usufruct to the object of lease and not the ownership, most often the temporary spouses do not establish joint households. This condition, legally and actually, minimizes a temporary husband's control over his temporary wife.

In a contract of permanent marriage the object of sale is "sold out," as it were. Generally, in exchanges of this kind, the vendor parts company with the object of sale after the transaction is completed. In a marriage contract, however, the woman accompanies the object of sale: she carries it within herself. Ideologically, a permanent wife is associated with the object of sale, and therefore, it is presumed only natural that she ought to be more stringently controlled in this form of marriage.

In a contract of temporary marriage, a woman is *both* the lessor as well as the object of lease. She is the one who negotiates the terms of her marriage contract. This is of course technically no different from any other contract of lease where people are hired on the basis of their particular expertise, exchanging their labor for some money. In the case of a contract of temporary marriage, however, what is exchanged is not a woman's labor, but the "right" to her sexual organ. Although *mut'a* shares this feature with permanent marriage, it does not entail the wife's total submission to her husband because the exchange is not finite. In this form of marriage, legally, a woman has greater autonomy and control over her own activities. The monetary values thus vested in the female sexual organ translate into the different sociocultural values, meanings, and prestige invested in each form of marriage.

The Sociocultural Dimension

Conceptually, Shi'i Islam views women's sexual and reproductive organ as an object, a commodity — actually and symbolically — that is separated from the woman's persona and that is at the core of an individual, social, and economic transaction — an object that is abstracted, reified, and then treated as a separate entity. Sexuality though thus isolated from a woman's body is perceived by the dominant male ideology to represent her whole being; woman as a person metamorphoses into woman as an object. Women are thus ideologically perceived not only as symbols of sexuality but as the very embodiment of sex itself; woman and "it" become almost indistinguishable. Collapsing the symbol into what it stands for, Shi'i Islam views women as objects to be owned and to be jealously controlled, objects of desire to amass, to discard, to seclude, and to veil, objects of indispensable value to men's sense of power and virility. In Iranian society, therefore, sexuality comes to be a cultural cynosure (LaBarre 1980), because of which, it is simultaneously perceived as precious and treacherous to its original master.

From the perspective of Shi'i law, a Lévi-Straussian binary model of culture/nature seems to provide a perfect theoretical analogy for the male-female relationship. Men are perceived to represent law and order and to be the upholders of cultural tradition. Women, on the other hand, are representative of nature and thus are perceived to be irresistible, indispensable, capricious, powerful, and fearsome. The sexual power thus attributed to women is reinforced by the legal prescriptions and cultural beliefs that strongly warn — even forbid — men to look at their wife's vagina, for otherwise their progeny will be born blind (Hilli SI, 434; Tusi 1964, 490; see also Vieille 1978). It follows not only that women ought to be controlled and segregated but that they ought to be guarded against (Freud 1918).[23] Like the rulers and kings Freud reflected on, women are presumed to be "the bearers of that mysterious and dangerous magic power" (56) that satisfies and controls male sexual pleasure, as well as ensures the continuation of his descent. So, while men derive their authority from a divinely inspired legal and political system that locates them at the apex of sociopolitical hierarchy, women, as projected by the dominant male value system, derive their power from within themselves.

Significantly, even as Shi'i law and ideology relegate women to the realm of nature and because of which consider them to lack self-control, it also acknowledges the urgency, vulnerability, and unpredictability of male sexuality by legitimizing sexual gratification through various institutions such as permanent marriage, temporary marriage, and slave ownership. Female sexuality, however, has not been subject to legal and ideological elaboration, in and of itself. Even when women are granted certain rights, such as the right of intercourse every fourth month, these rights have really little to do with a recognition of female sexuality. The logic behind this right, in my view, rests on the legal distinction made between the recreational and reproductive aspects of sexuality, as differentiated in the objectives of temporary and permanent marriage, respectively, and on the perceived differences between the nature of male and female sexuality. Although it is hard to imagine that the Shi'i legal scholars are unaware of the interconnectedness of the two dimensions of sexuality for both men and women, the law presupposes that men enjoy sex while women enjoy having children or, in their absence, being financially compensated.

The right of intercourse is therefore an occasion to provide women with opportunity to conceive; it is not due to a "fear of unrestrained female sexuality" (Mernissi 1975, 25) — at least, not as far as the Shi'i law is concerned. A temporary wife does not have the right of intercourse every fourth month (according to the majority view), and she may be let go at any time, even immediately after intercourse — a situation forbidden in a contract of permanent marriage. Further, should she happen to be past her menopause, she is legally permitted to contract another temporary marriage, even immediately after the termination of her marriage. Because a woman is perceived as an object of lease in the first instance, her sexual satisfaction is of no concern of the man or the lawmakers. In the second case, because she is incapable of bearing any children, her sexual activities do not pose a threat to a man's purity of seed, nor are they of any concern of the law. As long as she does not transgress certain prescribed legal boundaries (e.g., marry four husbands simultaneously), a menopausal woman can marry as frequently as she likes.

In the light of the above, the thesis that Islamic ideology perceives female sexuality as "active" (Mernissi 1975) needs to be reevaluated. Shi'i Islamic ideology, as I have pointed out, does not have a clear and unambiguous notion of what constitutes female sexuality per se. Its position is not based on an intimate understanding of or a subjective feminine view of female sexuality. Rather, it is derived from what it *signifies* to men and what it most likely ought to be in *relation* to male sexuality. If Shi'i Muslim men are sexually as helpless as the Shi'i doctors legally make them to be, then it follows that the power to satisfy them, excluding homosexuality, rests with women, who possess the object of male desire. It is because of this inextricable interconnectedness that the Shi'i ideology imputes a strong sense of power to female sexuality, not as something powerful in and of itself, but powerful in the sense of what it signifies to men and in the reaction it presumably provokes in them. What the nature of female sexuality actually is and how women themselves feel or think about it, or whether female sexuality is active or passive, dormant or dynamic, is legally and ideologically left ambiguous. One can even argue that on the surface the Shi'i law appears to be negating female sexuality by placing emphasis on reproduction in permanent marriage or financial compensation in temporary marriage. Whether female sexuality is perceived to be passive, active, or ever-responsive to male needs, the underlying Shi'i assumption is always that it possesses the potential power of provoking men.

Part Two

law as local knowledge

4

THE POWER OF AMBIGUITY
Cultural Improvisations on the Theme
of Temporary Marriage

> Law . . . is local knowledge; local not just as to place,
> time, class, and variety of issues, but as to accent—
> vernacular characterizations of what happens connected
> to vernacular imaginings of what can.
> —Clifford Geertz, *Local Knowledge*

tHE LEGAL AMBIGUITIES discussed in part one find their articulations in Iranian culture in rather ingenious and innovative ways. The cultural improvisations on the theme of temporary marriage in Iran require closer scrutiny. My compilation of such improvisations is not exhaustive; rather, it consists of those that I have been able to identify in my fieldwork. Although the description of the organization and terminology is partly mine and partly indigenous, the descriptions of *sigheh* variations are entirely indigenous. By identifying variations of temporary marriage I wish to bring to light: (1) the internal diversity of the institution, reflecting the entire spectrum of male-female relationships; (2) a culturally meaningful context for negotiations of rules and ethics in a society organized around the paradigm of sex segregation; (3) the many innovative and ingenious ways some Iranians cope with ambiguities in the law and ambivalences in relationships; and (4) the ways Iranians use their ideological "maps" to guide their behaviors in a highly gender-differentiated "territory" (Bateson 1972, 180).

The term *sigheh* literally means the legal form of a contract. Colloquially, it may be used to mean the form, the way, or the formula for doing something. It may also imply a transitory situation. When, why, and how the terminological change from *mut'a* to *sigheh* took place is not quite clear. The shift may have occurred, suggests Dr. Ja'far-i Shahidi, the director of the Dihkhuda Institute in Tehran, in the mid-nineteenth century when *mut'a* had become quite popular because of the indulgence of the Qajar royal family in the custom. He postulates further that the change might have come about because of the populace's penchant for abbreviation. Instead of saying *sigheh-i mut'a*, the legal form of a *mut'a* contract, those who practiced it might have dropped the ending and gradually referred to it as *sigheh* only (personal communication 1981). In its current usage, *sigheh* has a pejorative connotation and is popularly applied to a woman who is temporarily married, but not to the man. Moreover, a temporarily married couple is seldom, if ever, referred to as married, *izdivaj kardih*, but is said to be a *sigheh*. Following an Iranian practice, I shall use the term *sigheh* as both a noun and a verb.

RULES FOR GENDER RELATIONSHIPS:
THE *MAHRAM / NAMAHRAM PARADIGM*

Islamic law conceives of gender relationships within the two categories of lawful, *mahram*, and unlawful, *namahram*. Men and women must not associate freely with each other unless their relationship is prescribed either by blood or by marriage. A *mahram* relationship is formed either through birth or marriage. Consanguineously, it involves ego's immediate family, paternal ancestors, maternal and paternal siblings, and siblings' children. Outside this limited circle of consanguineal *mahram* relationships, the only legitimate medium for establishing cross-sex relationships is marriage. Affinally, a *mahram* relationship includes parents, parental ancestors of ego's spouse(s), spouses of children, and their children. In these categories veiling is not required for women, and men need not keep their distance (see figure). Any gender relationships outside of these two *mahram* categories are unlawful, *namahram:*[1] women have to veil and rules of segregation apply.

　　　The *mahram/namahram* paradigm, or rules for segregation and association of the sexes, is one of the most fundamental and pervasive rules of social organization, social relations, and social control in Iran. Through the processes of socialization, enculturation, and education, these rules and their related principles are inculcated early in life, leaving lasting imprints. Elaborate etiquette, rituals, and local customs to further control and contain male-female relations have evolved. Symbols of segregation are evident everywhere. Walls and veils are omnipresent: from the architecture of traditional homes that distinguishes the women's quarter from that of the men's (Haeri 1981, 215–16), to public arenas that are demarcated by partitions, to

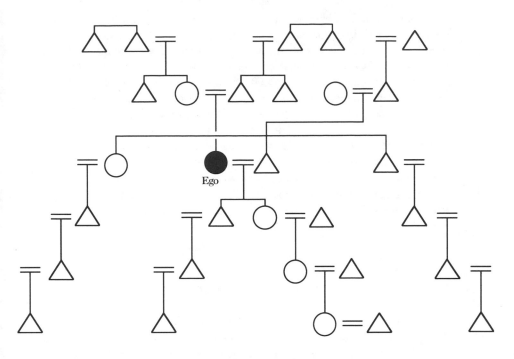

KEY: = Marriage   − Sibling | Generation
      ○ = Female   △ = Male

Mahram relationships to ego in ascending and descending order.

prescribed garments worn by women since the revolution. Walls and veils are constant reminders not only of the prescribed places of men and women in the public and private domains, but of where they stand in relation to each other. The paradigm of *mahram/namahram* and its symbolic manifestations color people's social world, informing their behavior in their daily actions and interactions. In everyday life the principle of segregation of the sexes, however, constantly poses pragmatic problems and moral dilemmas for men and women caught in various cross-cutting networks of relationships, associations, and acquaintances.

Many Iranians readily identify two distinct types of *sigheh:* sexual and nonsexual *sigheh.* Anthropologically, one may refer to these forms as actual and fictive, respectively, though natives themselves do not utilize such terminology. Shi'i ulama of all eras have written extensively on sexual *sigheh,* describing it as a divinely recommended solution for the gratification of un-avoidable sexual drive, or more precisely, male sexual drive. On the other hand, they have been generally mute on the subject of nonsexual *sigheh* and treated it, if at all, with passing comments. A few have even considered it invalid (see Langarudi 1976, 3). A nonsexual *sigheh* fulfills an entirely differ-ent purpose in interpersonal male-female relationships and communica-tions. Through an elaborate fictitious replication of kinship relations, non-sexual *sigheh* provides meaningful solutions to pragmatic problems created by the law of segregation of the sexes. Although sexual *sigheh* has a legal structure, however vague, and may be argued to be law "imposed" from above, nonsexual *sigheh* is truly a product of popular "imagination." It is con-tinually improvised by people who come face to face with moral barriers im-posed by the paradigm of sex segregation. Let us look at each type of *sigheh* in some detail.

SEXUAL *SIGHEH*

What motivates men and women to *sigheh*, and why they do it, depends on a host of variables and circumstances. The Shi'i doctrinal view has been, all along, that men contract a *sigheh* marriage motivated by sexual desires. Why women *sigheh*, however, seems to have escaped the concern of Shi'i sages. It became an issue only in the past few decades. Basing their thinking on the logic of contract, the ulama have assumed that women ought to be contract-ing a *sigheh* for financial motives. These gender-differentiated, officially for-mulated motivations were echoed repeatedly by many of my informants. Al-though such popularly held beliefs contain an element of the truth, the range of factors motivating the sexes, particularly the women, are much more com-plex and extensive than that formulated by the religious ideology.

Sigheh Associated with Pilgrimage

As Curzon observed of the city of Mashhad in 1891:

Perhaps the most extraordinary feature of Mashad life . . . is the provision that is made for the material solace of the later pilgrims during their stay in the city. In recognition of the long journeys which they have made, of the hardships which they have sustained, and of the distance by which they are severed from family and home, they are permitted, with the connivance of the ecclesiastical law and its officers, to contract temporary marriages during their sojourns in the city. There is a large permanent population of wives suitable for the purpose . . . and I should be sorry to say how many of the unmurmuring pilgrims who traverse seas and lands to kiss the gratings of the Imam's tomb are not encouraged and consoled upon their march by the prospect of an agreeable holiday and what might be described in the English vernacular as a "good spree." (1892, 1:164–65)

The city of Mashhad still enjoys the same reputation it had a century ago, if more discreetly and secretively, and much to the dislike of some high-ranking religious leaders. "In the old days in Mashhad," said Amin Aqa (a *rawzih khun*, a religious preacher) to me in 1981, "there was an old man, a shaikh, who had a worn-out scrap notebook in which he would record names and addresses of women who were interested in becoming a *sigheh*." Male pilgrims, or even some inhabitants of the city, would go to the old shaikh in the hope of finding a temporary mate during their sojourn in the city. By helping them, he would gain some *savab* (religious merit) for himself as well as for the pilgrims. Amin Aqa said that he himself vaguely remembered the shaikh, for he was just a little boy then. He assured me, however, that he did not know whether another person had continued the shaikh's vocation after his death.

Although many mullas in Mashhad and Qom are reluctant to admit that such semiorganized networks of matchmakers exist, they do not hesitate to emphasize the religious merit of *sigheh* and the fact that many people do indeed approach them to be introduced to a possible *sigheh* mate. Mulla Hashim, another religious preacher from Mashhad, told me that not only was he frequently propositioned by women pilgrims but he was also approached by men who would seek his mediating capacity to find them a *sigheh*. For the past twenty-five years he himself had contracted a *sigheh* every other week, he said, all unknown to his wife.

In the shrine of Mashhad I asked a mulla whether there was any truth to Mashhad's reputation as being a *sigheh* city. He laughed and said no, adding, however, in the same breath that a few weeks prior to our meeting he was approached by two young women on a ten-day pilgrimage who claimed to be teachers from Tehran. They told him of their vow to *sigheh* a *sayyid*, that is, a presumed descendant of the Prophet. Not being a *sayyid* himself, he instructed them to go to the Guhar Shad Mosque, a mosque adjacent to the shrine—reputed to be a place for finding *sigheh*—and to see a certain mulla whom he knew to be a *sayyid*.

Muhsin, one of my male informants, told me about a friend of his who is from a small town near Qom. Under the pretext of performing his religious duties, he would go to Qom at least twice a month, where during his pilgrimage he would arrange a *sigheh* for a couple of days before returning home. He is married and is thirty-seven years old. Oftentimes, according to Muhsin, he *sighehs* the same woman, and other times he gets a reference from a female matchmaker whom he has known for some time.

Sometimes older women, or even some men, who because of physical impairments cannot embark on the pilgrimage to Mecca, hire another person, usually a *sayyid*, to undertake the journey on their behalf. They arrange a *sigheh* marriage with the *sayyid*, often of the nonsexual type, before dispatching him on his proxy pilgrimage. According to Islamic law, spouses can perform essential rituals on behalf of each other (for another variation on the same theme see Wishard 1908, 159).

Sigheh Associated with a Vow: Sigheh Nazri

In the early days of Islam, with the Prophet Muhammad's rapid ascendance to prominence and power, more and more women sought him out and "bestowed" themselves on him without asking for or receiving any "dowry." Though Stern (1939, 155) states that it is impossible to determine if this was a form of *mut'a* marriage, the tradition of women bestowing themselves, or *hibbih*, is also recorded by Muslim theologians and historians, who held that only the Prophet was worthy of accepting such offers (Hilli SI, 438; Dashti ca. 1975, 50).

Sigheh associated with a vow, *sigheh nazri*, bears a close resemblance to the tradition of *hibbih*, except that sometimes a woman may receive a brideprice, but at other times she may offer to pay the man whom she approaches. *Sigheh nazri* seems to occur primarily around the shrines of religious leaders. Believing that *sigheh* incurs religious merit, a woman may make a vow, either for herself or on behalf of her daughter, that should her wish come true she would then contract a *sigheh*, often with a *sayyid* (many mullas are *sayyids*) who is held in great esteem. Usually the woman approaches a mulla directly and conveys her message to him. Mullas, it is believed, are generally more approachable and agreeable than others. For instance, Mulla Hashim, a religious preacher from Mashhad, claimed to have been propositioned by a woman pilgrim who made a vow to *sigheh* a *sayyid* and to pay him one hundred *tuman* (some twelve dollars). Mulla Hashim said, "I refused her because she wasn't my type. She was old."

Variations of *sigheh nazri* abound. A fifty-five-year-old custodian— not a janitor — of the shrine in Qom told me that a few months before our meeting, he was approached by a woman who told him that she had made a vow to *sigheh* her sixteen-year-old daughter to a *sayyid*. She then offered the custodian to *sigheh* her daughter in exchange for a fifty-*tuman* brideprice. The custodian said that he took a look at the little girl and refused her request. Not all women are refused, of course.

What is significant in this form of *sigheh* is that women often take the initiative and negotiate the terms of the marriage contract themselves. The activities of these veiled Iranian women challenge a Levi-Straussian model in which women are perceived as merely precious objects, exchanged by men in order to create kinship alliances.[2] On the contrary, in this type of *sigheh* women are active subjects in control of the object of exchange (their sexuality), negotiating the terms of its exchange personally.

A *sigheh nazri* and *sigheh* of pilgrimage may often coincide. Either a vow, *nazr,* is made and then the pilgrimage is undertaken, or the pilgrimage itself becomes the object of a vow, during which a pilgrim may gain added spiritual rewards by contracting a *sigheh* marriage.

Sigheh Associated with Travel

One of the objectives of *mut'a,* from the ulama's point of view, has been to provide a man with a wife at times when he is away from home, at war, on military service, or engaged in trade (Levy 1957, 116). "Men who go on trips," writes Kashif al-Ghita', "cannot take their wives and children with them. Nor can they marry permanently, because permanent marriage requires a lot of preparation. Besides, these men are often at the peak of their youth and have the rebellious rush of sexual impulse. If temporary marriage was forbidden, then what could they do?" (1968, 278–79).

There are some *hadiths,* or religious sayings, to this effect. In one attributed to 'Abdullah ibn-i Mas'ud recorded in Mussallam, it is stated, "We had gone to war. No Woman was with us. We asked the Prophet to allow us to castrate ourselves. The Prophet did not permit that, but instructed us to *mut'a* women for a piece of cloth and a specified period" (cited in Yusif Makki 1963, 12). In another *hadith* it is reported, "When the Prophet went to Mecca to perform the out-of-season pilgrimage, Meccan women adorned themselves and left their homes. The Prophet's companions complained about the length of their celibacy. He then ordered them to *mut'a* those Meccan women" (Yusif Makki 1963, 27).[3] It is still assumed to be natural that men want to — or should — marry in case they happen to be away from their wives. A *sigheh* associated with travel or trade may follow one of several variations. Sometimes a *sigheh* may be contracted when, in pursuit of his profession, a man travels from city to city. He may engage in a short-term *sigheh* in one or more of the cities he will have to frequent. He may *sigheh* a local woman and visit her when he is in that city. One of my informants told me that her father, while residing with his wife and children in Tehran some twenty-five years ago, was sent to Esfahan on assignment. While there, he contracted a *sigheh* marriage with a local Esfahani woman. This was not revealed until some time after his death, when one of his sons from his *sigheh* wife tried to locate his half-siblings. Similarly, describing his expedition into Iran in the company of some Indian Muslims, Sir Arnold Wilson writes, "All they [the Indian Muslims] need to make them perfectly happy is a wife (sigha) in every village or town we visited" (1941, 290).

A traveler may take a *sigheh* to accompany him on his trip(s). The Qajar royal family often set the trend for their subjects. When on short trips, Nasir al-Din Shah (1831–96) and some of his courtiers would leave their own wives behind in the harem but would take along one or more *sigheh* wives. Citing Aqa 'Ali Amin Huzur, I'timad al-Saltanih (the Shah's official translator and minister of communication) writes, "Today I [Aqa 'Ali] told the Shah, it was customary for your father and your grandfather to give their servants one of their wives. What harm would come of it if you give me one of your old *sigheh[s]* who would accompany your harem during the day, and would come to my tent at night?" (quoted in "Fath 'Ali Shah" 1968, 122).[4] Like his grandson, Fath 'Ali Shah's lust for female companions would even prompt him to "kidnap" them! "One night sneaking in the house of Muhammad Khan-i Davvalu," writes Pizhman Bakhtiari, "the Shah kidnapped his daughter by hiding her under his long robe, *'aba.* He immediately *sighehed* her, and then sent a message to her father that 'according to our custom I have stolen your daughter. Why don't you do likewise by stealing, *sirqat,* one of my daughters for yourself or one of your sons?' " (1965, 156).

Non-Iranians, too, sometimes availed themselves of the custom. According to Sir Arnold Wilson, "Our Indian officers and some sergeants have acquired a *sigha* who unobtrusively accompanies the luggage like a *viviandiere* and is referred to politely as a 'cook' " (Wilson 1941, 290). Likewise, with a little help from matchmakers, some Europeans who passed through Iran in the late nineteenth and early twentieth centuries contracted *sigheh* with local women. Formerly, these matchmakers frequented places such as caravansaries, offering "decent and pretty" women to the newcomers.[5]

Sir Arnold Wilson again gives us a taste of the tradition: "some ladies of unconventional virtue whose society was pressed upon me by the hospitable captain who had spent many years at sea, and assured me, knew the English and their taste. 'You do not drink,' he said, 'or smoke, but you will enjoy her'—pointing to the largest. 'She is returning after a long engagement with a very prominent Russian, and he is not . . . tired of her . . . she would make you comfortable after so long a journey' " (Wilson 1941, 10–11).[6] Sir Arnold Wilson politely refuses the captain's offer of a temporary marriage. However, his Indian guides enjoy their privileges in a far-off land (see also Mehdavi 1953, 135–47).

Natiq claims that in the late nineteenth century there were "special matchmakers" who would solicit the various embassies and consulates. Ob-

taining the names and the length of the visit of Europeans, these matchmakers would then arrange a compatible *sigheh* match for them (1975, 60). She
further claims that often Armenian and Assyrian young girls were used for
this purpose, with the knowledge and consent of their families, who viewed
the practice as a sign of prestige (59; see also Ker Porter 1821, vol. 2).[7]

Master-Maid *Sigheh*

According to Islamic law, a marriage contract may be concluded
with a slave, provided that his or her master's permission has been secured.
Cohabitation with one's own slave girl, however, is legitimate. Although
slave ownership and slave marriage appear to be all but obsolete in Muslim
societies, some aspects of it seem to have persisted in Iran and have reap-
peared in the form of a *sigheh* between some men and their house maids.

As an unrelated and unattached woman, a maid is religiously required to veil herself before all adult males in the household. For the same
reason, many Iranians believe that having a virgin maid in the household is
morally problematic, the assumption being that her presence is a constant
source of temptation for men in the household. It is, at the same time, im-
practical to carry out household chores while observing rules of segregation
and avoidance. One way of resolving such a tension between rule and practice is to perform a *sigheh* (of sexual or nonsexual type) either between the
master and the maid, or one of his sons and the maid. Having done so, the
master and the maid are considered lawful, *mahram,* to each other: the
maid may loosen up her veil before her employer and master without any fear
of moral impropriety.

It also happens that some traditional and affluent families may
sigheh their young maids to their young sons, with two purposes in mind.
The first is to follow the guidelines of propriety by making the maid lawful,
mahram, to men of the household, and therefore to allow her to carry on
with her household duties unveiled. The second and more important is to
prevent the young maturing boys from frequenting some undesirable quarters of the city. One informant told me of her husband's shock, when, as a
student, he had gone to his room one evening and found a half-naked, apprehensive teenage girl in his bed. He had returned to Iran for a summer va-
cation from France, where he had been studying. His mother had arranged
a *sigheh* for him with one of their young maids and ordered her to go to his
room and await his return (see Wishard for another variation 1908, 211–12).[8]

On their part, some maids start their jobs on the condition of being
made a *sigheh,* often of the nonsexual type, to the master of the house. What
they gain has not only pragmatic results but also symbolic consequences.

The daughter of a well-known Mashhadi ayatollah whose father had *sighehed* a few of their maids put it unambiguously: "These maids are pleased to be elevated to the status of a *sigheh*. They gain respect in the eyes of the community where they work, as well as in the eyes of their fellow villagers back home." This ayatollah is long deceased, but his wife, Bibi Jan, and her *sigheh* cowife maid, Nanih Jan, are now living together. Bibi Jan is bedridden and is being nursed by Nanih Jan; both of them are provided for by Bibi Jan's eldest son. Nanih Jan was barren. I observed, and was also told emphatically by different members of the family, that there was greater love and affection between Nanih Jan and the grandchildren than between Bibi Jan and her own grandchildren.

Another well-known ayatollah made a *sigheh* contract with one of his maids some thirty-five years ago, much to the displeasure of his wife. They had five children already. After the maid gave birth to a little boy, the first wife persuaded her husband to dismiss the maid, and she herself assumed responsibility for the boy's upbringing. The maid was given some money and was sent away. In this case, too, the relationship between the *sigheh* child and his siblings was quite cordial, defying the popular stereotypical perception of animosity between such mixed siblings.

Among the many service agencies that sprang up during the last few years of the Pahlavi regime was the so-called Maid Agency, *azhans-i mustakhdim*. The agency is still functioning under the Islamic regime, though it has fewer international maids. Nowadays, it is run by a certain hajji[9] and provides household services by maids of all types, ranging from daily to monthly to live-in maids. One particular middle-aged maid was asked why many of the would-be maids were the hajji's *sigheh*. She responded, "Because it is more respectable to be a *sigheh* than just a maid."

Whether she actually was the hajji's *sigheh* I do not know, but the point is that by claiming the status of a *sigheh* wife, she seems to realize at least three objectives. First, she creates the illusion of being more than just a maid—an occupation perceived as demeaning in Iranian society—by giving the impression of being a *sigheh* wife. Second, she lessens the chances of sexual harassment and abuse. Most places in which she will work are unknown to her, which can be anxiety-producing. By claiming the status of a married woman, albeit of a *sigheh* type, a maid is creating a sort of security wall around herself; she can presumably ward off many unforeseen problems, including a proposition of a *sigheh* marriage from an employer. Furugh Khanum, one of my informants, also a divorced maid but not from the hajji's agency, put in earnestly: "Everywhere I go, men want to marry me. They say, 'Khanum, you don't have a husband, why don't you become my wife'" (i.e., *sigheh*). Finally, she legitimizes her association and cooperation with the hajji and his organization. This last point is particularly important in view of the puritanical and punitive attitude taken by the present Islamic regime in discouraging many public forms of male-female association, and in enforcing the traditional Islamic codes of conduct.

Not all *sighehs* between masters and maids are done with the consent of the wife and the acquiescence of the maid. A man may deceive his maid(s) with a promise of marriage of either form without attempting to fulfill his promise later on. Muhsin, one of my male informants from Tehran, described the following case.

Akbar, a man in his late thirties, was married and had two children. They had a young peasant teenage maid, left in their guardianship by her parents. Taking advantage of his wife's absence one evening, Akbar seduced the maid by getting her drunk. The next day the maid panicked, but Akbar consoled her and directed her to follow his instructions. He told her to wait until his wife returned home and then to go to her crying, saying that he had spoiled her reputation by deflowering her and that she would have no choice but to sue him. The maid followed his instructions and broke the news to the unsuspecting wife, threatening to take her husband to court. Not only did the wife feel betrayed, she became alarmed at the thought of having her husband jailed. In the meantime, Akbar convinced his wife that if she did not give her consent for a marriage to the maid, she would complain, and he would be jailed.[10] The wife played into his hands but demanded that he should *sigheh* the maid rather than marry her. This he was only too happy to comply with. Presently, Mushin told me, he has bought a duplex and each wife and her children live in a separate unit. There is constant tension and fighting, however, between the cowives and between the half-siblings.

Perhaps the most unusual variation of this form of *sigheh* occurs when a wife takes it upon herself to find a *sigheh* wife for her husband and a maid for herself at the same time. A woman's motivations may vary widely, ranging from ingratiating herself with her husband to controlling his choice of whom he is having an intimate relationship with, to diverting his libidinal energy to another partner, to manipulating and controlling both the husband and the *sigheh* wife. Such was the case of one of the permanent wives of Muhammad Shah Qajar. Upon realizing that she had fallen into disfavor with the shah, she sold her jewelry, borrowed some money, and bought a Circassian slave girl whom she presented to her royal husband (Sheil 1856, 203–204). In contrast, Fati Khanum, one of my informants from Qom, arranged a *sigheh* marriage for her husband because she was tired of his incessant sexual demands.

Finally, in the last few years of the Pahlavi regime, as the traditional patterns of male-female relations got caught in the grip of social change, uncertainty in expected behavior sprang up. As the idea of temporary marriage was gaining more and more currency, to cope with the ambivalence they felt toward educated and professional women, some male intellectuals chose to have a *sigheh* rather than a wife. During my fieldwork in 1981, I was introduced to an aspiring writer. He was divorced, and I learned later that he had a live-in *sigheh* maid companion. He sounded bitter about "intellectual women," of whom his ex-wife was presumably one; evidently he associated me with such women. No sooner did I describe my research to him than he turned sarcastic and questioned my motives for having chosen such a topic. At first he did not disclose to me that he had a *sigheh* maid, but he did so when my other informant teased him about it and encouraged him to grant me an interview. He rejected this request, and after a lengthy and at times tense conversation, he said, "Women should stay home and take care of their children. May God save us from intellectual women! It is much nicer to have a *sigheh* who is proud of being your wife, than to have a wife who is full of expectations."

Religious Sigheh: *Sigheh Aqa'i*

Literally meaning *sigheh* permitted by the Master, *aqa*, *sigheh aqa'i* is not a form of *sigheh*, properly speaking. However, the fact that people refer to it as *sigheh* implies that it is perhaps not considered a perfectly proper marriage, either. Usually, it is done when one or both of the partners to a marriage contract are below the legal age. Under the Pahlavi regime (1925–79) on two occasions the Iranian legislature raised the age of first marriage for male and female, at first to eighteen and fifteen and then to twenty and eighteen, respectively. Additionally, all marriage contracts were required to be registered. These changes, however, left many religious families at odds with the law, particularly those parents who were eager to arrange a marriage for their children as quickly as possible. They therefore circumvented the legal age restriction by performing a *sigheh aqa'i*, or religious marriage, as the registration of *sigheh* marriages was not as strictly enforced as that of permanent marriages. For all practical purposes the couple was considered husband and wife, but because the marriage was not registered, from a legal point of view they were considered unmarried. Once the girl—or at times both partners—came of age, the marriage was then properly registered. The birth of any children likewise would not be registered until the parents' marriage was legalized. *Sigheh aqa'i* was probably more prevalent in the early days of the Pahlavi regime than it is today.

Sigheh aqa'i is apparently a response to a conflict between the civil law's requirements for a girl's minimum age of first marriage and the precepts of the *shari'a*. While not stipulating a minimum age for the genders' first marriage, the Shi'i law considers women nine years and above as mature, obliged to observe veiling, and thus capable of entering into matrimony (Tusi 1964, 475). Fathers are often advised to give their daughters in marriage prior to the onset of their menstruation. Imam Ja'far-i Sadiq once said: "An indication of a man's good fortune, sa'adat, is to give away his daughter before the onset of her menses" (see also Khomeini 1977, P#2459; Mishkini 1974, 42, 60). The average age of my female informants for their first marriage was thirteen and a half (see Khakpur 1975, 643–744).[11] Child marriage, though undergoing some legal modifications, is still a deep-rooted custom in many parts of the Muslim world, including Iran.

Sigheh for the Sake of Procreation

In many countries barrenness is perceived to be a misfortune and is usually believed to be the woman's fault.[12] Although this assumption is embedded in Iranian popular belief, legally Shi'i Islam considers barrenness sufficient grounds for divorce for both spouses. Should a man wish not to divorce his wife, however, he is permitted to contract another marriage of either temporary or permanent kind. In Iran women are restricted by rules of monogamy, but some married men do take advantage of temporary marriage to satisfy their desire for progeny while still married to their first wife.

One of my informants, a woman in her mid-forties, shared with me her painful discovery of her husband's secret sigheh contract for the sake of procreation. Iman was three years old when her father divorced her mother and placed her in the custody of his sister, whom Iman was led to believe was her own mother. Her father married soon after and conveniently forgot about his little daughter. Iman said that she never saw her mother again. She was hardly eleven years old when her twenty-three-year-old cousin, whom she thought was her brother, raped her and threatened to kill her should she tell anyone about it.[13] Iman was filled with terror and pain at being defiled and misled, yet she obeyed and remained silent. For some ten years she suffered the psychological and physical pain her cousin continued to cause her. Encouraged by her apparent helplessness, he abused her, even after he was married.

Finding life no longer bearable, Iman fled to Mashhad in the hope of ending either her life or her misery. Through the friendship and help of some women whom she happened to meet in Mashhad, she finished her last year of high school and eventually became a teacher. Her life began to improve, but her health started to deteriorate. Consulting a physician, she discovered that she had a venereal disease. Again her women friends came to her aid, gave her moral support, and nursed her to recovery.

At a gathering Iman met a retired army general, a colonel who became interested in her. A few months later he proposed marriage to Iman, and despite the twenty-year difference in their ages, Iman accepted his offer. She was excited but terrified, too, for she was not a virgin. Her women companions helped her to forge a document indicating that she was a divorcee. She then married the colonel, and they lived happily ever after — at least for as long as he was alive.

Not long into their marriage Iman realized that she was "fruitless," as she put it. But her husband exhibited magnanimity and love toward her and assured her that nothing had changed from his point of view. He was so kind and understanding that Iman, at a moment of ecstasy, decided to transfer all her savings to his bank account. That only brought them closer.

When he died of a sudden heart attack, Iman was devastated with grief. By the third day of the mourning, however, she and a few of her close friends noticed the persistent appearance of a woman stranger at the rituals. Nobody knew who she was. Like Iman, she also seemed to be stricken with grief, and she wept uncontrollably. Curiosity led Iman and her friends to a most shocking and heart-wrenching discovery. This stranger was in fact no other than the colonel's *sigheh* wife, whom he had married several years before his death and with whom he had two sons. Needless to say, Iman felt angry and betrayed. In addition to having lost a beloved husband and her sense of trust, she had lost a good portion of her belongings as well. According to the Islamic law of inheritance, children's share of their parent's legacy is more than that of their mother — or a wife. [14]

In another case, Mulla Amin Aqa, one of my informants from Mashhad, told me that because he strongly desired a son, he had "no choice" but to *sigheh* another woman. He was motivated to do so partly because his wife was no longer "fruitful," and partly because his three surviving children from his first wife were all girls, all three of whom were married and had children of their own.

Sigheh for the Sake of Financial Support

Many Iranians readily assume that a woman's motivation for making a contract of temporary marriage must be financial. The contractual form of marriage, the nature of exchange, and the religious rhetoric foster such a presumption. And some women do indeed contract a temporary marriage because of financial necessity. What has escaped attention, however, is men's economic motivation in making the contract.

In Kashan, where exquisite carpets of international fame are made, many women learn the art of carpet weaving very early in life. In fact, many homes have at least one loom where young girls and women spend hours daily to make carpets; they thus help with family income and sometimes contribute to their own hope chests. In this town some men may make one, two, or several *sigheh* contracts with women on the condition that they work for them as carpet weavers. Although such a contract may be financially beneficial to both, it is the man who benefits the most. Similarly, in the northern Iranian provinces of Mazandaran and Gilan, some men make seasonal contracts of temporary marriage in the hope of using their *sigheh* wives' labor in the rice fields (see also Khakpur 1975, 122–23).

NONSEXUAL *SIGHEH*

A condition unique to *sigheh* is an agreement for a nonsexual relationship, in which the temporary spouses agree to enjoy each other's company without having sexual intercourse. The earliest reference to *sigheh* contracted with this condition, according to Shafa'i (1973, 209), comes from Imam Ja'far-i Sadiq. This type of *sigheh* is also recorded by the eleventh-century Shi'i scholar Tusi in his *An-Nahayih* (1964, 502). The nonsexual *sigheh* is still valid today (Khomeini 1977, P#2421, 2423). The possibility of specifying such a condition in the contract allows the institution greater potentiality for ambiguity, while rendering it a more conveniently manipulable and useful institution in Iranian society. However, it increases the uncertainties in male-female relationships. And here lies an ingenious Iranian Shi'i response to dilemmas posed by the segregation of sexes, on the one hand, and the moral and pragmatic demands of everyday life, on the other.

Traditionally, Iranians have come to know the nonsexual *sigheh* as *sigheh mahramiyyat*, which may be functionally translated as "lawful association," that is, of the genders.[15] A nonsexual *sigheh* may take place between two consenting adults, an adult and a child, children, or even infants (arranged by their parents in the latter cases). The purpose of this form of *sigheh* "marriage" is to remove the legal distance between a man and a woman by creating a fictive "marital relation" between them or an "affinal kinship" between their respective immediate families. Having thus acquired a legalized circle of male "relatives," women may unveil themselves in the presence of their new "affines." The "affinity" thus created allows men and women to come together through a relationship similar, for example, to that between father-in-law and daughter-in-law, or between mother-in-law and son-in-law. Significantly, though the marital relation may be terminated by the end of the specified time, the affinal relation thus created remains valid for life. This ingenious stratagem enables the sexes to circumvent the law, to cross the forbidden boundaries of sexual segregation legitimately, and to interact more freely.

It is common knowledge among Iranians that a *sigheh mahramiyyat* is for the purpose of social interaction and not sexual relation. Similar to a contract of permanent marriage but unlike a sexual *sigheh*, nonsexual fictive *sigheh* is often publicly acknowledged, undertaken to integrate families, allowing its members greater flexibility and less restrictive association. This form of *sigheh* has been widely performed among the more traditional Iranians. It is not as morally stigmatized and culturally devalued as the sexual *sigheh*. Many Iranians assume that sexual and nonsexual *sigheh* are two distinct forms of temporary marriage, but in fact nonsexual *sigheh* is only a subtype of what I have called sexual *sigheh*.

The ambiguity inherent in a nonsexual *sigheh* may be systematically compounded by the fact that the nonsexual clause may be revoked by the woman (Tusi 1964), assuming that the contract has been concluded between two adults. Should she change her mind at any time, wishing to turn their nonsexual *sigheh* into a sexual one, all she has to do is to articulate her desire. On the other hand, having agreed to a condition for nonsexual intimacy, men are not accorded the same privilege, though of course they have the right to terminate the relationship at any time they wish. No further ceremony or procedure is required for either option (Tusi 1964; Khomeini 1977, P#2423; see also Murata 1974, 54). Culturally, however, the term *sigheh mahramiyyat* has come to indicate a *sigheh* without sexual intercourse.

For analytical purposes, *sigheh* and *sigheh mahramiyyat* are treated as two distinct forms of temporary marriage, but it ought to be kept in mind that in reality they are not mutually exclusive. Their boundaries are rather permeable, and there are many situations in which the two overlap. The following is a description of those variations that I have been able to document.

Sigheh for Convenience of Association

A nonsexual *sigheh* may be performed between an adult male and one or two or several prepubescent girls for the purpose of making the adult man and the mothers (or grandmothers) of the girls *mahram*, lawful to each other, which allows the involved parties greater flexibility in their association and socialization.

With the advice and help of his wife, Aqa Jalili, the husband in the family with whom I was living in Qom in 1978, had arranged a nonsexual *sigheh* with several little girls in their neighborhood. All these young girls were below the age of puberty, and the *sighehs* usually lasted for an hour or even less, with a brideprice of some candy or sweets. The whole ceremony would be performed amid much laughter and merrymaking. Although the *sigheh* contract itself would soon run its course, the affinal bond created between Aqa Jalili and the girls' mothers would last forever. This is to say, their relationship would fall under a lawful category, similar to that between a man and his mother-in-law. Therefore, these women were not obliged to veil themselves before Aqa Jalili every time he went to their homes, or whenever they visited his wife at his home. Although most of these women still kept their veils on, they did not cover their faces completely in his presence. Through similar nonsexual *sigheh* contracts between others in the neighborhood, virtually everyone in the whole neighborhood has become "lawful" to one another. Interaction was conducted under a more relaxed and comfortable atmosphere and without any feelings of moral or religious wrongdoing.

Meanwhile, Aqa Jalili's wife, Kia (widowed in 1981), asked me to perform a nonsexual *sigheh* between her and my little five-year-old nephew because she did not want to feel uneasy in the presence of my father. Kia was quite particular about the procedure. She wanted me to secure permission from my nephew's parents because he was underage and living with his parents in the United States. She gave me the power of attorney on her behalf. Once I had performed the *sigheh*, my father was then bestowed the role of Kia's grandfather-in-law, albeit fictively. Ironically, she had known my father for a long time and had never veiled herself properly before him, nor did my father care much whether or not she observed these rules of modesty stringently. She wanted, however, to *sigheh* because "deep down in [her] heart" she was worried that she was committing a sin. A nonsexual *sigheh* not only legitimized her habit of loose veiling, it also gave her a religiolegal basis for acting with moral propriety. She no longer felt like a sinner. Besides, she now had found a good explanation for her neighbors, who had become inquisitive about my father's frequent visits to Qom with me.

Sigheh for Sharing Space and Expenses in Travel

A person might arrange for a nonsexual *sigheh* in order to minimize the burden of veiling and avoidance on traveling companions who may happen to be outside of the permissible degree of consanguinity or affinity. It would be inconvenient for a woman to rush aside and veil every time she came into contact with a non-*mahram* traveler. The way to bridge the legal boundaries, maintain propriety, and resolve moral conflict is by performing a nonsexual *sigheh*. This done, the woman may loosen up her veil and the travelers may proceed, sharing space and therefore often the expense as well.

Mr. and Mrs. Kashfi were making preparations to go on a long journey to Iraq in 1957. In their company were their two young children and Mrs.

Kashfi's widowed aunt (her father's brother's wife). Religiously, the relation-ship between the aunt and Mr. Kashfi was in the forbidden category, and therefore the former was obliged to veil herself before Mr. Kashfi. Unless the family found a way of circumventing the rules, their journey would be not only inconvenient but costly as well: they would have to reserve two rooms in every motel. The nonsexual *sigheh* presented itself as a convenient and meaningful cultural solution. It would enable the aunt to remove her veil and to share with the Kashfis the space as well as the expense. Without hesita-tion, they arranged a nonsexual *sigheh* between the aunt and the two-year-old son of Mr. and Mrs. Kashfi for one hour. Having done so, the aunt became Mr. and Mrs. Kashfi's fictive daughter-in-law!

In another case, when Zarrin's husband died some thirty years ago, she became obliged, on account of the will left by her husband, to take his body to Karbala, Iraq, and bury him in the shrine of the Shi'ites' third imam, Hussain. As it was becoming increasingly harder to travel freely to Iraq, Zar-rin's family decided to use the goodwill of an influential and wealthy hajji, who was a friend of Zarrin's husband. He offered to accompany Zarrin and one of her married daughters to Iraq, but the problem was that the hajji was lawful to neither of them. Therefore, he arranged a nonsexual *sigheh* be-tween himself and Zarrin for three months, approximately the length of the trip, becoming thereby lawful to both mother and daughter.

Technically, Zarrin had to keep the four months' *'idda* of death for her husband and so could not remarry during this period. Culturally, too, it is unthinkable for a woman presumably in the state of mourning to get in-volved in a new relationship. Nonsexual *sigheh*, however, cut across both the legal and cultural barriers, enabling Zarrin to make the proper arrangements for her husband's burial in Iraq.[16] The influential hajji, who because of his trading enterprise already had a passport, smuggled out the tightly veiled Zarrin as his real wife, and together they transported the body to Iraq and entombed him in the shrine of the third imam. Even though the hajji's *sigheh* to Zarrin expired after three months, the affinal relationship that was created between him and Zarrin's daughter remained unchanged. Had Zar-rin and the aunt in the previous case still been married, they could not have arranged a nonsexual *sigheh* with anyone, regardless of age difference or the explicit agreement for a nonsexual relationship.

Perhaps it is not difficult to understand the prohibition of a nonsex-ual *sigheh* between an adult man and a married woman, but what about that between a married woman and a two-year-old boy?[17] What could possibly be threatening in a nonsexual *sigheh* relation in a case where all that the rela-tionship apparently entails is the creation of certain legitimate categories for a less rigid association between the genders?

A partial answer lies in the ambivalent nature of nonsexual *sigheh*, which can be transformed into a sexual one at the moment of the woman's change of heart. This is perhaps why in some nonsexual *sighehs* the age difference between the "spouses" is made intentionally so wide. It is to render any implication of a sexual relationship absurd, if not impossible. Most important, however, the answer lies in the contractual form of the marriage and the Islamic prohibition of plural marriages for women. The logic of the contract implies that a married woman is an exclusive "property" of her husband. Thus to give these fictive and symbolic kinship bonds legitimacy, rules pertaining to nonsexual *sigheh* are closely modeled after those of permanent marriage. A fictive nonsexual *sigheh* with a married woman is therefore perceived to be threatening because it symbolically infringes on the husband's exclusive right of ownership to his wife's wifely duties and, for that matter, poses a threat to the purity of his seed.

Sigheh to Facilitate Decision Making

A half-secret organization, the Marriage Foundation, *bunyad-i iz-divaj*, was operating from a small office in south Tehran during the last few years of the Pahlavi regime. Since the revolution of 1979 it has become public and is operating in one of the confiscated mansions in north Tehran. The function of this now enlarged, well-staffed, and well-organized institution, much like date-matching agencies in the West, is to bring together compatible men and women in matrimony.

Mulla X, one of my informants in Qom, said that this institution had been arranging marriages of both types for some time prior to the overthrow of the Pahlavi regime in 1979. He also gave me its current address in Tehran. The Marriage Foundation is segregated, maintaining different sections for men and women. The women's section is a small and dark room located in the back of the building, but the part devoted to male clients is large, spacious, beautifully decorated, and above all, it enjoys a generous amount of sunshine.

The two men in charge turned uncooperative and terse as soon as they found out that my objective was not to take advantage of their services. They were unwilling to discuss the specifics of their arrangements regarding *sigheh* marriages but did not hesitate to remind me of the social and religious advantages of such marriages, One of them finally said that more men than women were interested in arranging temporary marriages. They then permitted me to see one of their elaborate applications but refused to let me keep it. They also admitted to performing nonsexual *sighehs*. This, in fact, was printed on a procedure sheet pinned to the bulletin board displayed in the entrance hallway that separated male and female quarters.

Once a match is worked out through the mediation of the Marriage Foundation, a meeting is then arranged between the prospective partners. Because of the veiling requirement, a man is forbidden to see his would-be bride.[18] In order to facilitate the couple's decision making — most signifi- cantly, the man's — the authorities in the foundation perform a nonsexual *sigheh* between the couple for a few hours. This allows the woman to loosen her veil and to permit the man to take a glimpse of her face. If the parties do not find each other appealing, they depart and await another opportunity; their nonsexual *sigheh* is soon canceled. Should they find each other agree- able, however, they then follow the traditional patterns of marriage negotia- tions by allowing their families to negotiate the marriage payments and to make proper arrangements. Not always, of course, do individuals refer to the Marriage Foundation directly. Sometimes their families seek the founda- tion's assistance in finding a suitable mate for their loved ones.

According to common belief, the foundation's constituency is pri- marily religious men and women. The truth of this belief was evident from the clients who visited the foundation during the time I was there. Most of the applicants who use the Marriage Foundation's services prefer a perma- nent mate, though there are some who are interested in a *sigheh* marriage.

The Marriage Foundation and its newly established kindred orga- nization, the Martyr's Foundation, have gained the reputation of encourag- ing and facilitating marriages of either form between widows of the Iran-Iraq war and returning soldiers, or other men.[19] In the city of Kashan this policy reached scandalous proportions in 1982 – 83, leading to the forced resigna- tion of the head of the Martyr's Foundation. He had apparently arranged sev- eral *sigheh* marriages between himself and some war widows before arrang- ing other marriages for them with members of his staff or other suitable partners.

Nonsexual *sigheh* as a way to facilitate decision making is not unique to the Marriage Foundation. Popularly, the more traditional Iranian families have employed nonsexual *sigheh* as a way of giving a couple some degree of control — however minimal — to make decisions by seeing their intended spouses.

Sigheh for Cooperation

One of the more complex and puzzling phenomena that gained mo- mentum in the years immediately preceding the revolution of 1979 is the manner in which many young educated women rejected Western hegemony by donning the veil voluntarily. Secured and defiant beneath their veils,[20] yet eager to participate in the remaking of their society, many of them volun- teered to work side by side with men in various revolutionary projects, such as the so-called Struggle for Construction, *jahad-i sazandigi.* Under the auspices and close supervision of the revolutionary committees, young men and women were sent off to numerous villages to help with a variety of tasks. Because of the necessarily close association between the genders and the perceived ensuing moral problem associated with it, many of them, either on their own initiative or their supervisors' recommendation, arranged nonsexual *sighehs* — sometimes even a sexual *sigheh* — with their peers. Consequently, they continued their jobs, freed from rules of segregation.[21]

Paradoxically, many of these women had apparently realized that just as the veil created an actual or symbolic barrier between men and women, it could, under other circumstances, facilitate their close cooperation and association. By using the veil, they were able to share the public space that had been traditionally a male sphere of activity, and from which women have been barred historically.

The Shrine *Sigheh: Sigheh Bala Sar-i Aqa*

A prevalent form of *sigheh* in Mashhad is what the natives themselves call *sigheh bala sar-i aqa,* meaning literally "*sigheh* over the head of the master," referring to the Shi'i revered eighth imam, Riza, who is buried in Mashhad.

When two families have made all the arrangements for a couple's permanent marriage, they may then allow the couple to have a nonsexual *sigheh* in the shrine of the imam. This, in addition to enabling the couple some degree of privacy, gains them spiritual blessing from the imam. For this ritual the couple is expected to wear new clothes and, in the company of their representatives—often immediate family members—and relatives, to go to the shrine. Only the couple and their representatives enter the inside mausoleum and approach the area where the head of the imam is believed to be. Once inside, their representatives perform a nonsexual *sigheh* between them, and they all return outside to join the rest of their relatives, sharing sweets and candies with them. Depending upon the family tradition, shrine *sigheh* may take place a few days to a few months prior to the actual wedding, *nikah.* Despite the vagueness about the duration of *sigheh bala sar-i aqa,* the Mashhadis regard it as a genuine form of nonsexual *sigheh*, with the time limit understood to be until the actual ceremony of marriage.

Mr. and Mrs. Baba'i, my informants in Mashhad, had a shrine *sigheh* three days before their marriage. This, in addition to gaining them their parents' blessing, gave them some privacy and freedom to go shopping together without the constant chaperoning of their elders — especially the woman's.

This is a variation of nonsexual *sigheh*, where ambiguity and tension surround the relationship. But the tension is particularly masked in the case of a long-term shrine *sigheh*. In this situation, a girl's reputation could be seriously compromised as a result of the inherent ambiguity of the couple's status vis-à-vis each other, and the family and community expectations engendered by the shrine *sigheh*. On the one hand, the soon-to-be husband and wife are joined in a pseudo-marital relationship, but on the other hand, traditional expectations forbid intimate sexual relationship before the actual wedding. This is why many families who perform this form of *sigheh* often keep its duration very short.

NEW INTERPRETATIONS OF *SIGHEH*

Some of the most innovative and imaginative interpretations of a contract of temporary marriage are advanced by a handful of doctrinarians of the Islamic regime. Shortly after the revolution, the Islamic regime embarked on an intensive campaign to revitalize temporary marriage (the terms *mut'a* and *sigheh* are seldom officially used). The objective was to "purify" the institution of some of its negative cultural connotations and moral stigmatization, and to reintroduce it from a completely new perspective. The Islamic regime has shifted its strategy from defending *sigheh* as a legitimate form of marriage to that of upholding it as a progressive institution, and as "one of the brilliant laws of Islam" (Mutahhari 1981, 52) especially suited to the needs of a modern society. Most significantly, the objective is to reach the young adults as opposed to the middle-aged population, who have been traditionally the most frequent practitioners of *sigheh*. The officially formulated position now is that the concept of temporary marriage is one of the most advanced and farsighted aspects of Islamic thought, indicating Islamic understanding of the nature of human sexuality. The concept of temporary marriage is widely disseminated to the public through such different forums as mosques, religious gatherings, schools, newspapers, books, and radio and television. The Islamic regime is educating the public about its form, its function, and its moral superiority over the "decadent" Western style of "free" sexual relationships.

Of the following four variations, the first, trial marriage, has been best formulated by the Ayatollah Mutahhari (1974, 1981), one of the top-level revolutionary theoreticians prior to the overthrow of the Pahlavi regime, and it has been advocated rigorously since. The rationale and the procedure for this form of *sigheh* are published in the Iranian high school religious textbooks (Bahunar 1981, 37–42) and taught to students from the tenth grade up. The second variation was described to me by a mulla informant in Qom, and the other two variations are public knowledge, involving much rumor and controversy.

Trial Marriage: *Izdivaj-i Azmayishi*

Ayatollah Mutahhari, one of the more critically minded and influential ayatollahs during the Pahlavi regime, objected vehemently to an unfavorable article on temporary marriage that was printed in an Iranian weekly magazine during the late 1960s. In his article on the rights of women in Islam Mutahhari argues:

> The characteristic feature of our modern age is the lengthening of the span of time between natural puberty and social maturity, when one becomes capable of establishing a family. . . . Are the young ready to undergo a period of temporary asceticism and put themselves under the strain of rigid austerity till such time as there may arise an occasion for permanent marriage? Suppose a young person is prepared to undergo temporary asceticism; will nature be ready to forego the formation of the dreadful and dangerous psychological penalties which are found in the wake of abstention from instinctive sexual activity and which psychiatrists are now discovering? (translation from source, 1981, 52–53)

He then suggested that only two options are open to the youth:[22] either to follow the decadent Western path of "sexual communism," in which case "we have given liberty to the young men and young women equally," and so "have satisfied the spirit of the Charter of Human Rights," or to accept the legitimate course of "fixed-term marriage" and thus avoid a "leap into the valley of Gehenna." Accordingly, he concluded: "In principle it is possible that a man and a woman who want to marry permanently, but have not had the opportunity to get to know each other well enough, may marry temporarily for a specified period as an experiment. If they are fully confident and satisfied with each other, they may give permanence to this marriage; otherwise they can separate" (Mutahhari 1981; see also Bihishti ca. 1980:331–32).

This is indeed an intelligent, though culturally questionable, reading of the institution of temporary marriage, particularly in view of the actual and symbolic significance of the phenomenon of virginity in Iranian society. Taking their lead from Ayatollah Mutahhari, Dr. Bahunar (the late Iranian prime minister, d. 1981) and Gulzadih Ghafuri (a Majlis representative), however, have tried to temper Ayatollah Mutahhari's unconventional recommendations in a book they have edited for Iranian high school students. Acknowledging the importance of virginity in Iranian society, they suggest a more culturally palatable yet more ambiguous alternative, one that leaves more room for manipulation. This form of temporary marriage, while allowing a certain degree of sexual intimacy, does not necessarily involve sexual intercourse. Theoretically, therefore, it need not be threatening to young virgin women. These authors suggest:

> A man and a woman can in this type of marriage [*sigheh*] agree that their sexual pleasure be limited. For example, they can decide not to have sexual intercourse, and the man has to honor the terms of such agreement. Therefore, such marriage where nonintercourse is agreed upon beforehand can be an interesting experience during the engagement period. In fact, it can be a trial marriage, *izdivaj-i azmayishi*, and a way for the would-be spouses to get to know each other without any feelings of sin or guilt. (Bahunar et al. 1981, 40; see also Sani'i 1967; 'Alavi 1974; Hakim 1971)

It shall remain to be seen how openly or secretively young men and women will follow the prescriptions offered here. A positive response, however, may be inferred, based on the fact that the Islamic regime evidently has recalled its own manual from high school bookshelves. By 1984, when I revisited Iran, the religious textbook had been replaced with a new one. The idea of temporary marriage, however, is still very much alive, particularly because of the depletion of the male population during the Iran-Iraq war and the resulting imbalance between men and women.[23]

Although the effort to popularize *sigheh* as a form of trial marriage gained formal recognition after the revolution of 1979, it was conceived in this manner prior to this upheaval in Iranian political and religious structures. One of the high-ranking religious figures, a hujjat al-Islam and a college professor whom I interviewed in Tehran, spoke of his own contribution to cultivating the idea of temporary marriage in the last few years of the Pahlavi regime. His ideas are described in chapter 6.

Group *Sigheh*

An improvisation par excellence, group *sigheh* is apparently an amalgam of sexual and nonsexual *sigheh*. In an interview I had with a mulla informant in Qom, he graphically described this variation of *sigheh*. A group *sigheh* may be arranged between a woman and a few men, presumably serially, but sometimes even within as limited a period as a few hours.[24]

In one of Mulla X's trips to Tehran (some time in September of 1981), he was confronted by a group of young men at a gathering. The youths started to tease the mulla, who perhaps because of his religious robe appeared to them as a representative of, and an authority on, Islamic law and ideology. They challenged the mulla, claiming that Islam was restrictive of human pleasure, having no provisions, for example, for plural heterosexual relationships, for example, between four men and one woman.

Eager to prove to me, as to his challengers, that Islam has the answer for every conceivable contemporary problem, the mulla explained: "I told them that this act can be done very easily within an Islamic framework. In fact, there is an Islamic way for doing so." As if substituting me for his earlier adversaries, while addressing me, he said rhetorically "If you coordinate your actions according to Islam, soon you will find Islam." Mulla X then described the following procedure. "I told them, if one of you *sigheh* a woman and agree to a nonsexual type, then you may enjoy her company any way you please as long as you do not have penetration. In such a case, the woman is not bound to keep *'idda* when the *sigheh* is over and can remarry immediately. Next, the second man can make another nonsexual *sigheh* with her and enjoy her company but again without having intercourse. Then the third and the fourth man can repeat the same procedure." Finally, the mulla said, "I told them, 'You can then draw a lottery among yourselves. Lucky is the one who wins. He can then consummate the marriage, but he should be the last one, for this time the woman must keep *'idda* after penetration.' "

Though this variation of *sigheh* is perhaps the most novel interpretation of the custom, it does, nonetheless, follow the same general pattern of maintaining the form while improvising on the content. In a less dramatic but similar situation, Yaftabadi (1974) instructs male and female movie actors who have to appear in love scenes "that provoke instinct" to make a contract of *sigheh*. Having done this, the author argues, "They can become lawful to each other throughout the filming of the movie, and if they choose, they can do other things [i.e., have sexual intercourse] at other times. They have the right and it is not unlawful" (163).

Penance *Sigheh*

As one of the first measures to "purify," *paksazi*, Iran of Western "decadence," the revolutionary Islamic government bulldozed the red-light district, *shahr-i nu*, in Tehran and arrested, jailed, and even executed some of its female inhabitants. Many others, however, were taken to a huge confiscated mansion in northern Tehran for rehabilitation and purification. On the assumption that financial necessity is the culprit behind prostitution, the rehabilitation center provides room and board for the prostitutes and, in return, expects them to help with chores in the center: washing, ironing, sewing, and the like. Forbidden to leave the premises without permission, however, these women are under the constant surveillance of the revolutionary guards, who hope that through productive labor they will be rehabilitated. Money poured in from those who, under the cathartic feeling generated by the revolution, wanted to help the revolutionary programs. Two of my informants confided to me that they donated large sums of money to this rehabilitation center, hoping to help the "fallen" women to change their lives and start better ones.

The ultimate rehabilitation, however, is believed to be reached and penance paid when one becomes a *sigheh* to either a revolutionary guard or a soldier returned from the Iran-Iraq war. In metaphoric though not too subtle language, this is known as *ab-i tubih rikhtan*, "absolved [washed] through penance." Although reportedly some women choose this route to salvation, many others are forced into frequent *sigheh* marriages, much to their dislike. Usually these *sigheh* marriages are of short term, and after the expiration of the woman's waiting period, arrangements are made for her to have another short-term *sigheh* with another revolutionary guard or another newly returned soldier.

Penal *Sigheh*

As soon as the factionalism between the newly established Islamic regime and the opposition became clear, a massive purge of the opposition began. Since many of those arrested and jailed were teenage girls, their executioners were faced with a predicament. If these young girls were executed as virgins, according to religious beliefs, they would go to paradise. Before being executed, therefore, it is widely believed, these young virgins were forced to become *sigheh* to their jail-owners (Musavi-Isfahani ca. 1985, 199; Woman's Commission 1982, 3; Amnesty International 1986).

According to the specific teaching of Islamic law, the consent of both partners is essential for a marriage contract to be valid. Although legally no mature Shi'i woman can be forced to marry temporarily or permanently, under special circumstances this provision may be circumvented. Slave ownership entitles the master a right to contract a marriage on behalf of his wards, be they male or female. Other categories are those of captives and heathens. Since many of the executed women were accused of being "corruption on earth" and "infidels," they were therefore considered wards of the state and could be legally forced into a *sigheh* marriage. The objective of deflowering these young virgins was not only to humiliate them physically and psychologically but to prevent them from going to heaven.

Penal *sigheh* is almost the antithesis of penance *sigheh*, a fact that touches on the multiple qualities of sexuality as being purifying and polluting simultaneously. In one the sexual act is believed to absolve a woman's sins, whereas in the other it is believed to dissolve her purity and innocence.

DISCUSSION

I have described some of the many ways the institution of temporary marriage is understood by Iranians, the manners in which it actually functions
in everyday situations in Iran, and the various ways Shi'i Islamic ideology
could be employed to justify, rationalize, and moralize often conflicting practices, beliefs, and interpretations. Ideologically, in Shi'i Islam, the apparent
clarity of the law of *mut'a* marriage often masks ambivalences in its structure
and ambiguities in its meaning. The belief in the immutability of the law
has, paradoxically, set in motion a dynamic and lively world of meaningful
ambiguities, historically evolved to enable many Iranians to navigate their
way through the rough terrain of ideological beliefs, on the one hand, and
concrete realities of day-to-day life, on the other hand. Faced with such dilemmas, they tend to pledge allegiance to the law while improvising on the
contents. As long as people maintain the form, or give the impression of
doing so, they give legitimacy to a wide range of behaviors. Likewise, the
religious leaders justify their diverse interpretations of the institution of temporary marriage by couching their arguments within the same religiously
prescribed boundaries, while capitalizing on the inherent ambiguities of
the law.

By describing the variations of *sigheh*, I have had four objectives.
First, I have sought to illustrate the complexity of the concept of marriage in
practice in contemporary Shi'i Iranian culture. Marriage in this context does
not lend itself readily to reducible universal attributes—for example, the legitimacy of children—although it does share some characteristics with this
institution elsewhere. Despite its seemingly ideological and legal rigidity, its
form, content, and meaning are constantly being negotiated and reinter-
preted by men and women who seek socially and morally acceptable means
of establishing actual or symbolic relations with members of the opposite
sex. Although the officially stated objective of *sigheh* is male sexual satisfaction, it is, at the same time, a dynamic polysemic social institution evolved
to allow flexibility within presumably rigid and immutable boundaries. Its
variations are continuously unfolding and its definition is perpetually being
altered by the specialists who interpret its rules, as well as by the people who
use it.

This is shown by the fact that in the Shi'i worldview, sex for the sake
of pleasure — male sexual pleasure — is an accepted fact, but moral and
orderly relations between the sexes are possible only if they are restricted
to certain prescribed degrees of consanguinity or affinity. Thus, the most
significant and culturally meaningful role of *sigheh*, in both its sexual and
nonsexual forms, is to legitimize as "marriage" many variations of gender
relationships, enabling men and women to cross the boundaries of sex

segregation legally and to associate with one another unencumbered by moral dilemmas, guilt, and the actual or symbolic barriers of a veil.

I have also sought to underline the pervasiveness of the paradigm of sex segregation in Iran, simultaneously underscoring its malleability in rearranging and reorienting the genders' day-to-day activities. The ambiguities inherent in the form of temporary marriage and the multiplicity of meanings that it communicates make it possible for individuals of all walks of life to manipulate the parameters of the institution and at the same time to remain within legally and religiously prescribed boundaries. They forge the appearance of behaving according to some cultural ideals while sidestepping those very same ideals.

Further, I have sought to demonstrate that despite the restrictions of veiling and the apparent rigidity of the law of the segregation of sexes, viewed from the perspective of Iranians themselves, such precepts, though symbolically meaningful, are far from being immutable and unchanging, despite the stated belief to the contrary. Likewise, viewed within the larger context of Muslim societies, these restrictions are to be contextualized rather than treated a priori as a given in determining the life and behavior of peoples and cultures of the Middle East. The tendency to reify the institution of veiling and sex segregation in the Middle East inevitably leads to warped and stereotyped perceptions of gender relations in the region. On the other hand, just because some women may no longer wear the veil in these societies does not necessarily mean that veiling, as a conceptual paradigm for organizing social interaction, has also lost its significance or relevance. To appreciate gender relations in Iran, as in other Middle Eastern societies, we need to explore the "conceptual languages" by means of which gender differentiations are recognized and situated within a culturally specific social context. Marriage contracts, as I have attempted to show, provide one such conceptual language.

Finally, it remains to be seen what consequences the recent changes in the Islamic regime's attitude toward sexuality, association of the sexes, and *sigheh* (particularly, its advocacy of the institution as a form of trial marriage for youth) will have for a people who have become much more educated and aware of the concept and the uses of temporary marriage.

Part Three

law as perceived

5

WOMEN'S LIFE STORIES

The female subject . . . is on the basis of her
gender automatically excluded from all current
discursive fellowships. . . . She is consequently
deprived of the power and knowledge which those
fellowships imply, and is incapable of occupying
anything but the position of a *spoken subject*—that is,
of having anything but a passive relationship to
discourse as long as she "plays by the rules."
—KAJA SILVERMAN, *The Subject of Semiotics*

WHO ARE THE WOMEN who make *sigheh* contracts? What motivates them to engage in this form of marriage? What are their socioeconomic, professional, religious, and educational backgrounds? What is their marital history and their age range? What are the sociocultural and economic forces that might lead some women to choose a form of marriage imbued with cultural and moral ambivalence? How does the structural ambivalence in the two different marriage contracts influence women's sense of subjectivity? What is their perception of themselves, of the institution, and of the men? How and where do they learn about *sigheh*? How and where do they meet men in a society permeated with rules and norms of segregation of the sexes?

Views of women's status in Iran, and in the Middle East, often suffer from confusion associated with the particular perspectives taken by the observer and the observed; they are complicated further by specific theoretical worldviews and methodological applications. Such problems of perspective affect not only the conceptualization of women's status and worldviews but also the definition and analysis of social action and relations.

The most crucial methodological issue with which I had to grapple was finding a way of presenting my data that would reflect the multiplicity of

issues and the complexity of the lives of women who had treated me to a tour
of their worlds and enabled me to glance at them through their looking
glasses. I wish to reciprocate their generosity by letting them be the speaking subjects and to give them a chance to re-create their own histories. This,
in turn, will allow the reader to explore the worlds of these women, their
social reality, directly and intimately. Although I was in constant dialogue
with my informants, I have kept my voice in the background. It is the voice
of *sigheh* women I wish to put in the foreground in this chapter.

In the following pages eight *sigheh* women will speak about themselves. The form of our interviews enabled them to take a retroactive look at
their lives and to articulate — perhaps for the first time in their lives — the
course of the social events, personal motivations, inspirations, and actions
that led them to contract one or more temporary marriages. It further gave
them a chance to reflect on their feelings, desires, hopes, disillusionments,
and disappointments, evaluating them within the context of what they considered to be patterns of cultural ideal. I do not intend to imply here that the
women's life stories should be taken as the "truth," or that their narratives
have a one-to-one correspondence with independently verifiable social facts
and events, or that they have a perfect fit with "reality." Rather, I suggest that
they should be read as mediated histories of one's own life course, one's life
"story," in which the elapse of time from the moment of its occurrence to its
remembrance enables one to reflect, to rationalize, and to justify one's own
behavior and actions in the light of the cultural ideals and beliefs regarding
ideals of womanhood, motherhood, marriage, friendship, and the like.
Needless to say, boundaries between fact and fiction, fantasy and reality,
ideal and actual may become easily permeable and even indistinguishable to
both the actors and the observer.

The women's biographies are essentially written in the manner and
tone that were communicated to me, with some minor reorganization and
the elimination of some side stories. My intention is to convey a sense of how
information was originally presented to me, even though at times an informant's narrative may appear inconsistent. Some are more extensive and better articulated than others, and for some of them I was able to collect more
information from mutual acquaintances. The first three interviews were
conducted during the summer of 1978 in the cities of Qom and Tehran, and
the rest were concluded during my second field trip in 1981 in the cities of
Qom, Mashhad, Kashan, and Tehran.

Men and women, the orthodox Shi'i doctrine maintains, enter upon
a contract of temporary marriage with different motives. In the ulama's view,
men's prime motivation is sexual satisfaction, and on this issue they have
written ad infinitum, with great clarity and conviction of the "truth" of the
matter. Regarding women's motivation, however, they have been ambiva-

lent, never being certain of exactly what it is that a woman wants. Nonetheless, they have consistently and uniformly maintained that women's motivation ought to be financial reimbursement. This gender-differentiated primordial motivational objective has echoed repeatedly and resoundingly in the works of the Shi'i scholars and laymen, down to the present time. When viewed within the logic of a contract, the ulama's rationale makes sense; however, the women's motivations appear to be a lot more complex and unorthodox when the women articulate their own reasons for making a contract of temporary marriage. Let us hear from them.

MAHVASH KHANUM

I met Mahvash Khanum[1] in the Shrine of Ma'sumih in Qom during the summer of 1978. The first comment she made was that keeping 'idda is unfair, *bi insafi*, to women. "It is unfair," she said, "to expect women to *sigheh* for two hours and wait two months after that." Her candor was both enlightening and surprising. She openly admitted that she contracted *sigheh* for sexual satisfaction and wished that she could "*sigheh* every night."

I interviewed Mahvash three times: twice individually, and once in the company of a group of Qomi women in the house of my host. I met her by chance. As I was describing my research to two other women in the shrine, a soft and pleasant voice bid us to sit down. She had overheard our conversation, and her first comment, quoted above, was on the problematic nature of the waiting period for women. She volunteered information without much probing.

I was very excited that at last I had found my very first informant, a *sigheh* woman, and in my enthusiasm to record everything, I committed a great mistake. Eager to tape her, I asked her to wait until I went home and fetched my tape recorder from my house, which was only two minutes from the shrine. She agreed, and I ran out. But just as I was going out of the gate of the shrine, I saw Mahvash running out too. I hurried after her and inquired about her intentions. She appeared agitated, talking fast as she took her slippers out of her big shopping bag,[2] asking me to leave her alone, saying that she did not want to talk. I tried to reassure her about the nature of my research, but to no avail. She walked away, ending our short encounter with the proverb "She who has no headache doesn't wear a kerchief." I was devastated. Because of the tense and paranoid atmosphere in Iran, unwittingly I had frightened her away by suggesting that I tape our conversation.

In despair I walked out of the shrine and into the big crowded yard. I did not feel like going home and so walked aimlessly among the crowd, looking at people and trying hard to discern who might be a *sigheh* and also willing to talk to me. I kept thinking: how does one find a *sigheh* person?

It was getting closer to sunset, and rows of narrow straw mats were being stretched in the yard for the believers who were about to congregate for their evening prayers. Before reaching the other side of the yard, I spotted Mahvash sitting cross-legged on her little prayer rug with her shopping bag in front of her. She noticed me too, and smiled. I returned her smile but did not rush to talk to her. I wanted to avoid scaring her again. Much to my delight, however, she beckoned me to come and sit by her, and I happily complied. When I asked her what had frightened her away, she replied that it was not exactly a matter of fear, but there were things she could not say because she was "being watched." The "enemy, *dushman*," she said, "is trying to find excuses to put me in an asylum or to push me to commit suicide!" She talked fast and was hard to follow. Despite my growing curiosity, I assured her that she was free to talk or not to talk to me.

In our second interview she was friendlier, so I asked who the enemy was. She responded that it was the SAVAK, the Shah's security police. Asked why the SAVAK should be after her, she said, "Because I am a follower of the absent imam, *imam zaman*, and whatever he says I'll do. The enemy tries to push me into prostitution, or make me commit suicide, but I'll never do that."[3]

Although I never found out exactly what she was talking about, her paranoia began to seem justified to me when, upon leaving her, I was taken by surprise by a policeman who stopped me, wanting to know how I knew Mahvash, and why I had given her some money (which I had). He must have been watching us the entire time; I was unnerved. I told him that I had just interviewed her for my book and given her some money for her time. Upon hearing that, he simply walked away, leaving me pondering over Mahvash's comments and wondering about the objectives of such surveillance.

In a later interview Mahvash said that she had not wished to talk to me earlier because a quick divination, *istikharih*, she had made with her worry beads had proved to be negative. She asked me to wait until she could perform her religious ablution for the evening prayer, make a new divination, and then she would talk to me. Mahvash, however, never went to wash for her evening prayer. She just started talking and I was happy to listen and take mental notes.

Mahvash was born into a religious, impoverished family in Shiraz. She was only seven or eight years old when her father left his wife and six children for Tehran in the hope of finding a job. He never returned. Despite all the hardship, Mahvash, the oldest of the six, managed to go to school. "Because my mother was the daughter of a religious leader," Mahvash said, "she would never go to the well to fetch water or go out to buy bread. She thought these activities were beneath her. So I had to do all these chores for her while going to school at the same time. I did not have a nice uniform. The only one I had was torn in a few places. But I would iron it and wear it anyhow." Mahvash struggled through the six grades of elementary school and finally received her certificate. She showed me the document proudly. Soon afterward, at the age of thirteen, she was given in marriage to a man eleven years her senior, to relieve the family of some of its financial burden.

Her married life was a tale of unhappy events. Being a little indiscreet, unwittingly she had disclosed to their neighbors her husband's political affiliations. "My husband was pro-Mussadiq, anti-Shah, and used to badmouth the government and others. I was young and ignorant, and would talk about my private life, our sex life, and everything else." Consequently, the Shah's SAVAK found out about her husband and eventually persuaded his employer to fire him. He was so angry at Mahvash that he soon divorced her and kept the custody of their three children. He never again allowed her to see them, Mahvash said. She was twenty-one years old when she was divorced; at the time of our conversation she was forty-four years old. She said that she knew nothing of her children's whereabouts.

After her divorce Mahvash went to Najaf, Iraq, which like Qom, has had a reputation for being a *sigheh* city. There she married an Iraqi man whom she claimed was impotent. Sexually frustrated, she said, "I masturbated incessantly, to the point of nearly injuring myself." Worse yet, he would neither take her to his home nor provide for her. He would not divorce her either. Reaching the limits of her endurance, Mahvash left him and returned to Iran. She came to Qom, where one can easily learn about *sigheh*, find one or be one. She was very descriptive, leaving me amazed at the ease with which she described her whole experience to me. She was the only woman informant who told me she was masturbating.

In a group discussion with a group of Qomi women, Mahvash at times dominated the conversation.[4] Her approach was gentle but her tone was vindictive. Apparently, she knew she did not have a good reputation among these women. Refuting a young woman's criticism of temporary marriage, she said, "My first husband was young and handsome, but he divorced me. My second husband [the Iraqi man] was old, didn't like women, and wouldn't divorce me either! For sixteen to seventeen years he made me suffer; neither would he divorce me nor would he pay for me. I was so miserable, so depressed. I was deprived [of sex] all those years. I was young. I am a sayyid [who are believed to be sexually more potent[5]]. I wanted it. I was used to having it. But he did not have any need for women. All he wanted was someone to cook for him."

Mahvash at times sounded ambiguous and enigmatic. She became evasive when asked to be more specific on how she finally obtained her divorce from the old Iraqi man who refused to divorce her. In a roundabout way she implied that he died. I am not quite sure whether he actually died or she convinced herself that he must have died. In any event, she became a *sigheh* after that, and did it frequently. However, she stated that she *sighehs* in the hope of finding a permanent husband, which in her view is far better. In the absence of a permanent marriage, she prefers a *sigheh* for a long period, "three to four months and with a brideprice of four to five thousand *tuman,*" so that "I would be provided for, for at least a few months." For the time being she makes a contract of *sigheh* any time she gets a chance; they are usually short, one or two hours, or one night at most. In her words, "I want to get married [her euphemism for sex] all the time, every night."

Her most recent *sigheh* had taken place in a motel in Qom. She noticed a young handsome man who had come to Qom on a pilgrimage, in the company of his brother and father. She was taken by him, and compared him to Rakhsh in beauty and strength (Rakhsh is the name of the horse of Rustam, the ancient Iranian cultural hero). She approached them humbly and told them that she was alone and "without a protector," *bi sarparast,* using a term which colloquially means "unmarried." She added that she was afraid of the innkeeper, who would find excuses to go to her room. Appealing to their sense of honor, she placed herself in the protection of the three men. The young man evidently understood the underlying message and knocked at her door as soon as his brother and father went to sleep.

They made a *sigheh* agreement for one night. For her brideprice Mahvash asked for some Persian candy, *nabat,* saying that she did not care about the brideprice, but the young man paid her one hundred *tuman* anyhow. Who proposed the idea of a *sigheh* to whom is not quite clear here. Mahvash said that the young man suggested it to her, but my guess is that Mahvash herself must have introduced the idea to him, given the fact that she had targeted him, was twice his age, and knew all about *sigheh* rules and procedures.

At one point in our group discussion Mahvash championed the cause of men's rights. Much to the displeasure of other women present, she said, "God has privileged men [with sexual prowess]. It is good for men and they want it too. One [woman] is not enough for them. It is said in the Qur'an too. But men must treat their wives fairly. They can have as many *sighehs* as they want. It is good for men. God has given men permission to do so, but hasn't given women the same right. If a woman is good," preached Mahvash, "if she is pure, even if her husband does these things [*sigheh*] with a thousand other women, she would not lose her faith." Realizing that probably other women present perceived her as a potential threat to the stability of their marriages, Mahvash thus tried to underscore the "proper" way a Muslim woman ought to behave.

Mahvash told me that she is propositioned by men from all walks of life and age groups but emphasized that she chooses only those to whom she feels physically attracted. Asked whether she usually chooses pilgrims in the shrine as her temporary husbands, she shrugged, "God sends me my fate, *qismat.*" Asked whether her suitors were the religious students in Qom, she said contemptuously, "No. These donkeys do not have a room, and would want to take you either for a long walk or would want to make love to you in the cemetery behind someone's tombstone. There is no pleasure in such a marriage," adding in the same breath that sometimes she marries good-look-ing mullas. Her contemptuous tone was surprising to me, particularly at a time (1978) when mullas were gaining in popularity all over Iran, and in view of her emphasis on her religious convictions. Mahvash had a way of deflating my stereotypes regarding women in Qom at every turn of our long conversations.

Asked how she meets these men, Mahvash said, "It is incredible how many men want to have a *sigheh.* They are from all ages and back-grounds, young and old, rich and poor." Sometimes, she said, she approaches men herself, and other times men initiate a friendship. In the shrine a man may look at her eagerly and suggestively. If she finds him agreeable, she then walks to him and exchanges greetings, as if they have known each other for some time. This performance is for the benefit of all those ever-present on-lookers who might be mistakenly thinking that something fishy is going on! After that, "Things follow their natural course," said Mahvash smiling. Other times a man may signal to her by some facial gesture, or by exhibiting his keys discreetly, that is, by indicating that he is of some means and has a room of his own — apparently a much sought-after commodity in Qom. He may then point to a door, implying that they should go out of the shrine. Once out of sight of the omnipresent onlookers and eavesdroppers, they negotiate the terms of their temporary marriage and make appropriate arrangements. Al-though Mahvash said that she must have a clue from men before she would approach them, she appeared to know exactly what she wanted and how she should go about obtaining it.

According to Mahvash, none of her *sigheh* marriages have been ar-ranged by a matchmaker. She knew of a female matchmaker in Najaf, Iraq, but none in Qom. This Najafi woman, Mahvash said, had the names and ad-dresses of many women in the vicinity and would inform them if she heard of interested men. This matchmaker charged them a fee for her services by keeping a portion of the women's brideprice. Mahvash's admission of the nonexistence of matchmakers in Qom, I think, was perhaps self-serving. Her attitude was partly a reflection of the fact that matchmaking is regarded with ambivalence in Iran, despite the religious emphasis placed on it, and that matchmakers are sometimes viewed with suspicion. Mahvash was too poor to use the services of a matchmaker, and she was too clever to need the expertise of one. As a matter of fact, she was known to be a matchmaker herself.

Initially, negotiations of brideprice are done by the would-be temporary spouses themselves. Mahvash said that she preferred to receive the brideprice at the outset and before the consummation of the marriage; otherwise, there is the possibility that once "he takes me home, he may refuse to give me anything." She sounded uncertain on the issue of brideprice. At one point she told me that she did not care about the financial arrangements in *sigheh* marriage, but only the physical characteristics of her partner. At our group meeting Mahvash said rhetorically, "She who has faith has her eyes on God only. One should never support oneself through this kind of activity [*sigheh* for money]. God has said in the Qur'an that He will provide for all. God is the Provider. I expect support only from God." Another time, however, she made it clear that she wished for a permanent marriage that would give her greater security, both financial and physical, or in its absence, a long-term *sigheh.*

In our group discussion, when she was challenged by two young women who were against *sigheh* marriage, Mahvash, in her own gentle but preacher-like style, reasoned: "What if a woman wants to get married [meaning both to have sex, and permanently] but can't find a husband? Well, *sigheh* is better than nothing. It is not that she wants the money or wants to live off it this way; it is because of the instinct, *gharizih;* because she wants it so that she may not commit a sin. Now, if he paid her, fine, and if he didn't, well, at least she has been satisfied."

In the summer of 1978 Mahvash was using the shrine as her place of residence, for she did not have a room of her own. She said that homeowners would not rent her a room because of her reputation as a *sigheh-ru* (a woman who becomes *sigheh* frequently). Even her own siblings and mother did not apparently associate with her, yet Mahvash did not seem to be bitter. Aware of the ambivalence shown toward her and apparently resigned to her fate, she said, "There are all kinds of wrong rumors about me, like being a *sigheh-ru* or a matchmaker. But none of these accusations is correct. I am following the line of God and the Prophet."

She claimed to be very religious and, in fact, seemed to be well acquainted with the *shari'a.* She could read the Qur'an and other prayer books and used her skill by reading the Qur'an to women and charging them a fee. Several times in the shrine I observed her walking directly to women seated in the shrine, asking them whether they wanted her to read them the Qur'an or perform some prayers for them, or to "explain" certain religious issues for them in the style of the ayatollahs. Knowing the Qur'an and the *shari'a* and being assertive seemed to place her in a position of authority and power vis-à-vis other women. In our group meeting Mahvash backed virtually all her comments and opinions with a proper saying from the Prophet, or one of the Shi'i imams, and counteracted any challenger's remarks by the same technique.

Even though she knew she was no longer capable of bearing children, as the result of an operation, she claimed to keep her 'idda faithfully. She was, however, frustrated about the necessity of abstaining for nearly two months after each of her temporary marriages expired. She seemed to be caught between her religious convictions, on the one hand, and her sexual desires, on the other. Reversing our roles at one point, Mahvash said that she had a question but was hesitant to ask. Reassured of my interest, she said, "In a *sigheh* marriage where intercourse is done between a woman's legs or from behind, does she still have to keep 'idda?" I was dumbfounded: here was this tightly veiled woman, in the heart of a religious shrine in Qom, a place I had always associated with modest, veiled, and prudish women, disclosing to me her most intimate concerns! But I was enlightened by her question, too. Only then did I begin to realize the degree of her conviction over the issue of her abstinence after each and every one of her temporary marriage contracts, most of which lasted only a few hours. "Maybe if I can convince a man to do that," she continued, "not only would I be able to make a lot more money, I wouldn't have to wait for two months either." Having posed her question to me, and perhaps disappointed by not finding me knowledgeable in this respect, Mahvash giggled prudishly and then suggested that "we" should write to one of the ayatollahs in Qom for the answer. I declined politely.

Mahvash knew of other *sigheh* women in Qom and felt particularly envious of one of them. This woman, Mahvash informed me, was over fifty years old and past her menopause. Not being bound by legal requirements to observe a period of sexual abstinence, she could, theoretically, marry as frequently as she liked. Apparently, this woman was frequently sought out by men, who knew she was past her childbearing age.[6] But she would refuse them all! Mahvash found this most extraordinary and wished to be in her place. In exchange for some gifts and money Mahvash arranged for me to meet this woman; however, the woman was not in good health and refused to be interviewed.

Asked how she protected herself from getting venereal diseases and how she dealt with the issues of health and hygiene, Mahvash said that she was very careful and particular in selecting a man. She did not know about contraceptives except for condoms but said that she did not like the use of them by her male partners because "It takes out the pleasure, and besides, a flower needs rain."

MA'SUMIH

Mahvash also agreed to introduce me to Ma'sumiih, who was eager to talk. Unlike Mahvash, Ma'sumih seemed somewhat disoriented. She looked emaciated and appeared much older than her stated age of forty. Oblivious to her slipping veil and her surroundings in the shrine, Ma'sumih vented her pent-up grudge against some unknown enemies. She started by telling me about her dreams, describing them incoherently. Soon, I realized that for Ma'sumih the boundaries between dream and reality have been blurred, leaving her confused about fact and fantasy. Often it appeared as if she were using her own dreams—confusing though they were—to find causes for her misery, or to prophesy her future.

Ma'sumih was originally from Qazvin. Born into a traditional and religious family, she was the only daughter of three siblings. Her father was a low-ranking bureaucrat, and her mother, like the daughter, was illiterate. Like Mahvash, Ma'sumih was very young when she was married off to a man much older than herself. He was very bad tempered and used to beat her mercilessly. A low-ranking bureaucrat, Ma'sumih's husband was conservative in thought and deed, almost a replica of her father. Ma'sumih worked hard in his house, trying to please him and make life comfortable for him. She bore him three children but was seldom appreciated. "He was like a tower of snake venom at home, but was charming to others outside," she said.

Ma'sumih described herself as "gullible," *sadih*. She would, she said, share her previous life with many of her neighbors and friends without discriminating between sensitive private information and public knowledge. She would tell her friends about the corner store *kababi*, who would often smile at her and offer her some *kabab*. Since she was usually with one of her children, she would accept his offer and share the *kabab* with her child. She thought nothing of her actions or how they might be misinterpreted or misconstrued by others.

Under the pretext that she had dishonored him, one day her husband simply threw her out.[7] He accused her of having been seen "smiling at" the *kababi* at the corner store. "I begged him," she said, "to let me tell my side of the story. I begged him for the sake of our children to give me a chance, but he refused and threw me out." He did not let her see her children again, Ma'sumih claimed. She cursed those who had talked behind her back and ruined her life. Ma'sumih was convinced that she was bewitched and was a target of the evil eye.

Miserable and in disrepute, she went to the house of her father, who was so ashamed of her that he never again looked at her or returned her greetings. Ma'sumih's brothers, also ashamed of her because of her dishonorable divorce, lashed out at her verbally.

The *kababi* was indeed interested in her, and, realizing her predicament, he offered to *sigheh* her for three months. Ma'sumih told me that she did not know exactly what a *sigheh* was but accepted his offer because she could no longer bear the tense atmosphere in her parental home. During her union with the *kababi*, she conceived, but, terrified of her father's reaction to this, she fled to Tehran without ever telling her temporary husband about it. Just exactly why she was so afraid—or ashamed—of her father's reaction is not quite clear to me. My interpretation is that in addition to being aware of his strictness, she was perhaps unsure about the propriety of her *sigheh* marriage and therefore was ashamed of her pregnancy. In many rural areas or small towns in Iran, out of respect or perhaps shyness, young women customarily conceal the fact of their pregnancies from their fathers for as long as possible.

Ma'sumih lapsed back into the world of her dreams and became hard to follow again. She dreamed, she said, of holy men and women whom she asked for water. They gave her water. She wailed as she was narrating her life story to me, and it appeared as though she were reliving the grief, misery, and pain she had endured during the months of her pregnancy.

In Tehran, Ma'sumih lived in one of the ghettos in the ancient city of Ray, near the holy shrine of the Shah 'Abdul 'Azim, some three or four miles south of Tehran. Her struggle for survival forced her to beg in the streets until, through the help of a neighbor, she found a job as a domestic servant. When the hour of her delivery drew close, lonely and isolated, she dragged herself to the Firuz Abad Hospital. They refused to admit her, claiming that she was mentally ill. Ignoring her pain, the hospital personnel sent her to the Farah Hospital, and before she could be taken to the delivery room, she gave birth to a baby girl.

Regaining her strength after a few months, Ma'sumih and her baby returned to Qazvin in the hope of seeing the *kababi*, the baby's father. His lucky star, unlike that of Ma'sumih, was in ascendancy. He had expanded his small store and married his father's brother's daughter; together they expected the birth of their first child. When he saw Ma'sumih, he was startled and remained aloof and distant. He denied any relation to the child and eventually suggested that she should take her to an orphanage. Lonely and miserable once again, Ma'sumih yearned to see her mother but dared not go near her parents' house.

Ma'sumih went back to the city of Ray, but after a few months of hard work in a factory she decided to place her little girl in an orphanage. She was told she could visit her daughter once a week and was given a visitor's pass, which she, in her state of absentmindedness, subsequently lost. Every time she went to see her child thereafter, she said, they would not let her in because she did not have her pass. At last, in one of her visits, she was in-

formed that she could see her, but that she had to take her out of the orphanage because the girl was old enough (a year and a half), and that they no
longer had room for her. Ma'sumih pleaded with them to keep her longer, but
they refused. They gave her the child and led her out of the door.

Back in her neighborhood in Ray, Ma'sumih had a neighbor who
was a gentle, middle-aged opium smoker, *taryaki*. He became fond of the
mother and child and eventually offered to *sigheh* Ma'sumih for two months,
and she accepted it. He spent a considerable amount of time with them, and
every now and then, if some money was left from his opium expenses, he
would buy some candy or sweets for the little girl. They almost resembled a
happy family and meaning and order began to inform their lives. Their happiness, alas, did not last long. Ma'sumih's temporary husband died in an auto
accident, leaving the mother and child lonely and vulnerable once again.
Finding life in Ray no longer bearable and faced with her little girl's incessant asking for her "father," Ma'sumih packed her meager belongings and
went to Qom. There she joined the ranks of numerous others who use the
shrine as their "home."[8]

When I interviewed Ma'sumih in 1978, it was six years after her
flight. Nowadays she frequently makes *sigheh* contracts as a way to provide
for her little girl. For Ma'sumih herself, the clock had apparently stopped
some six years ago, and anything that happened to her after that did not seem
to matter much.

FURUGH KHANUM

Furugh Khanum was a woman in her mid-forties, plump and pleasant. I interviewed her in the summer of 1978 and had extensive talks with others who
knew her. Furugh was only twelve and a half years old when it was arranged
for her to marry an attractive twenty-year-old man. She was the only child
and did not have any objections to her marriage. She had seen her future husband the day he and his family came to her house asking for her. She had
served him tea and sweets and found him attractive.

Soon after their marriage, however, she discovered that her husband had a suspicious mind and was ill-humored too. Despite the fact that
he would mistreat her, swear at her, and even occasionally beat her, she tried
still harder to make a comfortable and happy life for him. Being literate, with
the equivalent of a sixth-grade primary education, Furugh assisted her husband in organizing his finances and even helped him in drawing charts and
graphs, which was part of his job. She believed that it was through her efforts
and prudence that he was able to amass some wealth. He, alas, became ad-

dicted to heroin and soon started spending their money for his habit and on other women. Furugh said that the more she tried to put things back together, the more careless he became. He beat her up and treated their five small children no less harshly.

With their resources drying up fast and her patience reaching its limits, Furugh finally left his house and went to that of an acquaintance, where she could work as a companion to one of the elderly members of the family. She took her youngest child, the only daughter, with her, leaving the rest with their father. When she left, not only did she not receive her meager brideprice of five hundred *tuman* but she also left behind all her belongings. She even gave him some money and "ran out of his house with only a flimsy veil, *chadur*, even though I had made him a millionaire." It was not until two years later that Furugh was finally able to obtain her divorce (see the section on *khul* divorce in chapter 2). Her four sons were placed in the custody of their father, while the little girl was left in Furugh's care.

From 1969 through the end of 1973 Furugh and her little girl lived with the same family. Furugh's pleasant manner and good looks were both an asset and a nuisance to her. "Everywhere I go men say, 'Khanum, you don't have a husband, why don't you become my wife?' " She felt exposed and vulnerable.

Furugh became animated when she began to recall her first meeting with her temporary husband. She remembered vividly the exact day and hour of her meeting with the hajji, a married man of some wealth. One of her friends, a seamstress, asked Furugh to go along with her to the main bazaar in Tehran to buy some fabrics. Instead, she took Furugh to the shop of a hajji who was an old acquaintance of hers. Laughing jovially at being complimented, Furugh said, "From the first moment he was giving me the eye." The hajji, interested in Furugh, asked them to have lunch with him at the corner store *kababi*, and with little hesitation, they accepted.

The hajji gave Furugh his telephone number and asked her to call him, but she did not use it, at least not for a while. At the hajji's instigation, however, and unknown to Furugh, her friend arranged another "chance" meeting between the two. This time the hajji expressed much interest in Furugh and begged her to allow him to meet her privately. She accepted. They continued to meet from time to time, and in one of these meetings the hajji informed her that he was preparing for another pilgrimage to Mecca. He then asked her to wait for him [not to get married in the meantime] until his return, and Furugh promised. As if to underscore the seriousness of the hajji's fear, Furugh said that in fact she had several other suitors during these two months, but that she refused them all.

The hajji returned in good health and the very next day went to see Furugh with all kinds of gifts from the holy shrine. He then posed this request: "If I give you ten *tuman* daily can you make do?" She responded, "There are times when one cannot make do with one hundred *tuman*, but there are times when one can make do with only two *tuman*. The money is not the objective. Courtesy and compatibility are the essence of a relationship. If these things are present, a man and a woman can live together; if not, they won't be able to be together even if they lived in a gold room." The hajji was evidently very pleased to hear Furugh's philosophy and promptly asked her to become his *sigheh*.

Their marriage ceremony was attended by Furugh's seamstress friend and a mulla friend of the hajji, but it was not registered. Furugh thinks her marriage is a religious one, and not a *sigheh*. However, she did not seem to be concerned one way or another. The hajji's explanation for his reluctance to register their marriage was a familiar one. He did not want his first wife to know anything about his new wife. Besides, in 1974 the Family Protection Law—passed in 1967—was in effect; no man was allowed to marry his second wife without a court's permission. Nor were notary publics at liberty to register a second marriage without such permission. To avoid penalties of up to two years' imprisonment, people usually did not register a second marriage, particularly a *sigheh*. Furugh was not afraid. She said that even if the hajji's wife were to find out about them and cared to sue them, she would have no documents to prove her claim. "Even if I was asked [by the authorities], I would say that the hajji is my lover, and nothing else. They couldn't prove a thing," that is, that they were married.[9]

"Nowadays," she reflected, "when two people love each other, registration of their marriage is meaningless. The first condition of a mutually meaningful relationship is love. I love the hajji and he loves me. What more do I want? I don't care whether or not I inherit from him." So, when the hajji gave her a check for 2,000 *tuman* as her brideprice, Furugh ceremoniously ripped it apart before his very eyes! Dramatizing her love for the hajji, Furugh recalled having said to him: " 'What do I want a brideprice for?' I told him, 'My brideprice is your love, my brideprice is your respect, my brideprice is your courtesy and humanity.' " Having had the experience of a failed marriage, Furugh seemed to understand the actual ineffectiveness of brideprice payment. For the same reason, she clearly perceived that her manifest lack of interest in money would make the hajji even more eager to reciprocate her love, pure as she presented it to him, with more gifts and promise of support for life.

By the time of our interview in 1978, the hajji's family had discovered their marriage and apparently did not bother to sue him. Although his mother and sister were on relatively good terms with Furugh and would visit her occasionally, they were much closer to the first wife and her children. Understandably, there was no socializing between the two cowives.

Furugh radiated with happiness when remembering the events that led to her *sigheh* contract with the hajji. Her life with the hajji seemed to have settled into a comfortable routine. He had rented an apartment for her and would go there regularly. Unless his first wife was away from the city, however, he would seldom stay overnight at Furugh's place. Again, Furugh seemed to have the last word. "I do not quibble about his comings and goings, and I welcome him anytime he comes here. Besides, most of his ablutions [i.e., those after sexual intercourse] are done here."

FATI KHANUM

I had heard about Fati Khanum in 1978 when I first went to Qom, but because of a chronic animosity between her and my host (who happened to be her sister-in-law), I was unable to interview her. Through the grapevine Fati had heard of my presence in Qom in 1981, and one day she just dropped by. Caught off guard, my host found some urgent errands to run and left us alone, and I, at long last, had a chance to interview Fati. We had a long conversation, and later on I interviewed some of her relatives and neighbors. She proved to be one of my most colorful informants. At the time of our interview her third husband (my host's brother) was being treated for cancer in a hospital in Tehran, and she was commuting back and forth between Tehran and Qom. Her in-laws did not know of her whereabouts when in Tehran, or even when back in Qom. She was seldom home, and I had a difficult time convincing my host to take me to Fati's house, because she was certain that "only God knows where she is."

Fati was in her mid-forties, although she claimed to be younger than that. She was vivacious and good humored but appeared to me to be a bit scatterbrained. She constantly referred to the time some five years ago when she first met her husband Isma'il—who was thirty years her senior—stressing how pretty she was ("fat, white, and blond"), and how she had lost weight in the past five years after she had married Isma'il (meaning that she had suffered in his house). She still seemed a bit overweight to me. When appearing in public, Fati not only wore the customary black veil, *chadur*, she covered her entire face with a black facial veil, *pushiyih*. Nobody could recognize her when she is dressed in this way. Notwithstanding her effort at modesty, however, the rumor in Qom is that she who wears a facial veil in fact signals her willingness to become a *sigheh*. Fati Khanum's rationale for wearing one was that her beauty might be tempting; she was afraid of being kidnapped by some men, taken to some godforsaken place, and raped.

Fati was only three years old when her father divorced her mother and retained her custody. Soon after, each of her parents remarried, and together they presented Fati with thirteen more siblings—nine from her father's side and four from her mother's side. Her life with a stepmother rivaled that of Cinderella, but without the happy ending. Fati repeatedly emphasized the fact that she was raised without a mother. Her father was a low-income merchant, very religious and conservative. For the most part, he ignored Fati's existence.

Perceiving her as the black sheep of the family, Fati's siblings did not seem to care much for her, said Fati's sister-in-law. She does not associate with her parental siblings but occasionally sees her mother and one or two of her maternal half-siblings. She exhibited an ambivalent attitude toward her family. At one time she almost bragged about the frequency of her visits with her family but in another context admitted that there was not much socializing between them. Other informants perceived Fati to be a little bit crazy, *khul*,[10] and they said that her family generally avoided her. It was known that she would still go to their homes every now and then, despite the cool reception she would often receive.

A child bride at the age of nine, Fati was married to her father's sister's son, who was apparently a bit retarded. She was given in marriage to him because their parents thought "it might be good for him," that is to say, bring him to his senses. Shortly afterward he contracted tuberculosis (he might have already had the disease when he was married to Fati—she did not know). She was barely fourteen years old when she was divorced by her ill husband, having discovered in the meantime that she was barren.

Her second marriage, to a rich seventy-year-old man, lasted only two and a half months. She was still incredulous, stating emphatically how he caused her embarrassment in the face of constant inquiries from friends and neighbors who wanted to know when she would go to the public bath to perform the ablution after sexual contact.[11] "He did not touch me," she declared. What he expected of her instead was to bring tea and sweets for his frequent guests and to prepare his opium paraphernalia. Ironically, despite the dissatisfaction Fati claimed to have had with this marriage, she said in the same breath: "From the time of my youth I always wished to marry an older man, because as long as he lives you have a quiet life, and when he dies you get his pension." She attributed this judgment to her "wisdom," *'aql.* Indeed, by the end of our interview it appeared to me that she was quite calculating insofar as her latest marriage was concerned. A few months after I left Iran, I received news of the death of her seventy-five-year-old husband, who left her his meager pension, in addition to a share of his small house.

By the time of her third marriage — or so she claimed — Fati Khanum had a good idea of what she wanted from a relationship. Through the shrine grapevine she learned about Isma'il, then a seventy-year-old twice-divorced man. Fati went to the home of the man's sister (my host) and told her and her mother that she was interested in meeting Isma'il. The mother and daughter, eager to find Isma'il a suitable wife, agreed to inform him and to set a date. The next time she visited, Isma'il was also present. Much to the amazement of his mother and sister, however, Fati asked them to leave the room! "Leave us alone so that we can interact freely," said Fati, supporting her request by some appropriate quotations from the Imam Ja'far-i Sadiq (see also Khomeini 1982a, 40). Isma'il's mother and sister left the room, annoyed and dismayed at her behavior—a grudge they still hold against her.

As soon as Fati was left alone with Isma'il in the room, she performed a nonsexual *sigheh* between them—supporting her act by some religious sayings once again—and quickly loosened up her all-covering veil. Finding Isma'il agreeable, she then suggested they should have a nonsexual *sigheh* for twenty-four hours to see whether they were compatible temperamentally. The next day, unlike Isma'il, Fati had concluded they were not compatible and wanted them to part. Faced with his eagerness, however, she suggested another *sigheh* for forty days, again with the condition of a nonsexual relationship. This time she moved into his house. They agreed to a third nonsexual *sigheh* before the desperate man suggested permanent marriage to her. This she accepted and received a large brideprice. My host believes that Fati manipulated her "raw" and gullible brother into paying her so much money.

Fati, it appeared to me, exhibited a calculating attitude toward her now ill husband. Lowering her voice so that her half-deaf mother-in-law, who at times was present in the room, could not hear her, she told me how her husband was dying, how her temperament was unlike her husband's, and how difficult it was living with him. Then raising her voice, she added how much she wanted him, despite all odds, and how much she had sacrificed for him. She conceded quietly again that they constantly argued over her extra-domestic activities. He wanted her to stay home, but she wanted to go to people's houses and to perform religious rituals for them, a service for which she was well known and apparently often sought out. Once he even divorced her, but regretting his hasty action, he tried for a reconciliation.

Fati had no qualms about telling me of her dislike for sexual intercourse (not unlike the culturally expected feminine behavior), but she admitted to tolerating foreplay. Shrewd as she was, she was well aware of the power of sexuality. She forced Isma'il to sleep separately from her, and told me that she would not let him become intimate with her more than once a month, or sometimes even less. She bragged about herself and seemed to draw a mischievous pleasure in describing how she tantalized him by moving around the house in her seductive lingerie. She would make life so difficult for her husband that he would offer to pay her "four to five hundred *tuman*" before she would concede to become intimate with him. She attributed this to her wisdom, also.

Fati Khanum described her husband as a very excitable man. "If I let him," said Fati, "he would want to take a bath three times a day" (i.e., have intercourse).[12] "Even now that he is sick and hospitalized," she continued, "every time I go to visit him he gets excited, jokes with me, and constantly wants to touch me." Addressing me, she emphasized, "Of course, he should want me. He is like my father, and I am so pretty, fat, and as white as snow." She claimed to dislike her permanent marriage, despite the fact that she was more secure that way, and indeed had maneuvered Isma'il to contracting one with her. She said that she would prefer to be a *sigheh* wife. In fact, she said she often begged Isma'il to divorce her and *sigheh* her instead, because, as she kept saying, "*sigheh* has religious reward, *savab*." Besides, she did not want to be tied down.[13] Fati Khanum consistently ignored her husband's objections to her outside activities and would spend most of her time away from him. Since he was an old and frail man, he could not prevent her from doing what she pleased.

Fati claimed to have a Qur'anic education and a good knowledge of the *shari'a*. She employed her knowledge to guide other women—and some men—and would perform religious rituals, preach, or read prayer books for them. Like Mahvash, Fati had a good knowledge of *sigheh* rules and regulations, but unlike Mahvash, she was not so much interested in its sexual aspects. She sounded more like a moralist and preferred to be a matchmaker of sorts. Fati went to great lengths to impress upon me how important the religious merit of *sigheh* was, and how frequently she had mediated a meeting between desiring men and women, thus preventing them from committing a "sinful act." So overwhelming was her enthusiasm for the moral soundness of *sigheh* that she even had a how-to *sigheh* pamphlet printed out for her. She distributed it among people, primarily men, in mosques, shrines, prayer gatherings, cabs, and buses. This pamphlet, according to Fati, contained a detailed description of the rules and procedures of *sigheh* marriage, specifically stressing how easily it could be contracted, how great was its religious and moral reward, and how satisfying were its personal benefits.

Fati Khanum took pride in her matchmaking capacity and in her own mediating ability to bring together interested men and women. Once on a bus trip, she recalled, a woman passenger appeared to her to be flirting with the bus driver, whom Fati described as very handsome. Perceiving their interaction as objectionable, Fati Khanum decided to teach them a thing or two about *sigheh*, and she so instructed them. They were then happily joined in a temporary union by no other than Fati herself. Not only did she perform the *sigheh* ceremony for couples, she often sought out likely men and women and encouraged them to *sigheh*, for, as she kept repeating, *sigheh* has religious merit.

Underscoring her convictions in the functional necessity of *sigheh*, Fati told me that she even arranged a *sigheh* for her own husband. Whether she was feeling harassed by his "incessant sexual advances," as she put it, or was trying to manipulate him further, or both, Fati one day went to the shrine in Qom in the hope of finding a *sigheh* wife for her husband. She said, "I saw this young woman sitting in a corner in the shrine loafing around."[14] Learning that she was from Tehran on a pilgrimage in Qom and without friends there, she then asked her if she would be willing to become her husband's *sigheh* for one night. The Tehrani woman expressed interest, and Fati took her home. Fati performed the *sigheh* ceremony between her husband and the woman,[15] and she herself "spent the night out in the yard." The next day, her husband paid the woman twenty *tuman* as her brideprice, and while bidding her good-bye, Fati instructed her to observe her required waiting period. In another instance, Fati once passed on a *sigheh* pamphlet to a cab driver, who subsequently became so interested in the idea that he asked her if she knew of any woman who would be willing to become his *sigheh*. She knew of one, fetched her, and performed the ceremony between them. For her services, Fati Khanum said she charged no fees and claimed even to pay some money to needy couples. She emphasized that she performs all these charitable acts to please God, hoping to gain more and more *savab* for herself in the world beyond.

As for her own *sigheh* marriages, for which she has a reputation, Fati was much more secretive. From her point of view, it was important for her to become the elderly Isma'il's *sigheh* first, to see if they could live together. Admitting candidly her dislike for sexual intercourse, she maintained, "If these men were willing to forgo sexual intercourse, I wouldn't mind becoming their *sigheh*. But alas, what man would want to do that?"

Once she attempted to do that, but it ended in chaos and confusion. Fati said she made a nonsexual *sigheh* arrangement with a married man, but when he took her to his house, his first wife fainted upon seeing them together, and Fati rushed away. Beyond this, Fati was not willing to disclose the nature or the number of her *sigheh* marriages. She, however, described her frequent trips to Mashhad, during which time she had negotiated and arranged *sigheh* contracts for this or that person. When I asked her why she would go to Mashhad so frequently, she shrugged her shoulders and said "pilgrimage." At one point she made the startling comment that if I [the interviewer] were not married, we could make a profitable business, *kasibi*, by becoming *sigheh*! In vain did I try to probe further. She laughed with abandon and said that she was only joking.

When I asked her what motivates women to *sigheh*, she replied immediately, "Women do *sigheh* because they need money. A lot of them are wretched, hungry, and have to find a way to satisfy these needs. But," she continued, "there are some women who do it for sex. It is very pleasing to become a *sigheh* wife, because the man wants to be with you all the time. He has paid for you. The time is short, and he doesn't want to miss his chance. His wife, he knows, is always there. Any time he wants he can go to her. No need to hurry."[16] I asked, if *sigheh* is so easy, why then are there not more women doing it? "Because," she said quickly, "a lot of girls look down upon *sigheh* . . . this used to be true at the time of the *taghut* [lit., an idol, a term coined by Ayatollah Khomeini to refer to the Pahlavi regime]. Nowadays more and more girls take advantage of it and do it. Even if there is sex involved, virgins do it from behind." Since the revolution of 1979, Fati believed, *sigheh* has become more prevalent. "During the *taghut* regime, people were discouraged from arranging contracts of temporary marriage. The inns and motels couldn't give rooms to *sigheh* couples," Fati continued. "Now even if certain activities go on in them, it is no one's business, since it is Islamic."

How do men and women find a *sigheh* spouse? What techniques do they employ to identify each other? I asked. Fati described several ways of finding a suitable *sigheh* mate. A most common technique—also described to me by other informants—occurs when a woman is pursued by a mulla (or a shaikh, as Fati referred to them); "the type of woman who hesitates in the street unnecessarily, loafing around, turning her head this way or that way aimlessly." Such a woman is usually followed and, at a suitable moment, is directly proposed to. Another approach, according to Fati, occurs when a mulla (or other men) follows a woman whom he has fancied, in the hope of locating her house and learning something about her marital status. Once certain that she is not married, he then approaches her directly and conveys his interest to her. Or, it may happen that a woman who is apartment hunting may be proposed to. Obviously, the belief is that such a woman is not married, for otherwise she would not be looking for a room; she would be living with her husband, or with her family, if she were a virgin. Fati said that an incident of this kind happened to her when she was looking for a place to rent. "Everywhere I went, everyone I talked to would say, 'Khanum, you who are so pretty, white, and fat shouldn't be looking for a room to rent. You should be getting married.'" On the other hand, searching for an apartment to rent may be a pretext by which a woman can communicate certain messages about herself, that is, that she is unmarried and available. Conversely, she can learn of the local gossip, which may then provide her with some leads (as in the case of Fati herself). Most of the people who propose *sigheh* are mullas, Fati maintained.

Still another method is through matchmakers. They can be mullas, old women, or men, or "those who have the ability to distinguish the type of woman who would *sigheh.*" These matchmakers, according to Fati, charge their customers a fee for finding them a *sigheh.* The amount of brideprice depends on the duration of the *sigheh* as well as on other agreements made at the time of the *sigheh.* The woman's age and physique are important factors. Most men, she said, have their own apartments and take their *sighehs* there.

Fati was adamant about the importance of keeping *'idda,* but she knew of some women in Tehran who were not as scrupulous about observing their waiting period. She found this most offensive. I posed Mahvash's question to her: whether sodomy required a waiting period. "Yes," she answered unhesitatingly. She knew it because she had asked a knowledgeable mulla about it and was told that "sodomy is like intercourse, and thus requiring the stipulated period of sexual abstinence."[17]

We set a date for the next day, and Fati prepared to leave. Just as she was going out of the house, she said jokingly that I should pay her for her "preachings." I had indeed wanted to pay her some money but hesitated because she was a relative of my host. Before I could get a chance to reach out for my purse, my host, who had returned a few minutes earlier, scolded her, saying that she should be ashamed of herself for asking for money. Fati laughed in her own shrill manner again, saying that she was only teasing me. Fati did not show up for our next meeting, and I was unable to reach her again.

SHAHIN

Shahin was born into a relatively well-off middle-class family. Her father was a military officer, and her mother was a daughter of a khan, a tribal leader. According to Shahin, both were authoritarian and ill humored, especially her mother. Shahin is the only daughter, and the youngest of three siblings. "My mother," said Shahin, "loves boys and dislikes girls. I don't remember my mother ever kissing me. In fact, I remember distinctly how she pushed me away with her elbow once when I tried to lean on her lap. I was only two years old. I still feel the pain in my chest. My parents never loved me. I never heard a nice word from them." It was her mother who ran the household, wielded greater power, and treated her most harshly.

"From an early age," said Shahin, "I was aware of men's presence, and would exchange glances with boys in our neighborhood any time I got a chance." Her first serious love affair began when she was only twelve years old. "One day when I was sitting at our balcony, I sensed the gaze of a young man who happened to be our neighbor. I smiled and threw my head back and ran into our house. The next day, I saw him throwing a matchbox into our yard; I ran to get it and found a love note in it." For two years they secretly conveyed messages to each other. She would use the services of their servant, and he his cousin. "Gradually, I became bolder and made a date to see him." They went to movies together and would walk in parks for hours. "We loved each other so much," she said nostalgically. They continued their secret affair until her mother became suspicious and discovered their forbidden relationship. Her mother was outraged. She taunted her husband into giving Shahin a good beating and punishing their servant. "My father was so angry with me that he said he did not want to see me ever again."

By then her lover, who was seven years older, had become a low-ranking army officer and was appointed to go to the northwest city of Tabriz. He wanted Shahin to go along with him, but she resisted, knowing that her "parents wouldn't agree to our marriage because his family was from Azerbaijan, and also not as well off as my family. I wasn't quite sure if I wanted to marry him, either. But when my father treated me so badly, I decided to run away." Having obtained the young man's address in Tabriz, Shahin dropped out of high school, packed a small suitcase, and took a bus to that city in northwest Iran. She was sixteen at the time. His family, she said, gave her a warm welcome and accepted her among themselves. In a few months they decided to get married. They returned to Tehran, to the house adjacent to Shahin's parents' house.

A direct approach to obtain her parents' consent seemed futile. Therefore, in accordance with Shi'i-Iranian civil law that required a father's permission for a virgin daughter's first marriage, the couple placed a notice of their intention to marry in a daily newspaper.[18] When after fifteen days they did not receive any response from her father, they went ahead with the arrangements for the wedding and held the ceremony in their house. Shahin's parents did not attend, and her two brothers were abroad in France and in Germany. Later on that year her parents sold their house for one-quarter of its market value, Shahin said, and left that neighborhood in order to avoid running into Shahin or her husband and his family.

The frustration of Shahin's parents was further compounded by the fact that Shahin had been betrothed to her paternal parallel cousin. In her view, her cousin was a nice man but was much older, and she liked him "just like a brother." Shahin, however, was not quite sure about her mother's feelings for her cousin. She described her mother's interaction with her betrothed cousin as an "infatuation with boys. My mother, I guess, was in love with my cousin. Every time he came to our house she would shower him with kisses. She would even kiss him on his lips. I was so ashamed of her flirtations with him."

Shahin's life with her husband was at first very pleasant, but it turned bitter gradually, as she became more and more possessive of him. He was, in her eyes, a handsome man, and she did not like seeing him being friendly with other women. She said she loved her husband very much, but that she was very temperamental with him. Their marriage lasted ten years. Shahin's decision to go back to high school and obtain her diploma, in her view, was the straw that broke the camel's back, as it were. He disliked the idea and "was afraid that I would get a job, and then he wouldn't be able to control me." She was ambivalent in her own feeling toward her husband, vacillating between being possessive and rejecting at the same time. He tried to prevent her from going to school, but she became more adamant. They argued constantly, and finally, "I asked him to divorce me." He obliged immediately, and soon afterward he married a woman whom he had apparently known secretly for some time.

Her husband took custody of their two daughters but permitted Shahin to visit them any time she wanted. After two years, however, he was transferred to Tehran, leaving Shahin behind in Tabriz. At the time of our interview, it had been some seven or eight years since her divorce,[19] but Shahin still regretted her hasty action and in a nostalgic mood said, "I still love him."

Shahin's loneliness led her to seek a job, and eventually she found a secretarial position at a private company. In her new environment she became acquainted with a young Frenchman with "big green eyes." They dated for a while, and eventually Shahin moved into his apartment. "Neither one of us knew the other's language," Shahin said laughing. "But with the help of a dictionary I managed to learn some French." They lived together happily for one year, before their relationship was disrupted by the Iranian revolution of 1979. The Frenchman's landlady, who, according to Shahin, was herself interested in him, reported them to one of the local revolutionary committees. They were arrested and taken to the committee. "We were both terrified," said Shahin. "He didn't know exactly what was going on, and was looking at me quizzically." Fortunately, it was in the beginning of the revolution, and they were not punished physically. However, they were warned not to see each other any more, and soon after his company transferred him elsewhere, outside Iran. "I don't have any information about his whereabouts now. I only know his name. I never got his address in France, thinking that we would go there together as he had promised. I miss him very much. I am such an unfortunate woman," Shahin reflected. "Anyone I love one way or another leaves me. But I keep hoping."

With the Frenchman gone, Shahin had no reason to stay in Tabriz any longer. She packed again and went back to Tehran, landing in her paternal uncle's house, the same uncle whose son had been engaged to marry her.

Not surprisingly, she was not really welcomed there. She was aware of that but had no other place to go. She could not go back to her parents' home. Her father was dead; her mother refused to see her; and her older brother, who was fifty-five years old and still unmarried, had returned to Iran and was living with their mother. If by chance he would meet her, "he would pierce [her] heart" by using sarcastic language and insulting her for her frequent liaisons and marriages.

Through a cousin, Shahin was introduced to an old man who wanted to marry her but who told her point-blank that he was impotent. Feeling like a "superfluous woman"[20] and faced with all kinds of familial and social pressures, Shahin agreed to marry him, but the marriage ended in divorce in less than two months. To her surprise, however, Shahin realized that during her union with the old man she was treated more respectfully by others. This she learned when one of her cousins admitted to her that "she felt more comfortable and proper to invite me to her house because I was not a single woman. My family didn't care whether or not we were suitable for each other, or whether I was happy. As long as I was married, that was enough for them. He was no husband for me. I didn't like him."

After two unsuccessful marriages, Shahin returned to her uncle's house again and lived there for several more weeks. "It was obvious," she recalled, "my uncle didn't want me there." It was then that she started looking for a job and found a position as a nurse at a private home. In exchange for room and board and a monthly salary, she assumed the duty of taking care of an elderly arthritic lady. Her employer told me that Shahin apparently never realized the seriousness of her job, that she would do anything but perform her duties, and that she was really looking for a safe and comfortable place in order to get out of her uncle's house. Soon Shahin became more of a burden than a help to the family and was asked to leave. Feeling sorry for her, however, Shahin's employer asked a well-to-do relative of hers to give Shahin a room where she could stay while she looked for another job.

This time Shahin decided to respond to an advertisement for a housekeeper. Her interview took her to a beautiful mansion in northern Tehran. She was stupefied by the amount of wealth displayed there and was charmed enormously by the appearance and behavior of her would-be employer, Zia. After the initial conversation, he told her, in Shahin's words: "You really shouldn't be looking for such a low position. You should be the lady of such a household." Shahin was overwhelmed by the attention she was receiving, but he did not hire her—at least not immediately—though he promised to phone her soon.

Weeks passed, and Shahin did not hear anything from Zia. A discouraged Shahin finally accepted a low-paying job at a boutique whose owner was a friend of her ex-employer. After two months, however, Shahin gave up all hopes of employment at Zia's mansion, quit her job, and went to Tabriz to visit her children, whose father had once again been transferred there. No sooner had she settled there than she received an unexpected phone call from Zia asking her to return to Tehran. Shahin complied happily, returning to Tehran immediately. But Zia still did not hire her, not as his housekeeper. Instead, he asked her on a date. She told me how perfect she thought Zia was for her; he was middle-aged, rich, and kind. He was also married and had four grown children.

Soon Zia promised to marry Shahin, to buy her a big house, and even take her to America. She had never been happier in her life. He went on promising without making any effort to fulfill his promises. In the meantime, his family found out about his affair. Somehow his sons learned Shahin's telephone number and placed threatening phone calls to her. Ignoring his sons' warnings and pressured by Shahin to come through with his promises, Zia fixed a date to take Shahin to a notary public's office and to register their marriage. Just before the ceremony was about to begin, however, he informed Shahin that because his divorce to his first wife was not yet final and because he did not want them to get into any trouble or to waste time by waiting for a court's permission, she should agree to marry him temporarily. Shahin told me that she was caught in a bind, worrying that she might lose him if she did not agree. Her ex-employer, however, said that from the beginning Shahin had sensed Zia's intention but had not wanted to admit it to herself. Not only that, her ex-employer had warned Shahin of her own suspicion of Zia's motives, but to no avail. In any case, upon the recommendation of the registrar, a mulla friend of Zia, he did not specify a brideprice for Shahin — or so Shahin thought — but instead agreed to give her fifty *tuman* per day.[21] Further, they agreed on a *sigheh* for life, *sigheh 'umri*, as Shahin was convinced by Zia that this was equivalent to a permanent marriage.

Shahin's happiness knew no bounds. For their honeymoon, Zia took her to the Caspian Sea and treated her to the best restaurants and hotels. Back in Tehran, he took her to see several houses that were for sale, but every time she expressed an interest in one of them, he would find some problems with it. However, he did not stop promising to find her a beautiful house, one appropriate to her new status.

Sometime toward the end of the first month after their *sigheh*, Zia decided to take Shahin to his house where his first wife and children also lived. Feeling shy and unwelcome, and out of "courtesy to his first wife," Shahin accepted Zia's suggestion that she sleep in a separate room. She was put in an upstairs room while Zia spent the night in another one downstairs. In the middle of the night his sons and their mother crept into Shahin's room, woke her up, and beat her unmercifully. Zia heard nothing and slept throughout the attack.

Promising revenge, Zia took Shahin to a guest house somewhere in northern Tehran. Her feelings for him remained unchanged. He rented her a suite and promised to buy her her very own house. He further assured her that the rent was paid, and that she could stay there for as long as she wanted. A few days later he returned, recalled Shahin, trying to coax her to go with him to the same notary public's office and to cancel their *sigheh* contract! His reasoning was that this way he could thwart his first wife's efforts should she try to sue him and demand concessions from him. In addition, this would protect Shahin from further attacks by his sons. He reassured her that nothing would change his feelings. Shahin was hesitant but, against the advice of her well-wishers, went along with Zia's scheme and let herself be deceived once again. She officially canceled her *sigheh* marriage and went back to her motel room, still filled with hopes and expectations. Shahin never heard from Zia again.

Before the month was over, the motel's management informed her that she was expected to move out because her occupancy was paid for only one month. In desperation, she tried to contact Zia, but to no avail. He never again returned her phone calls, and she dared not to go to his house in search of him. Once again, Shahin found herself heartbroken and lonely.

Perceiving herself as "gullible and naïve," Shahin now believes that Zia deceived her into becoming his *sigheh* out of vengeance against his wife. Shahin did not know exactly what was the point of contention between Zia and his wife but knew that she was "sacrificed" in the process. She was in a reflective mood toward the end of our long conversation and acknowledged that her ignorance of *sigheh* rules and procedures had worked against her in her temporary marriage. She said that she had only heard of *sigheh* but never liked the idea. After her disappointing *sigheh*, she said, she tried to learn more about it, and now she thinks she has a good understanding of the whole system. Asked if she would *sigheh* again, she responded negatively, adding immediately, however, "if there is some kind of guarantee in it, or if it is for life, I may do it again," apparently forgetting that there was no guarantee in her presumably *sigheh* for life with Zia.

At the time of our interview Shahin was involved in a lawsuit against her mother and older brother — the mother's favorite child, as Shahin kept saying. They were trying to deprive her of her rightful share of the inheritance left by her father. She was living with a family and was helping with household chores, but apparently she was unable to remain at any one job for any extended period. Shahin's inability to maintain any job commitments for long is understandable. As a middle-class woman she was expected to marry, to have a few children and a house, and to be supported for the rest of her life, all of which she had had and lost. In her social class, keeping a job, a menial job at that, is perceived as demeaning and beneath one's dignity. A few weeks before I left Tehran, I heard that she was seriously looking for a husband, often making suggestions to her employer to introduce her to some of the family's unmarried male friends.

NANIH

Nanih is a woman in her early fifties.[22] She has been a domestic servant for the past twenty years or so. I interviewed her at the home of her employer. Nanih has no formal education and seemed a bit amused at my interest in the subject of *sigheh* marriage in general and in her in particular. She did not volunteer much information, and her answers were relatively unelaborate. Often I had to probe several times to get responses longer than a "yes" or "no" or "maybe." Although she eagerly accepted the gifts and money I gave her, she persistently found ways to defer our subsequent interviews.

Nanih was born in a village near Sabzevar, in the northeast province of Khorasan. She never went to school and was married at a very young age to her paternal parallel cousin. She was happy with her marriage, but unfortunately it did not last long. Her husband died after a few years, leaving her alone with their only son. By then Nanih, like many other inhabitants of her village, was addicted to opium. "In our village," said Nanih, "everybody smokes opium; men, women, and even children. All are opium addicts."

Near where she was working as a domestic servant there was a small auto garage where she used to smoke opium secretly. In one of her excursions, Nanih made the acquaintance of the neighborhood garbage collector, Ahmad, who happened to be from the same village. Although occasionally smoking opium, he was not as addicted as Nanih was. Soon they became interested in each other, and when Ahmad offered to *sigheh* her for one year, she immediately accepted, even though he was a few years her junior. His first marriage had so far proved fruitless, and he had assumed that his wife was at fault. Ahmad contracted a *sigheh* with Nanih, specifying that should she become pregnant, he would then marry her permanently.

Nanih said that because she did not know what a *sigheh* was, she kept asking people about it. "I wanted to know," she said, "if I got pregnant whether he would get a birth certificate for my child." They went to a mulla to perform the rite for them. This marriage, too, proved fruitless, and much to Ahmad's dismay, they discovered that "it was not my fault. He was fruitless." By then, however, they had grown quite fond of each other and decided to renew their contract. Nanih was evidently quite popular in her neighborhood. Her employer told me that several neighborhood shopkeepers had approached her, asking her to persuade Nanih to marry them. Most of these offers, her employer said, were for a *sigheh* contract.

At the time of renewing their contract, Ahmad instructed Nanih to keep *'idda*. Thus, she said, she had to wait forty-five days before they actually signed a new contract for ninety-nine years.[23] "I did not ask for bride-price or daily maintenance," said Nanih, "but he would buy me gifts every now and then." He took her to Mashhad twice, where they stayed in a motel owned by an acquaintance of Nanih, who also provided them with some opium. It was during this trip that through Ahmad's patience and persuasion Nanih was able to kick her habit. "He never forced me to stop smoking," said Nanih, "but he was very good at giving me moral support and encouraging me to get rid of my habit." Nanih and Ahmad actually spent little time together, for they each lived separately: Ahmad with his permanent wife, and Nanih with her employer. But they enjoyed each other's company during the time they were together. "Before he became a hajji," said Nanih, "he used to take me to movies, but we don't go anywhere anymore." At the time of our interview Nanih and Ahmad were well into the sixteenth year of their temporary marriage.

Ahmad did not want his first wife to know anything about their *sigheh*, and likewise, Nanih was doing her best not to let her only son and daughter-in-law find out about it. They would meet each other in the house of Nanih's employer, who, being divorced herself, was quite supportive of Nanih's *sigheh* contract. Nanih and Ahmad continued their half-secret union for several years before Ahmad's wife found out about it and forbade him to see Nanih again or to go to her employer's house, for whom Ahmad, too, was occasionally working.

Despite his promise to his wife, Ahmad continues to visit Nanih every time he has a chance. Their families have never met. Her relatives are all back in her village, and nobody knows anything about her *sigheh*. "In our village," she maintained, "nobody *sigheh*s. It is shameful. Nobody knows I am a *sigheh*."

Asked what motivated her to become Ahmad's *sigheh*, she said, "Because I fell in love with him. I wanted him and was happy to be his *sigheh*, even though I was much older than him. After sixteen years my son still doesn't know about our relationship; even if he does, he pretends otherwise." Asked why her son may object to her marriage, she said, "He might object why I married a younger man who doesn't give me any money, or has not rented me a house. I did it because I liked him."

TUBA

Tuba is from Kashan and in her late twenties. I interviewed her twice, once for several hours, and the second time for an entire day when we shopped together, cooked lunch together, shared bread and salt, and talked.

Tuba was born into a poor family of seven children. Her mother is fifty-five years old and, according to Tuba, has become pregnant twenty-three times. Only seven of her children have survived to adulthood. Tuba is the fifth born and the third daughter. She did not go to school and, like her other sisters, was kept at home to help her mother with carpet weaving.

Her first marriage at the age of sixteen ended in divorce after six months because of her husband's preference for sodomy. He was a policeman from one of the villages around Kashan. "He was very nasty to me," said Tuba. "He wouldn't give me any money and used to beat me up. He would give me money only if I would let him have his way [sodomize her]. He stayed with me," recalled Tuba, "only for the first two nights after our wedding. After that he didn't want to have regular sex." Tuba remained a virgin, she claimed.

Her husband took Tuba to a house that had several tenants in its many rooms. He would torment her by ignoring her while at the same time lavishing attention on their female neighbors, with one of whom he had an affair. "Every time I objected [to his going to their neighbor's room], he would say, 'These women let me do what I want to.'" In order to force Tuba to comply with his wishes, he refused to support her altogether. Dissatisfied and frustrated, Tuba took her case to court several times. But feeling embarrassed and inhibited, she was unable to explain to the court the real reason behind her husband's refusal to provide for her. On the other hand, he, according to Tuba, would deceive the judges every time by promising to take care of her. However, once back home, he would mistreat her again and would not give her daily expenses. Tuba was finally fed up: "I let him keep my brideprice (set for 30,000 *tuman*), gave him 1,000 *tuman*, and got my divorce."[24] It took her four years to finally secure her divorce. Tuba believed that her husband had several lovers, one of whom had used witchcraft on her.

She went back to her parents' house who, in her belief, never cared much for her. For the next four years she continued helping her mother in carpet weaving and other household chores.

It was in a small bank in Kashan where Tuba met her first temporary husband, Aqa Rajab. She was in the company of a few female friends who were transacting some business there. While at the bank she noticed Aqa Rajab's steady gaze on her. She was overwhelmed by his attention. It was love at first sight. Commenting on their first encounter, Tuba said, "I was looking much prettier those days. I was plump, white, and blond."[25] He pursued her relentlessly and eventually, with the help of a neighbor, arranged to visit Tuba at the neighbor's house. There, he told her how much he "wanted" her and that if she did not respond to his request positively, he would make "trouble" for her. "He said, 'I'll do this for you,' 'I'll do that for you,' and I liked him too." Later on, in describing her interaction with her second *sigheh* husband, Tuba used similar language to indicate his intense love for her.

Aqa Rajab promised he would do anything for her should she accede to his wishes. "We fell in love," she said with a broad smile on her face. Soon afterward he offered to *sigheh* her for life. "I didn't know anything about *sigheh*," said Tuba. "I had only heard that it existed. My family didn't know much about it either, but neither one of us wanted to let go of the other." He gave her a promissory note, and they agreed on a brideprice of 50,000 *tuman*.[26] It was not until two months later that Aqa Rajab finally informed Tuba that he was married and that his wife and son were living in Esfahan. He told her, however, that he did not like his wife and was going to divorce her.

He rented her a house and paid her daily expenses. "We were together day and night," said Tuba. Her family, with the exception of her father, were happy with their marriage. They all treated them like "husband and wife" and would associate with them frequently. "Everyone was charmed by Aqa Rajab, even my father, who did not originally approve of our *sigheh*."

During the second year of their *sigheh* contract, Aqa Rajab was transferred to Tehran. He left Tuba without giving her any money or making arrangements for their one-year-old son. "I wanted him," said Tuba, "and I went to Tehran after him. There he deceived me once again. I got pregnant for the second time, but he still refused to pay me any money." Before leaving for Tehran, however, at a suitable moment Aqa Rajab had stolen the promissory note he had given Tuba on the day of their temporary marriage.

Discouraged and abandoned, once again Tuba went to court, this time to sue Aqa Rajab.[27] But she had no proof of the relationship or the money promised to her as her brideprice. Aqa Rajab, however, agreed to get birth certificates for their children, though he never paid for their daily expenses. "In the court, he told them he had *sighehed* me for four years. He lied, and I couldn't prove his dishonesty." The court, in turn, ruled that she had waited long enough and did not need to keep *'idda* any more. She was told she was free to remarry. It is not quite clear why the court did not make any arrangements for child support, which is legally binding on the father. In any case, Tuba claimed that Aqa Rajab had never paid anything for his children during the past seven years, and that this was the reason for her taking a job.

Forsaken by Aqa Rajab with two children and tormented by her parents' relentless verbal whipping, Tuba found a job at a day-care center. "I took care of other people's kids, and left my own kids in my mother's care." Tuba arranged to pay her mother some money in exchange for her babysitting services. "Unfortunately," recalled Tuba, "one day my little girl was found dead in the small pool of my parents' house." She held Aqa Rajab responsible for the tragedy and cursed him bitterly for abandoning his own children.

Some two years later a young police officer who lived in the neighborhood became interested in Tuba. Tuba said that she likes policemen: "Their uniform appeals to me," she said repeatedly. Because she was a young divorcee, her company was sought by many men, who would convey their messages to her through such intermediaries as mutual acquaintances, friends, or by letters or "chance" meetings. When one of her coworkers, herself temporarily married to a policeman, told Tuba of this particular police officer's interest in her, Tuba became excited once again. She agreed to meet with Riza at the home of her friend. He expressed his strong desire for Tuba and pursued her persistently. According to Tuba, he would literally block her way in the street, demanding that she should accept his offer of friendship. He would say, in Tuba's words, "If I can't be with you, I'll kill you."[28] Once or twice he offered to take her to her home in his police car, and gradually he found his way to her heart. As a token of his esteem for her, he borrowed some money from Tuba herself and bought her some fabric for a black veil. Tuba learned of the financial arrangement later.

Their mutual friends arranged several meetings between Riza and Tuba at their home. It was in one of these meetings that Riza and Tuba personally negotiated the terms of their marriage. Riza wanted to *sigheh* Tuba, but this time she was hesitant. She consulted her mother, and they decided that Riza should marry her permanently. Tuba discussed the issue with Riza and he promised to do just that. Riza's friend invited a mulla to their house and in their presence, but her family's absence, the mulla performed the ceremony for them. Riza gave Tuba a promissory note for 5,000 *tuman* and agreed on a deferred brideprice of 40,000 *tuman*. Noticing that the mulla did not register their marriage in his ledger book, Tuba objected but was told that he had left his big ledger at his office, and that he would document their marriage as soon as he returned to his office. "I learned then," reflected Tuba with resignation, "that he had pulled the hat over my eyes. My friend's temporary husband, the mulla, and Riza all had conspired together, and it was already too late." Tuba was so upset that for one week she did not pay him any attention, not until he promised to change their *sigheh* into marriage, *nikah*. Riza never did fulfill his promise once they consummated their marriage. He argued that he was afraid his father would have a heart attack if he were to hear the news of their marriage.

Realizing that Tuba's brideprices were all relatively large — all of them deferred, of course — I asked her how they arrived at these figures and who negotiated the terms of her contract in her three marriages. For her first marriage, because it was of permanent type, her parents conducted the entire negotiation and discussion. Tuba did not know anything about what was going on and waited in the wings for their final decision. But for the other two she performed the bargaining procedure herself. "Usually you bargain," said Tuba. "You say this much, the man says 'no.' Then the person who is present — in this case, their friends — would say 'neither her words nor his, but something in between.' The prettier you are," stressed Tuba, "the higher

your brideprice and your respect. If you are a virgin, pretty, young, and literate, then you can be sure to get a good brideprice. Beyond that," Tuba said
with resignation, "whatever they [men] give, you get."

Riza, unlike Tuba's first temporary husband, neither provided a
separate household for her nor paid her daily expenses, but he would visit her
at her parents' house every now and then. Nobody in Tuba's family liked
Riza, and none of her siblings ever invited them to their homes. Both of her
parents scolded her for her frequent *sigheh* marriages and for her inability to
find herself a suitable permanent husband. Her father was so angry at her
that he would constantly quarrel with his own wife, who would try to create
some sort of buffer between the father and the daughter. Tuba's parents finally stopped talking to each other altogether, even though they continued to
live in the same household. Her father also refused to support his wife any
more. This is one reason why, despite her conflicting feelings toward her
mother, Tuba continued to give her some money in exchange for her babysitting for her son.

"He did it," reasoned Tuba, "out of lust. If Riza really wanted me,
he would have married me [permanently]. I really suffered over him." After
their *sigheh*, he never again brought her any gifts. Worse yet, she was laid off
from her job because of him, for the authorities in the day-care center did
not like a *sigheh* employee who, on top of everything else, was pregnant.
Riza, too, did not want any children and asked Tuba to obtain an abortion. As
if talking to herself, Tuba recalled how her first husband's lover had used
witchcraft on her. She was certain that because of it, no man would care for
her beyond three months. "I don't want to get married again. I am afraid her
predictions might come true again," she said.

Barely a year into their *sigheh*, Tuba heard the news of her temporary husband's plan for a permanent marriage. "It was as if the whole world
was turning around my head. I felt as if the ceiling was closing in on me. It
made me so very unhappy. My friends would bring me the news of his wedding preparations: how big it was going to be, how fancy it was, and I became unhappier every day. He never threw a party for me. We didn't have a
wedding." Her friends advised her to make a fuss by her sudden appearance
at the ceremony. "I refused," reflected Tuba. "Something had been broken
in my heart. I was six months pregnant then, but I went and had an abortion.
I didn't want any more children." Using a popular Persian metaphor, she
said, "He burned me."

Despite being newly married, Tuba's temporary husband did not
wish to let go of her altogether. He would still go to visit her at her parents'
home. But every time, according to Tuba, they would end up arguing, and
he would depart on an angry note. Once, however, when he went to visit her,
he was in a good mood. "We joked and laughed," said Tuba, "but when he left

I quickly discovered that he had stolen the promissory note which I used to keep under the mattress." Furious, she went to him and demanded the return of the document. He refused, and she took him to court. She appealed to an influential bureaucrat, at whose house Tuba's mother was a part-time domestic. Through his help she was able to collect 20,000 *tuman* from Riza, with which she leased her present apartment. Their *sigheh* was canceled, and Tuba went back to work. Presently she is working as a low-ranking employee in one of the offices affiliated with a government ministry in Kashan.

Tuba believed that Riza still liked her, and that he did not really want to cancel their *sigheh*, but she was adamant about it. "He liked me and said so," Tuba said. "He didn't want to let go of me, but he wanted me to stay in the background. I was both his wife and not his wife." In her opinion, having a child affected her life in general, and her relations with men in particular. "If a man is but an angel," she said, "his wife's kid is like his cowife, *havu*." She was obviously in pain every time she recalled the agonies she felt during her *sigheh* marriage with Riza. She remembered how he had expressed his love and affection for her little boy before she became his *sigheh*, and how he would try to convince her that a boy needed a father. But once they were married, he changed his attitude completely, often beating the little boy unmercifully. On the only trip Riza ever took with Tuba, he became angry with the boy and beat him savagely. "My son fainted and later on had a seizure. For a while he was paralyzed. He is still very weak. I didn't dare say anything to him because I thought my son was somebody else's child, and that he had married me despite having a child. I didn't know what to do."

As if the suffering at the hands of her temporary husband was not enough, Tuba was psychologically tormented by Riza's new permanent wife. She would place harassing phone calls to Tuba at work, scolding her as being *sigheh* wife and calling her all names. Tuba complained to Riza but was told that she should do likewise. Riza himself was unwilling to talk to his wife and ask her to stop her obscene telephone calls.

Asked whether she would become a *sigheh* again, Tuba responded, "Until I die, I will never *sigheh* again. I never thought about becoming a *sigheh*. Even if someone had told me so, I wouldn't have believed it. I don't know how it turned out this way. The more you are scared of something, the greater the chance that it will happen to you. First I thought only bad women *sigheh*. Now I regret why I did it the first time. Both times I thought they were going to marry me [permanently]. Both swore to the Qur'an they would live with me, and both tricked me," she reflected. "I felt my rights were violated. But because I was a *sigheh*, I couldn't prove it. I should have tried to understand what *sigheh* was and what its conditions were." As if talking to herself, she continued, "I hate men nowadays. I even hate my own brothers. So, you can imagine how I feel toward others." She admitted, however, that some men, including Riza, have been solicitous of her company by sending her messages by phone, letters, or through intermediaries, but that she had refused them all. However, the family who introduced Tuba to me were skeptical of this claim. Their guess was that Tuba might be in fact making short-term temporary marriage contracts.

Like Fati Khanum, Tuba used the euphemistic phrase "going to bathe" when referring to the act of sexual intercourse. "Men," stated Tuba, "mostly want women for their baths. If their wives have their period for three days, they go and marry another woman. All Kashi men have a *sigheh*. Sometimes wives play it too coy for their husbands, and so men go and *sigheh*. Men," she went on, "like their *sigheh* wife more. They are proud to be known among people as having two wives. They want to go to their *sigheh* wife all the time. When you don't have much of something, you want it more than something you already have. A man's bath is mostly for his *sigheh* wife. My second husband [her first *sigheh*] wanted it every night. I loved it. He would wait for me. He wanted me to enjoy it too; otherwise it was no good. Sometimes, he wanted it three or four times a night. I never said I didn't want it. I just went along. I was embarrassed to go to the public bath so frequently. I would use the small pool in our own yard to do my ablution, *ghusl*. What would people say? But," changing her tone of voice, she stated, "not everything is rosy because of it. *Sigheh* is [like] an hour love [it is short-lived]." Tuba continued, "Most men play it coy for their *sigheh* wife, and women don't have any hold over them. They can simply leave them anytime they want."

Tuba's perception of women's sense of self, and their motivations for contracting temporary marriage, was ambivalent, underscoring the tension between social expectations and individual volition. She said, "Women are gullible. I was deceived. But even if he [her first temporary husband] hadn't *sighehed* me, I would have become his lover. It is not the money that concerns women. Men who *sigheh* don't pay much. Most women think their relationship will last. I thought we would never separate."

Tuba was aware of Aqa Rajab's extramarital affairs; he was not discreet about them, anyhow. She did not mind his excursions because he was good-natured at home. On one occasion, however, he brought two young women home and ordered Tuba to prepare dinner for them. Tuba clearly perceived this as an arrogant way to "humiliate me and to force me to lose my self-respect." When one of the newcomers began to flirt with Aqa Rajab, teasing him to buy her a winter coat, Tuba became very indignant and insulted them verbally. This in turn made Aqa Rajab very mad. So he took them home, and when he returned, he gave her a good beating.

Tuba lamented the fate of *sigheh* women, saying, "It is mostly employed, *idari*, women who become *sigheh*. Basically, less fortunate women have to work to support themselves so that, God forbid, they may not commit a sin," that is to say, be forced into prostitution because of economic necessity. "Their husbands might have died, divorced them or deserted them. So that's why they *sigheh*. Unlucky women either work or *sigheh*." Tuba was obviously upset about working. She literally perceived it as a "drag" and wished that some man would support her and free her from drudgery. Reflecting on the sociocultural values of her immediate society, Tuba said, "Being a *sigheh* woman is perceived as bad. People don't look at them as real husband and wife. Even if a man has ten wives, it is still better to be married [to him, and permanently] than to be a *sigheh*." Tuba said she knew of no *sigheh* woman who wouldn't prefer to be a permanent wife. "I prefer a blind husband to a *sigheh* one," immediately adding, however, "but we may have to *sigheh* anyhow."

Tuba spends her nights at her parents' house and her days at her own apartment. "I left my mother's house," said Tuba, "because I didn't want to be there. She scolds me in front of our neighbors, blaming me for my *sighehs*. She calls my son 'that bastard.' I hate it. It makes me so very upset. If my mother says those mean words to my face, just think what others would say behind my back." Her reliance on her mother as a babysitter, however, forced her back to her parents' house again. "It is not exactly what I had in mind when I moved out. It is my fate, *qismat*. It was meant to be this way," she said sadly. Tuba's apartment, however, provides some refuge for her. She entertains her friends there, though she said she seldom spends the night. She is afraid of being the subject of community gossip, though I gathered from others that her reputation is already somewhat tarnished.

Tuba spends her free time mostly in the company of two other women who, like her, are also temporarily married and employed. Their conversation often revolves around their situations. They commiserate over their "unlucky fates." "We say, why are we so unlucky? Why haven't we been married [permanently]? Why do we have to work, carry orders, constantly say 'salam,' bend right and bend left? Why didn't we get our own husbands who would be our provider and support us? We try to console each other." Asked what they do to entertain themselves, she said, "An unmarried woman doesn't go anywhere, but spends her time with her friends going to the public bath, or getting together on occasion, talk, make-up each other's faces, or dye each other's hair."

Tuba was familiar with contraceptives such as the pill and prophylactics but commented that pills are scarce in Kashan and prophylactics are not popular among men. Nor do they care, in her view, for coitus interruptus. She said, "From a hygienic point of view, women are defenseless. All they can do is to get sick. There are still a lot of bad women [prostitutes] in Kashan."

Knowledge of *sigheh*, in her opinion, comes primarily through friends or matchmakers, but never through one's own parents. Tuba herself knew nothing about *sigheh* until the idea was first suggested to her by her first temporary husband. She did not know of any matchmakers in Kashan, despite the fact that there were two very well-known female matchmakers, whom I also interviewed. Introduction between couples is also often done through mutual friends or neighbors. Depending on the length of a *sigheh* marriage, according to Tuba, the couple may spend their married life in the house of their friends, if it is to last one night, or make other arrangements, if the union is to last longer.

IRAN

In her early thirties, Iran[29] is the administrator of a small clinic in east Tehran. When I met her, she was smartly dressed and, much to my surprise, did not have a scarf on her head, as was required of all female employees by the Islamic regime. Her outward appearance defied any stereotyping of a *sigheh* woman. She received me warmly in her office and discussed her life history openly.

Iran's parents have six children, among whom Iran is the third-born daughter. Her mother is her father's second wife and is twenty years his junior. Iran's father is a sickly old man who used to be an opium addict. He has four children from a previous marriage. Both her parents are, Iran told me, quite authoritarian, but it is her mother who manages the household affairs and has things under her control. Iran's father owns a small business and is relatively well off, though a bit stingy, in Iran's opinion. Despite his conservative background, he evidently allowed his children some freedom. He was particularly lenient toward Iran, and she repeatedly emphasized that she is her father's favorite child. Iran and her other siblings all went through high school and obtained their diplomas.

Iran began her life story with her love affair with her first husband. "My first marriage," she said, "took place on account of a childish love. I was twenty-two years old and he was a few months younger. We had known each other ever since we were eleven years old." He was Iran's neighbor, and their families socialized frequently. When they announced their intention to marry, everyone was against it. But the couple resisted the pressure, insisted on the marriage, and eventually prevailed.

"From the moment of our engagement, I realized that there was no understanding between us," recalled Iran, "but we went ahead with the wedding." Feeling the burden of an independent life, they both had to work hard, even when Iran became pregnant soon after their wedding. From

Iran's point of view, their marital problem was primarily due to their living arrangements with her in-laws and not to monetary problems. She said, "Because they were friends of the family, I had assumed that they must have known me better. My mother-in-law, alas, treated me like a bride," that is to say, a stranger. "She had spoiled her son, and wanted me to follow her rules of propriety, whereas I thought she would be more understanding of my way of life."

Iran's son was barely three months old when she filed for divorce, against her husband's objections. The more he resisted the idea of a separation, the more obstinate Iran became. Finally, she granted him her bride-price, half of her belongings which she had brought to his house, and agreed to forgo the custody of her son in exchange for a divorce. "Because I knew he would try to take my son when he is three years old, I told him he could take his custody from then. I only wanted to get out," said Iran. After an unsuccessful attempt at reconciliation a year later, she completely broke away from her husband and moved back to her parents' home. Again, Iran perceived the problem to lie with her mother-in-law, who manipulated her son and interfered in their life. For the next seven years, Iran said, she worked, traveled, socialized, and enjoyed her life, until she met Amir.

Iran met her temporary husband, Amir, on a cold winter morning in 1980 when she was going to work. She described the incident in great detail, from the moment their eyes met as she was waiting in the bus station and he sped by in his sports car, only to back up to offer her a ride. She accepted it without hesitation. He took her to work and gave her his business telephone number. Two days later they had their first date. Attracted to each other, they quickly reached an agreement over the form of their relationship. Amir, a handsome man of thirty-three, told Iran that he was married and had two small daughters. Iran, too, told him that she was divorced and had a small boy in the custody of her ex-husband. In order to show his sincerity to Iran, Amir made it perfectly clear to her that his eagerness in establishing a friendship with Iran was not because his wife was "ill-tempered," in Iran's words, "or ugly," but that he saw it as his "inalienable right," *haqq-i musallam*, to have a "good friend" for himself. He added in the same breath, however, that since he was a "good family man, he would make the same sacrifices for [Iran] as he had done for his family."

A week later they flew to Mashhad for one day to solemnize further their love for each other. In the shrine of Imam Riza they exchanged vows "not to betray each other and to remain faithful in our relationship." He, however, gave her a warning: they should not let his wife know anything about their relationship, or else he would have to choose only one person. Iran said, "And I thought to myself, that person must be his wife!"

Their friendship began to sprout roots. Iran remembered how Amir would call her twice a day, wanting to spend more and more time with her. On two occasions they even traveled to Europe together. They were "just boyfriend and girlfriend," as Iran put it. It was after their second trip that Amir offered to *sigheh* her for six months. "First I thought it was a very stupid idea," said Iran. "Then I thought this was one way of living, too. I didn't know much about the details of *sigheh*, but I thought this was an escape." Apparently, they were worried about the frequent executions of alleged adulterers by the Islamic regime. Iran said, "I decided to do it because I didn't want us to run into any trouble." Although she articulated fear of reprisal from the Islamic regime as the motivating factor for their *sigheh* marriage, her real wish at the same time was an earnest hope in "strengthening our relationship."

Iran and Amir went to a notary public's office, where the head mulla happened to be Iran's new brother-in-law, who had recently married her second sister (his third wife, and her second husband). "In his office," recalled Iran, "I was amused when asked about my brideprice! I thought, before, when I was permanently married, I had to exchange my brideprice for my freedom. What's the use of a brideprice in this type of marriage?" Since brideprice specification is fundamental to a *sigheh* contract, she asked for one gold coin — a mere symbolic gesture — and Amir agreed to pay her one hundred *tuman* daily. He proved to be very generous. He lavished many gifts and much jewelry on her, and contributed much more than they had agreed upon to the household expenses. "He accepted all the expenses, but things were under my control," she commented.

Amir rented Iran an apartment near his jewelry store and arranged to visit her daily. On his way to work, he would pick her up from her parents' home in the morning and take her to their apartment, going to work himself. Not having a job then, Iran would busy herself in their house, cook lunch, and await his return. At lunch time, Amir would go back to Iran, have lunch there, and return to work after a short siesta. At closing time he would drive to their apartment once again, pick her up, and take her to her parents' house, himself returning home to his wife and children.

"As soon as we were married," said Iran, "it seemed as if our friendship came to an end, and all sorts of marital problems got involved." All through our conversation Iran kept emphasizing that, in addition to being lovers, they were friends, too; she prided herself for having the ability to be a man's friend, that is to say, not being just a wife. Articulating the ambivalence they both felt toward their new status, she said, "I am very independent minded and have certain opinions of things and life that nobody can ignore or take them away from me. Many times he would say, 'I am your husband.' He wanted to control me; wanted me to obey him. He would tell me not to go to this friend or that relative's house. But I did what I wanted."

Life was pleasant for Iran and her temporary husband until Amir's permanent wife found out about his temporary marriage. She was evidently tipped off by Iran's best childhood friend (Iran was not over the shock of this "betrayal" yet). The first wife confronted Amir and Iran unexpectedly one evening when they had just left their apartment to go to a party. She appeared suddenly and demanded to know what Amir was doing there, and who Iran was? Struggling to recover his composure, Amir tried unsuccessfully to deceive his permanent wife by leading her to believe that Iran was one of his friends' sisters to whom he was just giving a ride. The wife, for the moment, seemed to believe her husband's words and got into the car with them; the three of them drove away, with Iran being dropped off at her father's home. But the wife was smart and had her own game to play.

She arranged a dinner party and invited Iran, Iran's brother — presumably Amir's friend — and his wife in order to observe Iran and her husband — their husband — at close range. The wife was no fool, and at a suitable moment she whispered to Iran, in her words, "If my husband could betray me with two children, he can do the same thing to you." Caught in a vow of secrecy, Iran steadfastly denied any relations with Amir.

In the meantime Iran became pregnant, and this is where things started to go wrong, she believes. Amir asked her to obtain an abortion, but she wanted to keep the baby. It was "the biggest and most difficult decision in my life," she recalled. Against the advice of her friends, Iran let him convince her to get an abortion. He told Iran that he had no peace at home, since his wife had just given birth to their third daughter, and that he did not want Iran to take that comfort away from him. Besides, he argued, he could not provide for two households simultaneously. Iran finally conceded, but with the condition that he should marry her permanently. She had the abortion but he did not fulfill his promise.

On the day Iran had her abortion an extraordinary incident occurred that eventually led to the total breakup of their friendship and dissolution of their temporary marriage. Whether by accident or by design, Amir's first wife arranged to visit Iran on the same day that she was brought home from the hospital. Of course, she discovered her husband also present. Angrily, she demanded to know what business Amir had at Iran's home at that time of the day! Before Amir could get a chance to respond, Iran's mother intervened and retorted that he had all the rights to be there because he was none other than Iran's husband! Dumbfounded, Amir's first wife challenged them to show her proof of their marriage. Iran's mother happily complied and presented her with their *sigheh* document. Upon seeing the document, she fainted and had to be carried out by her husband. Lonely and depressed, Iran was left to her mother's care just at the moment when she needed Amir more than ever before.

The routine of Amir and Iran's life was interrupted. Their contract had expired, and they had to cut down on the frequency of their visits. This was partly because the first wife was now fully aware of the nature of their relationship and was making life difficult for them, and partly because he wanted them to cut down on their visits. He was "forced to choose only one person. It was getting to the point," Iran said, "where his wife would go to his shop and wait there till he was through with his work, and then they would go home together, so that he couldn't come to see me." Besides, even at times when he managed to go to their apartment and see Iran, he would put all the blame on her, saying that it was through her carelessness that his wife had learned about their relationship; otherwise, he would have never let her know. "I felt guilty," recalled Iran, "but thought how long can one play cat and mouse? I couldn't bear his unhappiness nor the guilty feeling."

Eventually, Iran gave up the apartment and once again moved back to her parents' house. She was disillusioned, and in a reflective mood she said, "I thought his wife's right [to a monogamous relationship] was taken away from her. But it was not my fault either. He was the culprit. He ruined the life of his three kids and the two of us." The whole episode was still fresh in her memory.

After a few depressing months, with the help of a friend Iran started on her present job. "It is two months now," she lamented, "that I haven't seen him at all. It is of no use. Even if he calls me, his wife will find out." In fact, she had called Iran a week prior to our meeting and accused her of placing harassing phone calls to her. Iran reassured her that she had done no such thing and that it was time they had a face-to-face talk. Iran went to her house, and the former cowives had a lively, if painful, encounter. There Iran described to her former cowife her version of their *sigheh* contract and tried to clear out some of the illusions Amir apparently had created about his relations with Iran. By the end of their candid conversation, the first wife told Iran that her life was "ruined," and that, in Iran's words, "after eleven years of marriage and raising three daughters in his house, Amir made me suffer so unjustly." Sympathizing with the wife, Iran said thoughtfully, "It might be true that I made a mistake by choosing a married man, but in turn I tried to help them, too. I could have kept the child that was growing in me. He did me wrong, too."

Before leaving her house and obviously setting herself apart from her cowife, however, Iran advised her, "Now that you know the truth and have a better understanding of Amir and have him back, then be content, and carry on with your life." Then addressing me, she said, "That woman doesn't understand the kind of life an Iranian woman has. Unfaithfulness is in the blood of Iranian men. She must have assumed that because she was pretty and had created a nice and comfortable life for her husband, he would never betray her. No matter how much you give a man, he will still go after other women." Yet in the same breath she continued, "She kept on saying that she couldn't forgive Amir for having made love to me. But I think she lies!"

"I had been divorced for seven years," reflected Iran, "I had a comfortable and organized life. I respected myself. I was not thinking about remarriage. When Amir came to my life he changed everything. He gave me so much hope and courage. I counted on him to make me a good life. After seven years he made me excited about married life once again. Unfortunately, it didn't last more than six months. He left me with a world of thought and all those phone calls from his wife. He wronged us both. On the whole," Iran argued, "a renewed life [remarriage?] doesn't exist for Iranian women. This is true for ninety percent of Iranian women [divorced or widowed]. I didn't think about marrying again. I don't know how it all happened. Well, I guess I did it. You see," she went on, "it is very difficult to be a divorcee in Iranian society. I thought he could end all my problems. I hated people calling me a divorcee, *bivih*."[30]

Iran's perception of Amir, though basically positive, was equivocal. She did not consider him a "chauvinist," *mard salar*, but said, "I don't know how he could upset both his wife and me." She regarded him as helpful and fun to be with and said that she agreed to become his *sigheh* "because I was in love with him." Asked what might have motivated Amir, Iran replied that he considered her a "good friend and companion," that he admired her slim physique, which is unlike that of his wife, and that he liked darker skinned women. Reflecting jovially she added, "*Sigheh* women have greater sex appeal."

I asked her whether she would *sigheh* again. Iran responded negatively, adding, "It was an absurd thing because no one makes a commitment. It is just a way of getting a woman. Women can never do anything, but men can do all they want." Pondering further her *sigheh* contract, Iran continued, "Very simply, he said because everyone had found out about us, we couldn't continue our relationship. Previously," she went on, "I never contemplated *sigheh*. I knew about it, but only that some women would do it in religious cities. I was one hundred percent against it. I think it is becoming more prevalent after the revolution."

Asked about her family's reaction to *sigheh*, Iran said, "My father loves me very much. When he heard I was going to leave our house and live with Amir, he felt very upset. He didn't know what to do. He told me I should try not to spend my time there. He said the same thing for my first marriage. My father didn't want me to marry Amir." As for her mother, Iran said, "She thought I was seeing him anyway and so there was no need to marry him. But I was afraid that his first wife might find out and complain to the revolutionary committees. Everyone in my family loved Amir and treated us like husband and wife. My extended family and relatives all are under the impression that we were married permanently, but they know that he had another wife and children. They know nothing about our *sigheh* or that it has been canceled."

Iran perceived herself to be an honest and kind-hearted woman, because of which she was often taken advantage of. As a case in point, she described in great detail how her best friend informed Amir's wife of their affair, thereby ruining their relationship.

Presently, Iran is dating a middle-aged married man with whom she had an affair before her *sigheh* to Amir. He is an uncle of her first husband and much older than she. Iran was aware that he could not marry her, but she was not sure if she wanted a serious relationship anyway—at least not then.

DISCUSSION

From the case histories presented here, one begins to get a sense of the complexity of women's motivations in making a contract of temporary marriage. This stands in stark contrast to the standardized official Shi'i view that assumes women's motivation to be monolithic and transparently financial. What is common in the life histories of these women is, rather, a dynamic and intertwined double dilemma: one is the conflict between the women's desire — however ambivalent — for being autonomous, and the sociocultural expectations of ideal female passivity; and the other is within women's own subjective understanding of what is ideally expected of them. Caught within these concentric dilemmas, women vacillate between being active subjects and passive objects of desire; between questioning the structure of their oppression and submitting to it; between negotiating the rules and making choices, and letting themselves be chosen. Being ideologically defined by their sexuality, women also come to define themselves, though not without ambivalence, in relation to their sexuality. They feel valorized and appreciated only if they are married, that is to say, desired by a man, paid for, cared for, and ultimately supervised.

In the following pages, I will discuss the stories of the women within the frameworks of three interrelated themes that seem to dominate women's sense of identity, coloring their lives with more or less intensity, the themes of liminality, ambivalence, and vulnerability.

Liminality

According to Victor Turner, "The attributes of liminality or of liminal personae [threshold people] are necessarily ambiguous.... Liminal entities are neither here nor there; they are betwixt and between the positions assigned and arrayed by law, custom, convention, and ceremony" (1969, 95). My data suggest that the greater frequency of *sigheh* marriages is among young divorced or widowed women of the lower socioeconomic class. Although no prohibitions exist against virgin women's making a contract of temporary marriage, for a variety of cultural and personal reasons they do not generally engage in this form of marriage. All my informants, and many others whose cases I have collected, are from such backgrounds. They are often poorly educated and not trained for any profession—save that of carpet weaving. Except for Iran, who was an administrator in a private hospital and gainfully employed, the rest of my informants were hard-pressed to support themselves. A divorce usually places a woman in a vulnerable situation in Iranian society. She is often perceived to be a moral and economic burden on her family and a threat to the stability of other marriages because she is believed to be sexually experienced. The underlying assumption is that once a woman gains carnal knowledge, she can no longer restrain herself, nor can she be controlled when in the presence of men. Presumably, this is because she cannot but yield to men's temptation, for it is in her "nature," and there is no physical impediment (hymen) to function as a check against her sexual activities.

It is not in women's nature, I suggest, that the rationale for women's presumable lack of sexual control lies, despite the ulama's all-purpose use of the term. "Nature" has been a most abused concept and category in the Shi'i vernacular. The root of the ulama's rationale is rather to be sought in the logic of contract and the nature of exchange in an Islamic marriage. Woman, as a commodified sexual object, gains in value only if she (it) is bought, paid for, and kept in the "safe deposit" of a veil. Sitting on the shelf, a commodity by itself has only a potential value. Its true value is actualized only when it is exchanged or bought. It is in the "nature" of commodities to "want" to be exchanged, bought, and maintained. Seen as an object of exchange and thus commodified, the woman "naturally," then, wants to be taken by the man who pays for her.

As long as a woman is married, that is, the commodity has been actualized, and her sexuality is legally controlled or supervised by her husband, she enjoys greater status and social prestige than do unmarried women in Iran. Her status is even more firmly grounded if she has also produced a few children, although as we learn from the women's stories, this is no guarantee for greater security or stability in marriage. Although the implications of divorce are not perceived uniformly by all classes or ethnic and age groups, a young divorced woman's relation with her family of orientation is often tense and ambiguous. Ambiguous, too, is her association with her family of procreation because of the potential for conflict over the custody of children, her financial support during her waiting period, and the chances for retrieving her brideprice.

The most significant unifying theme in these women's backgrounds is thus not so much to be sought in their socioeconomic class or their educational and professional backgrounds. It is, rather, to be sought in their precarious liminal status, in their betwixt-and-between transitional states. A young divorced woman in Iranian society is a liminal being in the sense that she becomes peripheral to both her family of orientation and her family of procreation; she is between family relations and marginal to kinship networks. A divorced woman, as most of my informants were, can neither fall back on her premarital virginal role in her parental household, because her whole experience has changed, nor can she continue to be at the center of her own family of procreation. Unless a husband agrees to let his divorced wife continue to care for their children, after a certain age the custody of children is automatically passed to their fathers. Consequently, a divorced woman's status represents both the negation of many features of preliminal social structure — virginity, marriage, control of women — and an affirmation of another order of things and relations—divorce, sexual experience, autonomy (see Turner 1974, 196; 1969, 125). An unattached divorced woman is culturally perceived to be a potential source of disorder and temptation.

Being young, divorced, and economically needy, my informants perceived themselves to be at the margins of their families, communities, and society. Either they were not welcomed back by their own families (Ma'sumih) or, if they were, tension and confrontation dominated their interactions with their parents and their siblings. Being identified as a divorcee, or someone who is willing to *sigheh* (sexually eligible), many of these women felt uneasy in their own communities. They were frequently approached by married or unmarried men, which not only jeopardized their reputation (as in the cases of Mahvash and Tuba) but put them in a potentially conflict-ridden position vis-à-vis their female friends and acquaintances (Shahin and Mahvash).

Ironically, however, a divorced or widowed woman enjoys greater legal and personal autonomy. She is no longer a child to require the protection of a *vali*, nor is she a married woman who needs to be controlled, nor does she have to submit to the jural authority of her husband. As a nonvirginal single woman, she distances herself, metaphorically speaking, from her commodified self. She has now the chance to manage her own affairs, arrange a contract, negotiate its terms, and conclude it without fear of legal interference on anybody's part. This is the closest a Shi'i Muslim woman can come to having legal autonomy and independence. She has the legal capacity, in theory, to exercise her decision-making power, to negotiate the terms of another marriage contract for herself, or to turn down a matrimonial offer. A divorced woman's capacities of execution and obligation seem to merge more closely now than at other stages of her life cycle. Besides having legal control over her activities, she also has greater freedom to go and come as she pleases.

Autonomy, however, is not a trait approved of for Muslim women. Ideally, in Iranian society, as in other Muslim societies, women are to be protected (guarded and veiled), financially supported (not earn wages), and sexually controlled (married and kept under male supervision). It is, however, the potential, and often actual, exercise of autonomy and the power implied in it that place divorced women in conflict with their social surroundings. The institution of temporary marriage provides young divorced and widowed women with an opportunity to sidestep the limitations of the formal structure, to negotiate on their own behalf, to choose their own marital partner(s), and to exert greater control in the outcome of their lives. All my informants arranged and negotiated their temporary marriages personally without involving their immediate families. Because of this exercise of power in the sexual domain, however, women alienated their families and communities, further pushing their status to the periphery of their society. Not all of them, of course, had a clear idea of the legal objectives of temporary marriage or its long-term implications for their individual or married lives. Their liminality, coupled with their legal autonomy, afforded them greater power to cross forbidden boundaries and to engage in activities normatively contrary to the ideal and the traditional feminine model of passivity and submissiveness.[31]

Not only do these women's activities provide a "countermodel" to the traditional ones (Safa-Isfahani 1980, 46), their motives for making contracts of temporary marriage also place them at odds with the society at large. They point to an appreciable divergence between the ideal and the actual. Contrary to the Shi'i assumption that women's primordial motivation is financial, what motivated *sigheh* women to engage in this type of marriage is *not* primarily a desire for money. This official and stereotyped belief, though logically deduced from the contractual form of marriage, is simplistic, missing the range of factors that may lead women to make contracts of temporary marriage. Most *sigheh* marriages—short-term ones in particular —are not economically advantageous, particularly since women have to abstain from sexual intercourse for at least forty-five days after it ends. Although the financial arrangement does temporarily assist some women in

precarious economic circumstances, money is not the only, or even the greatest, impetus for most of these women's *sigheh* contracts.

The unifying motivational theme for all these women is complex and
double-edged. On an intimate, personal level, their objective is a desire for
attention, affection, and belonging, which they all (with a possible exception
of Iran) so desperately lacked, both in their families of orientation as well as
in their families of procreation. With the exception of Iran, the women
whom I interviewed all remembered their childhood as unhappy. Child
brides at the time of their first marriage at an average age of thirteen and a
half, most of my informants were still in their early twenties when they were
divorced, with or without their own consent, and were barred from seeing
their children.[32] Born into impoverished and large families, many of these
women received little emotional support, formal education, and professional
training during their developing years. Initiated into married adult life at
such a tender age, they were denied the opportunity to mature emotionally
and to develop meaningful relationships with their parents or with their husbands later on.

More importantly, but perhaps less consciously, many women contracted a temporary marriage in the hope of being integrated into another
family group, to shed the marginality that had eclipsed their lives. A contract of marriage simultaneously provides a legitimate channel for an erotic
relationship and a framework for the control of women and their sexuality,
however momentarily. It is by the submission to the structure of their own
control that women are in turn integrated into a group and granted status
and recognition. Confused by the rhetoric of the religious leaders as to the
absence of fundamental differences between the two forms of marriage,
however, these women assumed that temporary marriage would provide
them with the same refuge (precarious though it may be) that a contract of
permanent marriage would. They sought not only to establish meaningful,
enduring, and humane relationships in which pleasure and friendship would
be reciprocated in kind but also to anchor themselves in their communities.

Ambivalence

The built-in logic of exchange in Islamic marriage constitutes the
scaffolding that supports the structure of uncertainties and ambivalences the
sigheh women experience in their marital relations. I argued earlier that Islamic ideology has a double image of woman: one as a person and the other
as an object. These images are metaphorically collapsed together at the time
a marriage contract is concluded. Women can be easily divorced, deserted,
or refused support altogether. The tension and uncertainty in the lives of

these women, and others in their situation, lie precisely here. From their life
stories, we can come to appreciate the profound sense of ambivalence and
uncertainty they feel in their daily lives, both personally and in relation to
men. They seem to be experiencing a sense of split self, vacillating between
perceptions of themselves as subjects and objects — as autonomous whole-
some subjects who are erotically, economically, and socially motivated, and
as objects of desire whose values are recognized only if they are exchanged.
On the one hand, they appreciated the independence and autonomy they
gained after their failed marriages. They had a better sense of their own desires, as well as an awareness and a cherishing of their sexual appeal to men.
They rationalized it, pragmatically, as a "law" of supply and demand: "the
less one has of something [coitus], the more one wants it." Becoming increasingly aware of the capriciousness of the marital relationship (both forms),
however, women experienced intimately the sense of ambivalence and uncertainty that is likely to develop as a result of a marriage contract, more specifically, a contract of temporary marriage. Repeatedly, my female informants expressed a wish to have a "protector" or a "buyer," *kharidar*
(Mutahhari 1974, 232) for the precious "object" that is so structurally posi-
tioned at the core of the marriage contract and is thus so culturally valorized.
It is within this context that we may appreciate many of these women's reluctance to seek or to maintain a job.

The tension and uncertainty in women's sense of their own autonomy and of what is ideally expected of them are likely to lead to a chronic
sense of insecurity in their married lives: tenuous relationships, a mistrust
of their husbands, which may be displaced unto other women (particularly
of unmarried ones), helplessness, and a resort to cunning, perhaps as a
means of coping with an essentially hostile universe.[33] Persian literature is
riddled with such presumably "innate" feminine characteristics.

Vulnerability

Any discussion of worldviews inevitably involves perceptions of self
and other, perceptions that are gradually engraved, and that may become
more complex and dynamic as one goes through different stages of one's life
cycle. These perceptions, though not easily identifiable, are at the same time
in constant tension with a society's ideal images of men and women, which
are promoted through various cultural and symbolic means. Iranian wom-
en's perceptions of the world surrounding them involve a wide range of views
and values, often not in congruence, though overlapping, with that of the officially formulated Shi'i worldview. The most dominant and recurring theme
in the life stories of the *sigheh* women was that of vulnerability. Ideologically,

female vulnerability is actively promoted and rewarded in Iranian society. Ideally, men defend women's honor, support them financially, and protect them from all kinds of foreseen and unforeseen problems. Women in turn are rewarded depending upon how well and how completely they subordinate their wishes to men's discretion. The weaker or more vulnerable they are (or pretend to be), the more they prompt men to value, respect, and protect them. In fact, some women use a manifested sense of vulnerability as a strategy to attract men (e.g., Mahvash).

Whereas within marital relationships female vulnerability is rewarded, subtly or overtly, for those women not "lucky" enough, in Tuba's words, to be married, vulnerability is a liability and punishable. Repeatedly, and even in opposing contexts, my informants stressed how vulnerable they felt, be it in their relationships with other women who had presumably betrayed them (Iran's childhood friend, or Ma'sumih and Mahvash's neighbors) or in terms of their experience of deception by the men with whom they fell in love. The formulaic way with which they attributed cunning to other women and deceit to men fit uncannily the dominant perception of feminine cunning, *makr*, and masculine aggression, *tajavuz*, which in relation to "unprotected" women translates into deception. Although not articulated as such by my informants, it is clear that women's intensified and formulaic explanations of vulnerability are a result of their not living up to the cultural ideal, that is, being married and protected. Further, it seems to me that this is also a side effect of their actual autonomy, toward which, as we learned, they feel quite ambivalent. In other words, autonomy seems to prove too burdensome for them, both personally and culturally, and they wish to escape from it. Not fully conscious of the dynamics of their circumstances, however, they displaced the "evil" that had befallen them onto others, sometimes onto other women. Their misfortune, in other words, was primarily seen in terms of what others had done to them: whether they were the subject of gossip, witchcraft, or betrayal, and the like. By identifying their predicaments in terms of their vulnerability, not only did they displace the evil onto the other, they also rationalized and justified their stigmatized and unfavorable sociocultural standing.

6

MEN'S INTERVIEWS

No one can deny that most, if not all, married men have
had sexual relations, legitimate or illegitimate, with other
women. Is it wise then to forbid married men from having
relations with other women? Is such law just and in
accordance with human nature? Of course not. Such law
has not been practical and will not be so!
—A. A. MUHAJIR, ["Polygamy and *Mut'a*"]

HIS CHAPTER, like that dealing with the women's stories, explores some men's perceptions of the institution of temporary marriage. It includes the perspectives of men who have practiced the custom of *mut'a*, as well as those of the contemporary Shi'i ulama from before and after the revolution of 1979. By presenting some biographical data on the men, I wish to bring to light the differences and similarities in the genders' worldviews, the primacy of eroticism in motivating men to make a contract of temporary marriage, the incongruity between the prescribed rules of sex segregation and the actual relations between the sexes, and men's conceptual distinction between their family life and their erotic desires.

The interviews with Mulla Hashim and the ayatollahs Najafi Mar'ashi and Shari'atmadari were done in the summer of 1978 in the pilgrimage centers of Mashhad and Qom, respectively; the rest were done during my second field trip in 1981. In keeping with the format I used for the women, I have also let my male informants guide us through their own world — or the part of it they were willing to show. This way, not only will we be able to compare the articulation of men's and women's expectations, perceptions, interpretations, and experiences of *mut'a* marriage, we will also be able to compare their contrasting styles of presentation and narration. The interviews are presented here in chronological order. Not all the men I interviewed had contracted a *mut'a* marriage, or at least the higher ranking mul-

153

las did not wish to share that information with me. All of them, however, told me of cases and stories they knew at first hand. The names of all my informants except for the two grand ayatollahs are fictitious.

"A man is approached by a woman who is totally cloaked in a black veil and is unrecognizable. She asks him whether he would want to *sigheh* her for a month (this time-limit varies in different versions). He is hesitant yet does not want to miss his chance. He asks her to remove her veil and to allow him to see her. She refuses, saying that if he is willing to *sigheh* her, he should do so without seeing her unveiled. She assures him that he would not be disappointed. He agrees to a *sigheh* for three nights.

"The black-veiled lady takes him to a house that is as beautiful as a palace and instructs her servants to bathe him, give him fine clothes to wear, and then bring him to her room. Washed, perfumed, and clothed, he is brought to a most charming room where the black-veiled lady is expecting him. She is still in her veil, and though he is excited, congratulating his own good fortune, he is impatient to see her face. When they finally perform the *sigheh* ceremony and the woman takes off her veil, he is enthralled by her beauty and charm. When after three days and nights their contract is over, the man, regretting his own time restriction, begs her to extend their temporary marriage longer. But she refuses, saying that he had his chance in the beginning. She then asks her servants to see him off."

I heard this account of *sigheh* marriage over and over from my male informants, whose versions differed slightly but agreed in the fundamentals. Initially, I did not know exactly how to classify it, or where to fit it in my typology, so I left it out. Rereading my male informants' stories and interviews for this book, however, I decided to describe it at the beginning of this chapter. I was struck by the close resemblance between features of this account of *sigheh* and the stories of my male informants. I call this version of temporary marriage the "*sigheh* myth." I am using "myth" in its general sense, and as a "sacred narrative" (Dundes 1976, 279), which explains certain ideal origins, behaviors, or relationships. None of my informants, including those who told me variations of this myth, actually claimed that this myth had happened to them, but their narrations of their own life histories led me to believe that history and myth were often interwoven in their stories (see also Crapanzano 1980, 7).

PREREVOLUTIONARY INTERPRETATIONS

I interviewed the ayatollahs Najafi Mar'ashi and Shari'atmadari, two of the Iranian Shi'ites' "Loci of Imitation," in the summer of 1978, shortly before the unfolding of the Iranian revolution. Unlike the Ayatollah Shari'atmadari, the former did not have an open house, and those who were interested in seeing him had to obtain permission by telephone. My interview with the Ayatollah Najafi Mar'ashi therefore was arranged after some negotiations and telephone calls by my father, who informed him of my bilateral genealogical relations to two grandparental ayatollahs. He apparently knew my maternal grandfather and agreed to grant us an audience on a Tuesday afternoon at four o'clock.

My interview with this ayatollah was short, culminating in his repetition of the traditional official Shi'i view on *mut'a*. He spoke precisely and deliberately; his answers were short and unelaborated. He did not address me directly but occasionally looked at my father, who was sitting next to me. Because this was my very first interview with such a high-ranking ayatollah, I felt shy and was too inhibited to engage him in a dialogue and to maintain a fruitful conversation. At one point he even became annoyed when I asked him whether there were more *sigheh* marriages taking place in Qom. Tersely he said, "Qom is not a *sigheh* city."

I have incorporated his view into earlier chapters and therefore here describe only the views of the Ayatollah Shari'atmadari. My objective in presenting his interview in detail is to provide a basis for comparing continuity and change in the pre- and postrevolutionary official interpretations of the institution of temporary marriage.

Ayatollah Shari'atmadari

Ayatollah Shari'atmadari's residence, unlike that of Ayatollah Mar'ashi, was open to the public.[1] A crowd of men from all walks of life were present in the outside quarter, *biruni*, of his residence compound. When my father and I arrived at his house, we found two policemen guarding the gate. Apparently, they were stationed there by the SAVAK to control the great ayatollah's associations and to report on, or to prevent, possible eruptions of antigovernment activities, which were quite prevalent in the summer of 1978, just before the Iranian revolution. The policemen, aside from being obviously bothered by the intense summer heat, appeared to be oblivious to what was going on around them and did not prevent anyone from going in or coming out of the house. The thought of meeting the then highest-ranking religious leader in Iran was both exciting and frightening to me.

Inside his compound we were first taken to a large rectangular room with floor-length windows opening onto a medium-sized yard. Thin and narrow mattresses were spread out on all four sides of this room, and many pillows and cushions were leaned against the wall, providing support and comfort for visitors. As soon as we entered the room, however, our attention was focused on a shattered window in the corner of the room. The pieces of glass were scattered all over that corner, and there was a smattering of blood on the dusty and dirty mattresses there. In the middle of that chaos, standing in sharp contrast to the neatness of the rest of the room, a white, dusty, and bloody turban lay on the floor. This turban had been left there, we were told by mullas present in the room, to remind visitors of the "martyrdom" of a young mulla three months before our visit to Qom. We were told in great detail of the heroism of mullas who fought against the shah's regime, their participation in the mourning rites of their fallen colleagues, and how the SAVAK raided the ayatollah's residence, killing this young mulla in that very same room. As a way of paying tribute to the "martyred" mulla and of protesting the shah's policies, they had kept the dead man's bloodied turban in that public room.

After more than thirty minutes we were taken to the ayatollah's private residence, which was connected to the first yard by a narrow ground-floor hallway with a low ceiling. This yard was a lot smaller, but much more charming. It had a small concrete pool in the middle, shaded by several pomegranate trees all around it. We had hardly settled in the guest room when the ayatollah and some of his entourage walked in. The ayatollah Shari'atmadari was a very pleasant and courteous man in his early seventies. He exchanged greetings with my father as well as with me, and, unlike Ayatollah Mar'ashi, who averted his gaze from me, he did not avoid looking at me directly. He appeared to be quite at ease, smiling at times, and even humorous about the subject.

He exhibited knowledge of the pre-Islamic origins of *mut'a* (which I found wanting in the case of most Iranians) but specified, "The way it existed at the time of the Prophet Muhammad was different from its pre-Islamic form." He began by describing the rules and procedures of the institution of temporary marriage and in great detail enumerated the reasons for its legitimacy. In his opinion *mut'a* was permitted for several reasons: (1) "When men were away from their families during the time of war, the Prophet permitted *mut'a* marriage with easy conditions so that illegitimate relations would not develop among the warriors." (2) Such marriages would not shake the ethics and principles of the group. (3) It would prevent disease. And finally, (4) it would satisfy sexual needs. He condemned 'Umar for outlawing the custom and argued that the second caliph's action was illegitimate and unbinding.

I asked him, if the purpose of *mut'a* was to satisfy sexual needs legitimately, then how was it that the Islamic law had discriminated between men and women, since the sexual instinct is evidently present in both sexes? The ayatollah did not address my question directly but in a rhetorical style described how *mut'a* is intrinsically good, *bih khudi khud*, and how it is advantageous because "anything which facilitates an important act [satisfying libidinal drive, preventing fornication] is good. That *mut'a* is a good thing is not in question. But any good thing under certain circumstances may not be beneficial to all. For example," he continued rhetorically, "permanent marriage, which itself is considered beneficial in all societies, may not be possible under some conditions. There might be one who is not willing to marry permanently. This has nothing to do with the law. The law is strongly standing on its own place." He then gave a few analogous examples on the nature of economic reciprocity and barter, which are "intrinsically good" but "not good at all times." Relating his analogy to *mut'a*, he said, "There might be one who does not have great sexual need, but there is another who may need one, two, or twenty women. Or there might be women who are willing to go along. This has nothing to do with the weakness of the law." He emphasized, "The law is good and credible. *Mut'a* has been set as a limit to combat moral corruption and decadence. Of course," the ayatollah stressed again, "no matter how good a law is, under certain circumstances it may not be beneficial to all."

The Ayatollah Shari'atmadari objected to the activities of people who abuse *mut'a* by using it frequently, or who take advantage of their wealth or position by *mut'aing* a few girls and then deserting them after a few days. Repeatedly he stressed the "emergency" aspect of *mut'a*, that it should be resorted to only as "medicine," and that it has to be used when one is "sick" and in need. He objected to the view that maintains *mut'a* as abusive of women. On the contrary, he defended the institution, arguing that *mut'a* is particularly beneficial to women. He concluded that if it had not been for the legitimacy of temporary marriage, economically needy women would have to resort to prostitution to support themselves.

I objected to his comments that the law is clear and that it did not leave room for manipulation or abuse. He responded by saying, "As I said, it is because of its emergency aspect. It is a medicine, not food. But some people have assumed that it is food. This is not correct. This is why it is customarily stigmatized." He challenged the views of a certain Russian writer (whose name he could not remember) who has alleged that *mut'a* is legalized prostitution. The Ayatollah Shari'atmadari maintained this to be an erroneous understanding, typical of what foreigners think about *mut'a*. "*Mut'a*," he stressed, "is a form of marriage, a different form of marriage, a light marriage, a temporary marriage."

Asked about the network of male-female introduction and the role of matchmakers, he said, "Nowadays this is not as prevalent as it used to be. Even if there are some matchmakers, they are not well known." He then commented on an Egyptian writer (no name given again) who had alleged that in Mashhad there used to be a mosque frequented by women and that there was a certain shaikh who knew of these women and some men who were referred to him. (The Egyptian was evidently referring to Gohar Shad Mosque, which still enjoys the same reputation.) The ayatollah deplored this situation and said that such activities were no longer going on in Qom or Mashhad. "Even if there are any," concluded the Ayatollah Shari'atmadari, "they are very private."

Mulla Hashim

I met Mulla Hashim accidentally in the shrine of Imam Riza in Mashhad during the summer of 1978. It was late in the evening, and the shrine yard was bustling with enthusiastic worshipers and pilgrims. The big veranda on which we were sitting was packed with men, women, and children. A young mulla was sitting near me, and since the dense crowd had pushed us to sit so close together, I decided to start talking to him. Finding him agreeable, I began by describing my research to him briefly and asked if he would be willing to talk with me. Much to my delight, he turned out to be very talkative and generous with his views. Looking back, I now think that the prerevolutionary mood of the time had filled the air, providing a catharsis that facilitated our conversation.

Mulla Hashim was born forty years ago in one of the northern villages in Iran in a family of five children. His father was a farmer, whom he helped until he was eighteen, at which time he moved to Mashhad, aspiring to become a religious preacher, an *akhund*. At the age of twenty-five he married an eighteen-year-old Mashhadi woman, with whom he has six children.

Mulla Hashim had no qualms about admitting that ever since he moved to Mashhad he has been contracting *sigheh* marriages frequently, regularly, and secretively. "In my village up north," said Mulla Hashim, "nobody performed *sigheh*, because it was shameful." However, once in Mashhad, he joined the ranks. He appeared to be bragging about the frequency of his temporary marriages, which he contracted once or twice a month, all unbeknownst to his wife. When asked, however, whether he would allow his sixteen-year-old daughter to contract a *sigheh* marriage, he said emphatically, "Never."

Mulla Hashim believes that women most often initiate an offer of a *sigheh* marriage. In great detail he described the feminine techniques in communicating their messages to him. Women, he said, stare at him or ask him to read them verses from the Qur'an, to recite religious prayers for them, or to perform Qur'anic divination.[2] If this first stage of communication fails, some women may then resort to a more direct approach by saying, in a mutually understood code and, in Mulla Hashim's words, "that which shall remain a secret between you and me." He said, "Many women do this [*sigheh*] for its religious reward, and sometimes they don't even receive any money for it." To validate his statement, he continued, "Yesterday a woman asked me to perform a divination for her, and I did that. She then asked me for another one. After the third divination I asked her what she was there for. She said that she wanted to gain some religious merit [by making a contract of temporary marriage] and would pay one hundred *tuman*, too. I said no. She was not my type. She was old."

Mulla Hashim also claimed that there are also women who *sigheh* to support themselves. For instance, recently a woman had approached him and asked him to *sigheh* her for 300 *tuman*. He recalled having rejected her offer, too, telling her he would not *sigheh* for that much money. He did not say, however, that he always refused women's offers. Once he was asked by a woman to go to her house and to perform a religious prayer. After he completed the ritual, she asked him to stay a while longer. Not knowing exactly what was her intention, Mulla Hashim finally told her that he had to leave. The woman then uttered the formula: "that which shall remain a secret between you and me." He told her that he could not stay overnight but said, "Two hours are okay." At the time I was interviewing the men I neglected to ask them how, if at all, they negotiate brideprice payment when women offer to pay them.

Mulla Hashim was quite pleased with his religious profession and on several occasions said that he would not "refuse God's blessing," that is, an offer to a *sigheh* marriage from women. All his *sigheh* marriages have been for only two or three hours. He said that he usually visits women in their own homes but said, "Nowadays [1978], I don't go to their homes because it might be a trap." He was apparently referring to the then rising conflict between the Pahlavi regime and the religious establishment. He was worried that this would be used as an excuse to shame mullas.

In Mulla Hashim's opinion, a view supported also by my data, *sigheh* was more prevalent among the religious groups, *ruhaniyun*. "Nonetheless," he concluded, "all come to the shrine in Mashhad for that purpose," to find a *sigheh*. As we were talking, he pointed out one man after another whom he claimed were in the shrine in the hope of finding a *sigheh*.

Women who want to *sigheh*, said Mulla Hashim, gather around the Steel Latticed Window (see above, introduction), communicating their intentions to the pilgrims. And "that's why," he said, "if lust and concupiscence are divided into ten portions, one portion would go to men, the other nine would go to women." He was among a few mullas who cited lust as women's primary motivation for contracting a *sigheh* marriage, forgetful apparently of his earlier comments on women's religious merit making or financial motivations. Mulla Hashim believed that the number of *sigheh* marriages has increased in the past fifty years, owing primarily to a rapid growth in the population.

POSTREVOLUTIONARY INTERPRETATIONS

Hujjat al-Islam Buzurgi

My first meeting in Tehran during the summer of 1981 was with the Hujjat al-Islam Buzurgi, a high-ranking official in the Ministry of Education and the director of a publishing company. His views on *mut'a* represent a significant shift of emphasis in the interpretation of the institution of temporary marriage: from that of justifying its legitimacy on the basis of its functional benefits for individual health and social order, to one of viewing it as symbolic of Islamic foresight and progressiveness in matters of human sexuality. This interpretation becomes particularly meaningful when understood as a reaction to the Western hegemony over and cultural dominance of Iranian culture for the past several decades.

Hujjat al-Islam Buzurgi, like Mulla X and other high-ranking religious officials I interviewed after the revolution, argued that the existence of the institution of *mut'a* indicated the Islamic keen understanding of the nature of human sexuality. He found it ironic that while under the Pahlavi regime Iranians were busy aping the West, some Western thinkers, such as Bertrand Russell, discovered the Islamic temporary marriage, recognized its importance, and even advocated its use for the European youth (see Russell 1929). In my view, however, the irony lies with his almost unconscious appeal to a Western philosopher for the credibility he sought to establish for this Islamic tradition. He stressed, "It is important to note that we, as an Islamic society, are much more advanced than the Swedes regarding sexual matters. Fourteen hundred years ago Islam realized the significance of satisfying sexual needs and devised temporary marriage to deal with them." Referring to the religious education textbook for high school students, he said, "We have been ahead of the Swedes for providing solutions [suggesting temporary marriage] for our youth's sexual problems in high schools."

Before the revolution, as a professor at one of the teacher's training colleges in Tehran, Hujjat al-Islam Buzurgi would give his students lecture notes (of which he promised to provide me with a copy) about the advantages of *mut'a* for the individual and the society. In our subsequent meeting he apologized for not being able to find a copy of his lecture notes but instead gave me two small how-to booklets in which procedures for temporary marriage were clearly and simply printed (Kiafar 1981; Shirazi n.d.). In these manuals Russell's views on "trial marriage" were repeatedly invoked as a justification for temporary marriage and a valorization of Islamic principles. Russell's opinion and his "recognition of Islamic superiority" were frequently referred to in many conversations I had with mullas (see also Mutahhari 1974, 29–32, 119).

Much to my surprise, the Hujjat al-Islam Buzurgi, like many other mullas, was very straightforward in his views on sexuality.[3] He repeatedly referred to the "animalistic," *hayvani*, nature of sexual needs and the fact that it had to be gratified, often on demand, or great illnesses could result. "Between the ages of eighteen and twenty-five," said Buzurgi, "men and women are animals caught in their uncontrollable and unsatiable sexual desires." As a case in point, he described how during his learning days in Qom, and later in Najaf, Iraq, many poor religious students had to take camphor to neutralize their sexual appetites. In his view, such an unhealthy atmosphere prevailed because "*sigheh* women were demanding one *tuman* for their brideprice while we didn't even have two *rials.*"[4] He deplored the situation. It became gradually clear to me that Buzurgi, like most men I talked to, heaped the blame on women's shoulders, holding them responsible for men's well-being or lack of it. He said he now instructs his students in the teacher's college to use *mut'a* as a way of preventing such suffering.

He believed that every woman who went to college under the Pahlavi regime must have prostituted herself by having a "free" relation with her male colleagues, since such behavior is in the nature of the situation.[5] Therefore, he was teaching his own students about *mut'a* because it is "Islamic, morally acceptable, and it prevents the relationship from being tainted with feelings of guilt and sin."

He was forthright about his own *sigheh* relationships, without being specific. Putting his argument in a hypothetical sense, he said, "For example, if I know of a chaste and unmarried woman, I see no problem in proposing to her." He repeatedly emphasized the religious merit of *mut'a* marriage and eventually gave me the name and telephone number of a woman whom he praised highly for her piety as well as her skill as a female preacher. He said that she contracts *sigheh* herself, suggests its religious merits to others, and encourages them to make *sigheh* contracts.[6] It was not clear whether or not he himself had made a *sigheh* contract with her.

Mulla Pak

Mulla Pak is a notary public, and his official duties are similar to those of a justice of the peace in the United States.[7] He has an office in east Tehran. Through the grapevine I heard that Mulla Pak, who performed the wedding ceremony for an informant's daughter, was giving out what I call "*sigheh* documents." He would provide his male friends with these signed documents, enabling them to use them as proof of their *sigheh* contracts in case they were detained and questioned by the puritanical revolutionary guards.

As a policy to combat Western "decadence," the revolutionary guards arbitrarily detain couples and ask them for proof of their lawful relationship. Faced with such strict policies, many couples now claim to be temporarily married, even if they really are not. Caught by one of the unintended consequences of its advocacy of *mut'a*, the Islamic regime has thus been confronted with an overabundance of unverified claims of *sigheh* relationships. Since *sigheh* contracts traditionally have not required witnesses or registration, the regime's agents have had to accept such claims at face value. However, the government is now trying to put an end to these claims by requiring that all *sigheh* marriages be registered. Faced with this new ordinance, many urban Iranians have come up with yet another way of satisfying the government's requirement for a "proof" while pursuing their own affairs. Some notary publics, most of whom are mullas, sign a form — a "*sigheh* document" — leaving the space for the names of the spouses blank. Men who obtain these documents keep a supply of them in their pockets. Every time a *sigheh* marriage is contracted, they simply fill in the blanks, quickly informing the mulla in case the revolutionary guards decide to press charges.[8]

I asked one of my informants, who knew Mulla Pak, to arrange an interview with him, and he agreed to do that. The following day he took me to the mulla's office, where he received us warmly. Mulla Pak is married and has two children.

Knowing that he was a notary public, I began the interview by asking about the frequency of *sigheh* marriages. Mulla Pak said, "After the revolution *sigheh* has become more popular, partly because there are so many war widows, and partly because people are scared of the regime and need some sort of document." He estimated that "*sigheh* marriages are approximately ten percent of permanent marriages" but said that this refers only to those who care to register their temporary marriages. For instance, he continued, "last month I registered four such marriages." All of the women who cared to register their *sigheh* marriage, he said, were employed (having some kind of income), and most of the men were married. "Unmarried men are more inhibited than we married men. We are experienced," he said smiling. In his view, women often prefer a permanent marriage, but not men. "If women had a say, they would not choose *sigheh* because it lacks status, stability, and security. Men, however, do it because they don't want women as their partners, and women have no choice but to go along with them." Mulla Pak argued, "People who come to me to register their *sigheh* don't do it because of financial needs. In fact, seventy percent of them are financially secure. They do it to satisfy their sexual needs. Women want companions while men want to gratify their sexual desires."

Asked how men and women meet for the purpose of a *sigheh* marriage, Mulla Pak smiled and said: "A heart seeks a heart. For example, one of my friends gave a ride to a veiled lady whose face was completely covered. She asked my friend to *sigheh* her, but he hesitated. My friend wanted to see her face and so asked her to lift her veil and let him see her. But she refused. She said, 'You *sigheh* me first, and if you are not satisfied [when you see me] you can cancel it.' And my friend obliged." He added, "Often, however, matchmakers play the role of intermediaries between couples." In his view, men learn about the institution of temporary marriage by attending mosques, religious prayers, and the like, and that on the whole they know more about the institution than women do. However, he believes that women usually initiate a *mut'a* marriage. "Among the religious establishment, *ruhaniyun, sigheh* is more prevalent, and that is to prevent corruption. They do it more because they are better informed of the laws."

Most of the *sigheh* marriages, according to Mulla Pak, are for six to twelve months, and "before the first wife comes to know it, the time is over. Nowadays," he continued, "even if the first wife finds out and complains to the court, the law won't hear her out, even though the old law [the Family Protection Law of 1967] technically hasn't been replaced. In effect, the religious precepts take precedence."[9] He was one of the few mullas who did not approve of polygyny, despite his nearly conspiratorial compliance with other men to contract additional *sigheh* marriages. His own father had made his mother suffer unjustly when he brought home his second wife. "Men shouldn't get involved in plural marriages. God is one, lover is one," he said smilingly, apparently not including *sigheh* marriages in this category.

Mulla X

Mulla X is in his early forties and is dark in complexion. Through the neighborhood grapevine I had learned that he was very popular among women and was something of a Don Juan. He was divorced, and his four-year-old son was in the custody of his wife. He was living alone in a large house with a traditional Persian garden in its courtyard. He turned out to be a most colorful mulla.

Like other religious leaders, Mulla X was surprisingly forthright in talking about sexuality and took it for granted as man's "natural right." He was eager to share his beliefs with me. I interviewed him twice: once at his own house, and the second time at my residence. Both times my father was present. His presence gave legitimacy to my inquiry and I believe was helpful in encouraging Mulla X to be open and uninhibited. Unfortunately, because of a few political mishaps, including the assassination of President Raja'i, several later attempts to see him failed.

He started by telling me about the rules and procedures of *mut'a*, but once assured of my knowledge, he opened up and fully answered my questions. He claimed to have twenty years of experience in this matter and agreed to tell me not only of his own experiences but of the stories of people whom he knew to have made *sigheh* contracts. Mulla X admitted to having performed *sigheh* frequently himself and claimed that there are many people who do it. Later, however, when I asked him to introduce me to some of his acquaintances, he backed off. Expressing surprise, he said: "What do you want to learn from these people? I am telling you all you need to know. I have twenty years of experience myself.[10] People would get mad if one were to refer to them as *sigheh'i*. They don't want to be interviewed."

In answer to the question of why people *sigheh*, he reiterated the religiously formulated and culturally perceived notion that women's motive is financial whereas men's is sexual. On another occasion, however, he suggested that some women may be more passionately inclined than men. Subscribing to a causal relationship between climate and eroticism, he argued that the "amount and intensity" of desire and passion are based on one's geographical location on the globe. "Because we [Iranians] live in the hotter climates than do the Westerners," he reasoned, "we are more passionately inclined and have greater sexual urges." He believed in variations in libidinal intensity even within Iran. "For instance," he continued, "Rashtis [northern Iranians] are too languid, and therefore aren't much interested in sex. But in Qom [bordering on the desert], no one can escape this animal need."

Mulla X is an administrative assistant of one of the great ayatollahs in Qom. He is in charge of many activities, including being an adviser, or a counselor of sorts, to the newly accepted female students in Qom religious centers.[11] From the knowledge of his advisees' problems, he specified the following as motivations for a *sigheh* marriage: sexual gratification, financial need, psychological complexes, and envy of others' wealth or beauty. He particularly emphasized the role of ignorant and conservative parents in creating or intensifying their children's inadequacies, especially those of their daughters. He argued that some fathers and brothers are unnecessarily harsh, depriving their daughters and sisters—and sometimes their sons too—of certain individual rights. Particularly vulnerable, in his view, were unmarried women who have to bear all kinds of limitations and humiliations at the hands of their parents and relatives. However, he said, until the revolution of 1979, virgin women did not *sigheh* as much as nonvirgins, except for girls raised by a stepmother! Even while I was interviewing him, some of his female advisees phoned, and a young woman came by, whom he turned away because of our presence.

Some of Mulla X's most intimate and firsthand information came from his experiences as a student counselor in Qom. According to him, in

1981–82 there were more than five hundred female students in Qom, studying under the tutelage of one or another ayatollah. He said that since the revolution of 1979 more and more unmarried virgin women make *sigheh* contracts. Some may make several serial contracts during their educational and
religious training in Qom. "Out of five hundred female students in Qom," he
estimated, "more than two hundred are either a *sigheh* to one of their teachers or a fellow religious student." I asked him where these *sigheh* couples
reside during the term of their marriage. He replied, "Anywhere they can;
often at the man's house." Emphasizing the religious reward of *sigheh*,
Mulla X, like many other mullas I interviewed, frequently underscored the
advantages of a *sigheh* marriage over the Western form of "free love," which
he perceived to be tantamount to "fornication."

He then described the case of a young woman who had made a contract of *sigheh* with one of her professors without the knowledge of her parents. This couple used to meet at Mulla X's house for their reunions. Every
time she went back to Tehran to visit her parents, they suggested a desirable
suitor to her, but she would reject them all. Mulla X expressed fear for her
safety should her father find out about her secret *sigheh* marriage, adding,
"The last time they wanted to use my house again, I refused them." Pointing
to his throat with his index finger, he said, "I don't want to get involved with
an angry father." Although he casually said that many of these women performed *sigheh* several times, he was unwilling to divulge details of these
teacher-student *sigheh* marriages. When I asked to be introduced to some
of his advisees, he wavered a while and eventually said that they would get
upset if they were identified.

Such reluctance to identify those who contract *sigheh* marriages was
expressed by many people but was especially pronounced in the case of mullas. At the level of theoretical abstractions they all went to great lengths to
underline the legitimacy of *sigheh* and its religious reward for the believers,
but at the level of individual action they became evasive and were reluctant
either to talk about their own experiences or to introduce me to others who
practiced *sigheh*. They became secretive, appearing to share the negative
cultural perception of *sigheh* marriage. This ambivalence was more evident
during my initial fieldwork in 1978.

When I asked Mulla X for the reasons behind such moral ambivalence, he responded: "This is because of the policies of the Pahlavi regime
that encouraged free male-female relationships and viewed that as progressive. But they discouraged this Islamic tradition, viewing it as old-fashioned
and demeaning to women. The problem," he emphasized, "is not to be
sought in the Islamic laws, but in such decadent policies."

It is true that the Pahlavi regime maintained a negative view of
mut'a marriage, though never formally outlawing it. But it is equally true

that even though the Islamic regime has endorsed the custom, many still do not want to be known as being temporarily married.[12] Placing, or misplacing, the problem with the Pahlavi regime's policies, Mulla X ignored the fundamental distinction he was making between the private and the public aspects of *mut'a*. Public policies regarding the moral value and cultural prestige of temporary marriage in Iran have fluctuated drastically from one regime to another. Correspondingly, public opinion has been divided as to the moral propriety of the institution and the integrity of those who make use of it. Consequently, many practicing Iranians prefer to keep the fact of their *mut'a* marriages to themselves. The problem, therefore, from his point of view, seemed to rest with merging the private with the public by making public knowledge of what is a private act. As long as a temporary marriage is kept secret, or nearly so, it is all right. But once it becomes public knowledge, such information may be appropriated by different people for questionable purposes.

Mulla X made no secret of his own frequent *sigheh* marriages. Like Mulla Hashim, he claimed that women always initiate the relationship. Once in the shrine, he recalled, he was approached by a woman who asked him to perform a Qur'anic divination. She then asked him to *sigheh* her because the divination had indicated a good omen, presumably for her to make a contract of temporary marriage. He complied, and they decided on a one-hour *sigheh* contract and a twenty-*tuman* consideration. Another time, a woman approached him, asking him to *sigheh* her virgin daughter for one night for a brideprice of fifty *tuman*. In both of these cases, Mulla X said, "They needed money." On the other hand, he said, there are times when women initiate a relationship because they are physically attracted to men. "Many women," said Mulla X, "approach young men, particularly handsome ones, directly and frequently." Women, according to Mulla X, pursue these men either directly or indirectly through letters, messages, or intermediaries.[13] Contrary to the popular belief, he viewed these young men to be in a more vulnerable situation than women. "They might be easily tempted and stray from the right path," by which he meant men find it difficult to say no to a feminine proposition. His view was echoed in interviews I had with other men.

In our second interview Mulla X almost contradicted himself by asserting that men always make the first move. When asked if women take the initiative too, he said, "Those women who come to you and ask for divination are in fact prostitutes."[14] He was of the belief that women's motivations for making contracts of *sigheh* marriage run along a continuum. On one end there are those women who are "outright prostitutes," he said, but who veil their activities under the cloak of a *sigheh* marriage. These women are indiscriminate and do not observe the period of their sexual abstinence properly. "This kind of *sigheh* marriage," he stated, "is primarily found in motels or inns [around the shrines or in the urban centers] where the innkeeper usually knows of several women whom he or she introduces to the inquiring visitors. Most pilgrims know where to go to find a *sigheh.*" At the opposite pole, he maintained, there are those women who contract *sigheh* "just for God's sake and for its religious reward. They do it," he said, "to disobey 'Umar's [the second caliph] order of prohibition of *mut'a,* and to please God." In his estimation, only "three percent" of women make contracts of *sigheh* for God's sake; the others' motivations fall somewhere in between the two extremes he described.

Asked what group or class of men do *sigheh* more frequently he answered: "All are busy. Everyone who has the money and desire will do it, but the clergy, *ruhaniyun,* get all the blame." I asked him what then had prompted such a popular perception of the mullas' indulgence in contracting *sigheh* marriages? Without really disputing the point, he said, "Well, because they are more religious and better informed of the laws."

I asked Mulla X whether there are networks of people who act as intermediaries, matchmakers, and brokers: who introduces whom to whom? Although he admitted that often matchmakers act as intermediaries, he became evasive when asked to facilitate an interview with some of them. He, however, referred me to the two best-known and well-established organizations in Tehran, which are prospering under the Islamic regime and have branches in all major cities in Iran. These are the Martyr's Foundation and the Marriage Foundation, described above, chapter 4. As for individual matchmakers, he made an astute observation, saying that "each class or group has its own matchmakers," that is, merchants, mullas, poor people, and so forth. "But," he emphasized, "at the higher echelons matchmakers are useless. These people don't leave their affairs in the hands of matchmakers."

Mulla X aired the official Shi'i view on *sigheh* marriage, emphasizing particularly the contemporary relevance of Islamic law and its progressive ideology. "Islam has recognized the importance of sexual desire and has devised *mut'a* to take care of this animal need." He repeated this statement several times during our interview, commenting each time on how in each other's presence men and women are incapable of controlling themselves. Further, he argued that Islam has answers for "all human problems, past, present, and future." More than that, he stressed, "Islam has provided the most convenient way of gratifying sexual desires." To substantiate this assertion, he described how four men may *sigheh* one woman in a relatively short time (see group *sigheh,* above, chapter 4).

Mulla Amin Aqa

Amin Aqa, a mulla in his early to mid-forties, was introduced to me by one of my informants in Mashhad. She took me to her aunt's house, which was located at the end of a long and winding alley in the ancient and impoverished part of Mashhad known as *pa'in khiabun*. The aunt was a striking seventy-year-old woman whom I call Qamar Khanum. Qamar Khanum shares her house with her senior cowife, Kulsum Khanum, seven of their married children, along with their children, and a few other unrelated tenants — twenty-one in all. Their husband, a certain hajji from Afghanistan, has long been deceased, but the two cowives continue living together not because of mutual desire but because of economic necessity. Qamar and Kulsum were once best friends, but their friendship gradually turned into animosity when the hajji secretly married Qamar after her husband's death. Much to Kulsum's bitter disappointment, the hajji eventually brought Qamar to live with Kulsum and her children at their house.

As a way to appease Kulsum, however, the hajji arranged for Qamar's fourteen-year-old son Amin, from her first marriage, to marry one of their daughters, Zainab, also the same age. This was also done for pragmatic reasons: because Amin had reached puberty, he could no longer share the same space with Kulsum and her daughters. The latter had to veil before the former because his relationship with them did not fall in any of the permitted categories. Therefore, the cowives' children were married off to each other in order to realize the two objectives at once.

Amin Aqa was not home when we arrived, and so I talked to Qamar Khanum (his mother), Kulsum Khanum (his mother-in-law), and his first wife, Zainab (Kulsum's daughter). This turned out to be a very revealing, though painful, recounting of these three women's life histories. The two cowives, together and intermittently, recalled their life stories for me, from the time when they were each other's best friends to their life together as cowives.

Amin Aqa arrived toward the end of my long talk with the women in his household. I interviewed him twice, once in the company of his mother and his mother-in-law, and the second time in the company of his womenfolk.

Amin Aqa is soft-mannered and pleasant. He has a permanent wife, Zainab, with whom he has three married daughters, and a temporary wife, with whom he has a son and a daughter. He started by explaining to me the different types of Shi'i marriages, describing in detail the rules and procedures of each. In his opinion there are many "distorted rumors" about *sigheh* activities in Mashhad, particularly those supposedly happening under the Steel Latticed Window. Wishing to demystify activities regarding *mut'a*, he described the correct procedure: "For example, a woman comes to Mashhad for pilgrimage; she might take a mulla, like myself, into her fancy. She then goes to him and expresses interest in becoming his *sigheh*. If he has a place, he may agree to it. The woman may even suggest giving him some money. They then decide on how long they want to be married, and the brideprice."

Where, I asked him, do people find each other? He smiled and recited a famous Persian adage: "He who searches, shall find." Probed to be more specific, he said, "Men and women find each other in gatherings and meetings, in the homes of their families and relatives, in the shrines, or in the mosques. For example, this man is walking along and a woman passes by." Changing his tone of voice, he said to me, "One can guess from a woman's appearance whether or not she wants to *sigheh* [e.g., the way she walks, looks around, or manipulates her veil at a critical moment to convey certain nonverbal messages to a man]. The man then expresses interest and the woman accepts. Sometimes, a woman who is not married [divorced] may initiate an interest and the man agrees." But how exactly is this done? I insisted. Amin Aqa laughed and said, "God creates everything with its means." He then told me of the following incident.

"One of my friends, who is a sayyid, and I were standing in the shrine yard [in Mashhad]. A woman walked toward us. The wind blew her *chadur* open. She was pretty." Changing his tone of voice again, he said smiling: "We are *akhunds* [mullas], we know the type." He realized that his friend was favorably inclined toward this woman. He continued, "I asked her whether she was with her husband. She said 'No.' My friend the sayyid asked her whether she would be willing to become his *sigheh*, and she said 'Yes.' From then on," he concluded, "every time my friend saw me he would thank me." In addition to his own improvisational matchmaking role, he told me about the cases of a few old men whom he knew when he was a little boy. These matchmakers apparently used to occupy the upper chambers of the shrine in Mashhad and would act as intermediaries between the Mashhadi women and interested pilgrims. [15] Asked where the *sigheh* couple reside during their union, Amin Aqa said, "They either go to the home of one of their relatives, or friends, or their own home, or they may stay in an inn, or the like." He added, "The main thing is to find the object, *jins.* He who finds meat knows how to eat it." (*Jins* in Persian means both a gender and an object.)

He was still not very specific about his own latest *sigheh* marriage, which had created an uproar in his household. But at an opportune moment, as soon as his mother and mother-in-law left the room, he whispered to me, "Well, in the mosque I found a *sigheh* for myself," but before he could tell me his story, the two women walked back in. He straightened his posture once again, changed the subject quickly, and in his own professional formal tone said, "Because of my position as a mulla many people refer to me. I know who wants what. Sometimes I guide them and give them directions." He added, "If a man comes to me and wants me to find him a *sigheh*, I would say to him, 'You go and find the woman yourself and then come to me and I shall marry you.' " Admitting that some inns and motels have reputations for

being meeting places for *sigheh*, he stressed that these might be more rumors than facts. "It is possible," he reflected, "that the innkeeper or the
cleaning ladies who work there may know of some people who would want to
do that, but this is not very prevalent.

"Islam has permitted *mut'a* marriage," said Amin Aqa, "and there
is nothing wrong with it. Islam wanted to prevent corruption and prostitution in the society, and that's why it has permitted *mut'a*. *Mut'a* is for the
people who can't marry permanently and who are in need, or are afraid that
if they don't do it they will commit a sinful act [fornication]. It is to prevent
sinful homosexuality, *lavat*, masturbation, *istimna'*, and the like." He sub-
stantiated the legitimacy of *mut'a* with a saying from the Shi'i Ninth Imam:
"God has prohibited wine drinking but permitted *mut'a* instead." He emphasized its emergency aspect and repeatedly said, "Because Islam is an
easy, *sahl*, religion, and because suffering [celibacy] is not permitted in Islam, *mut'a* has been sanctioned."

Articulating the orthodox Shi'i view, he argued that 'Umar's motive
in banning *mut'a* was his personal animosity toward the Prophet's son-in-
law, Imam 'Ali. Citing the book of *Luma'ih*, Amin Aqa narrated the following anecdote: "'Umar ibn-i Khattab [the second caliph] was holding a grudge
against His Holiness Imam 'Ali, who had claimed to have intercourse with
one of his wives every night. Deciding to prove the Imam 'Ali boastful,
'Umar invited him to come to his house for dinner. 'Umar instructed his servants to delay serving the dinner, scheming to oblige 'Ali to spend the night
at his house. His Holiness 'Ali played into 'Umar's hands and agreed to sleep
over. At dawn, under the pretext of awakening him for his morning prayers,
'Umar rushed to 'Ali's chamber. Addressing His Holiness 'Ali, 'Umar said:
'Do you remember to have claimed to do such and such act every night?'
Imam 'Ali says, 'Yes.' 'Umar says, 'Well, last night you were at my house and
had none of your wives with you.' Imam 'Ali disagrees and says 'Ask your sister.'[16] 'Umar becomes so enraged that he rushes out of the house and immediately orders the banning of *mut'a* marriage and the stoning of those who
continued to practice it."[17]

It was getting near the evening prayer, and Amin Aqa told me that
he had to go back to the mosque to perform the evening prayer. I had to
leave, too. He offered to walk me to the main street. Once outside their
house and out of earshot of his mother and mother-in-law, he felt more at ease
and eager to talk about his own experiences. He told me about the circumstances that led him to marry his first wife, Zainab. He said that he was really
interested in the hajji's second daughter, who was prettier and younger. But
when she became terminally ill, the hajji and his mother decided that the
young Amin should marry Zainab, whom Amin Aqa claimed was five years
his senior, a claim vehemently denied by Zainab. Amin Aqa lamented the fact

that while he was still in his prime Zainab was no longer "fruitful." He tried to impress upon me how fair he had been with Zainab, how desperately he tried to obtain her consent for his several attempts for remarriage, which she obstinately refused, and how he was yearning to have a son. He sounded genuine, repeatedly stressing the point that he made a contract of *sigheh* because he wanted to have another child, which his wife was incapable of giving him. Earlier that day he had said that *sigheh* was in essence prescribed for men who were not married, or who were really in need, sexually. He presented his own motivation as different, however. Zainab had borne him five daughters, three of whom survived, reached adulthood, and were married. She never agreed to his request for permission for a second marriage (she told me this, too), even though she knew she could no longer conceive.[18]

Amin Aqa said, "Finally, I gave up on her." Unbeknownst to her, he made the acquaintance of a woman with whom he later made a *sigheh* contract for five months. When Zainab and his family found out about his *sigheh* marriage, they made his life so miserable that he had to cancel the contract. "But," he continued, "I was still searching. In my position [as a mulla], many women for many reasons come to me. They make the excuse of asking me to read them a religious prayer, make divination, and the like. I was being pressured to marry again by my friends and women clients. Finally I gave in. I met the daughter of a friend who was divorced and had two daughters and a son. My friend introduced me to his daughter, and I made a *sigheh* contract with her." Zainab, however, told me that Amin Aqa made this *sigheh* because she already had a son; otherwise, "She was very ugly, lacking one eye."

Amin Aqa offered to *sigheh* her for one year with the condition that, should she present him with a son, he would marry her permanently. Before the year was over she gave birth to a son, Amin Aqa's son. Much to her disappointment, Zainab discovered the bitter truth soon after the little boy was born, but she was no longer a match for a younger cowife who had fulfilled her husband's lifelong desire for male progeny. An overjoyed Amin Aqa extended their *sigheh* marriage for life.

After his wife found out about his *sigheh*, it was a "hard life" for Amin Aqa for quite a long time. "She made it such that I couldn't go to the house of my *sigheh* wife even once a week." However, her prohibitions and objections had apparently worn thin by the time of our interview, for he admitted spending most of his time at his *sigheh* wife's house. He would stay with Zainab every other night and sometimes even less often. They no longer had an intimate relationship, though he appeared to be quite respectful toward her. He promised to talk privately with me some more. We made an appointment and parted.

When I arrived at his house promptly at ten-thirty in the morning for our second interview, he had not yet come back from his *sigheh* wife's

house. Zainab and two of their daughters were cleaning the house and preparing lunch. It was a precious opportunity for me to talk with his eldest
daughter who, upon discovering her abusive husband's frequent temporary
marriages, had obtained her divorce, against her father's and her husband's
objections.[19]

Amin Aqa finally arrived at twelve-thirty and apologized for being
late. At once the mood of the meeting became more formal, as all five women
in the room sat silently, in deference to him. He sat down and opened a big
book of *Muntahi al-Amal* written by Shaikh 'Abbas-i Qomi (d. 1941), and instructed me to take careful notes while he read some passages from the book.

I found the formality with which he greeted me this time and his
preaching manner inexplicable. He was not the only mulla who behaved that
way. Such behavior had become a predictable pattern for some mullas. Only
later, however, when I could compare the behavior of all the mullas I interviewed, did I realize that the mullas who were more gregarious, open, and
spontaneous in our first interview would generally become formalistic, rigid,
and pedagogical in our subsequent ones. My guess is that the novelty of our
initial meetings prompted the mullas to disclose aspects of their private
lives, or to express their unguarded views of religion, which they later regretted having expressed and did not wish to repeat, once they had had time
to reflect.

Having formally established the legitimacy of *mut'a* once again, he
then said that I could start the interview. But before I had a chance to begin,
he pointed to the women present in the room and said authoritatively, "Is
there no problem in talking in front of these ladies?" It was a tense moment.
Apprehensively, the women awaited for my response. I wanted to interview
him privately, and I knew that the presence of his womenfolk, especially his
first wife, would inhibit our conversation, but I could not bring myself to let
him dismiss the women at that particular moment. I knew that none of them
would disobey, were he to order them to clear the room. But what would they
think of me? I thought I could not betray those women, especially since for
the past few hours they had been sharing with me some very private
moments of their lives. I resolved that they could stay, and he made no
objection.

Hoping that Amin Aqa would speak of his personal experiences regardless of the women's presence there but not wishing to embarrass him, I
posed my first question in a general form. What is the age at which men and
women typically learn about the phenomenon and practice of *mut'a?* He replied, not addressing my question directly, "For some men it is not possible
to marry, even if they want to; they can't afford it. Either they themselves
find a *sigheh,* or someone else will find it for them [a veiled reference to his
own case]. For the more mature people, and for those women who are di-

vorced or widowed, it is easier to *sigheh*," because they have some experience with the opposite sex. As to whether there is any age discrepancy between men and women for their first *sigheh* marriage, Amin Aqa responded, "There is not much difference between them, although men are more aggressive, and women are more inhibited than men. Young women [virgins] don't do this." Asked what motivates people to contract a *sigheh* marriage, he ventured, "A variety of reasons. Sometimes a woman may not want to marry permanently; she has greater freedom in a temporary marriage. Other times she may not find a man who is of her status."

At this point Amin Aqa's eldest daughter, Bilqais, interrupted him and said, "Or, it might be for the sheer experience. Or like in the case of my father, it might be for the want of a son." I became alarmed, expecting an abrupt reaction from Amin Aqa, but he appeared tolerant and let his daughter continue. "My father wanted a son," Bilqais went on, "and my mother was past her fertility period. So, he got himself a *sigheh* wife, and God gave him a son."

I found this incident extraordinary, because, in the presence of her parents—and others—the young daughter skillfully articulated the family's lifelong point of contention. She was not sarcastic or irreverent toward her father; she seemed to care for him genuinely. Nor was she unduly sympathetic to her mother. She was taking advantage of the opportunity presented at that moment to voice out, to let everyone *hear*, what was a fait accompli, hoping in the process to ease the tension between her parents. How her parents interpreted her words I do not know. The point is that both her parents, especially her father, whom I perceived to be authoritarian, remained silent and let Bilqais act as intermediary in this family conflict. He even appeared quite respectful toward his daughter.

Amin Aqa resumed his talk: "The fundamental objective in Islam is to lessen human hardship and to solve problems; therefore, people resort to *sigheh* marriage for a variety of personal reasons." To the question of where *sigheh* occurs more frequently, and whether or not couples generally come from the same city, Amin Aqa answered, "It happens everywhere, but it occurs more in Mashhad because it is a pilgrimage center. Couples may be from everywhere, but they are not usually from the same city." Asked whether or not *sigheh* couples establish a household, he said, "Not usually. They commute. It might be once a week or more, but it is not like a permanent marriage household."

Now it was Zainab's turn to express her point of view. She said, "Many women complain about their husbands' frequent *sigheh* marriages." An unveiled reference to her own situation. Once again Amin Aqa remained calm, and Zainab proceeded to describe in some detail the case of a young woman who had been abandoned by her temporary husband ten days before she gave birth. Aware of the dynamic tension between himself and his wife, however, Amin Aqa, though nodding his head in apparent agreement, displaced the conclusion she was driving at by stating, "If a woman is unlucky, he would leave her!"

As I reflect on the unfolding of this family drama before me and the other women present in the room, I begin to realize the mediating role that was assigned to me by their unspoken agreement. Conflict resolution and mediation, particularly within families, are tasks often performed by wise old men, the so-called white-bearded men, in Persian vernacular. In the absence of a white-bearded man, sometimes a "wise woman," 'aqilih zan, assumes the role of a mediating agent. "Wise woman" means not only a knowledgeable woman, it also means a middle-aged woman who has gained knowledge through age and experience. That I was not a white-bearded man or a middle-aged woman was obvious to all—or at least I so hoped. What I shared with these two categories of mediators, I now think, was my knowledge of the *shari'a*, which in their eyes endowed me with the authority to judge, to mediate, and, perhaps, to render an opinion if not a resolution. I performed, of course, none of the above, at least not in the way they presumably expected it of me. Although intimately sensitized to the subtle ways in which this family communicated some otherwise difficult messages, I had not quite grasped the dynamics of our group, particularly that of my own strategically marginal yet potentially powerful position within it. I was an outsider, I assumed, and expected to remain so. But being a world traveler and a Persian-speaking woman who was also a knowledgeable teacher, both men and women of this family included me in their stories and saw in me a capacity to mediate, a capacity for which under other circumstances, I would have been considered too young, *kham*.

I asked Amin Aqa how familiar he thought men and women were with *sigheh* rules, procedures, rights, and obligations; and whether there was any difference between them. Amin Aqa replied, "While both men and women know about *sigheh* and its related rules, mature women [married several times] are better informed." The women in the room objected at once and argued that men were better informed. Bilqais ventured again, "Religious people are more inclined to do it, especially since they know that fornication is a sin and forbidden, and so, they go and do *sigheh*."

Amin Aqa resumed unperturbed: "For example, a young man comes to Mashhad and wants to *sigheh* a woman. They come to me to perform the rite for them. Should I refuse them, the man would say, 'If you don't marry us, we would sin.' So, I do it reluctantly, because I am not always certain that what people tell me is the truth; that the woman might not have been married before [might be a virgin], or that a girl has her father's permission." In another context, he had told me he would not perform a *sigheh* ceremony for a young virgin woman who did not have her father's permission.

Regarding the prevalent negative perception of *mut'a* and the moral ambivalence surrounding it, Amin Aqa posited, "Because the brideprice is less in *mut'a* than in marriage, *nikah*, it is therefore less culturally valued." The women presented another perspective once again. They argued, "A woman who respects herself won't *sigheh*. An ugly woman, a divorced or widowed woman, or one who doesn't know any profession, or doesn't have a son, would relinquish her self-respect to become a *sigheh*." Bilqais continued with the popular belief: "Most *sigheh* women are from lower classes and don't have much self-respect. Financial insecurity is the main reason for becoming a *sigheh*. Men do it because they must gratify their sexual needs." When later Amin Aqa left the room, Bilqais became more specific, "My father's *sigheh* wife did it because she was poor, but now that she has a son and my father spends money on her, she has become conceited."

It is significant to note here that while Amin Aqa stressed the legal and transactional principles behind the cultural stigma associated with the institution of temporary marriage, the women emphasized the moral and cultural values placed on the custom. Whereas he identified the problem (however vaguely) with the institution of temporary marriage itself, the women associated it with individual women who practice it. Further, the women did not seem to question the validity of the institution of temporary marriage — at least, not openly. Zainab was quite vociferous against the institution of temporary marriage in a private conversation I had with her, but she showed considerable restraint while in the presence of her husband. However, even she did not dismiss the institution totally, but emphasized that only unmarried men should be allowed to contract it. Whether these women genuinely believed that "other" women are to be blamed for the precariousness of their marital relation, or whether they prudishly chose not to challenge Amin Aqa in front of me, is not quite clear to me. What is clear is the fact that they really are much more aware of the dynamics of the situation than they pretend to be.

As for how financial arrangements are made in a *sigheh* marriage, Amin Aqa said, "The man and woman first agree on the amount to be exchanged. For example, they may decide to *mut'a* for one month with a brideprice of one hundred *tuman*. It is customary for the woman to receive her brideprice first."

Muhsin

From one of my informants I learned about Muhsin, who has reputedly had extensive *sigheh* experience. I interviewed Muhsin twice, the second interview lasting an entire day. Muhsin's wife, Razi, who apparently knew of most of her husband's affairs, at times participated in our conversation, but for the most part she left us alone. Muhsin is thirty-nine years old. He dropped out of high school and joined the street-corner gang of high school dropouts. He fell in love with Razi and married her at the age of nineteen. They have five children.

During the Pahlavi regime he joined the much hated and controversial Iranian secret police, the SAVAK, and quickly climbed the ladder of success and financial prosperity. When the regime was toppled by the revolutionary forces in 1979, Muhsin was jailed but was released after only three months' incarceration. At the time of our interview, though claiming to having been unemployed since the revolution, he was obviously quite well off.

He started by telling me about one of his early experiences with temporary marriage. He was very descriptive, having a penchant for details. "Ten years ago," he started, "as I was praying in the shrine in Mashhad, I noticed a very beautiful, tall woman walking toward me. She gestured to me to approach her. One could not ignore her," he said. "I walked toward her and said, hello, *salam*. She introduced herself and said that she had a question to ask me but was hesitant. I was getting curious and wanted to know what she wanted of me. I told her to go ahead. She then said that I should swear to the Imam Riza [in whose shrine they were meeting] to keep my answer secret! I promised her; I didn't know what she wanted of me. She then asked me to *sigheh* her for three days. I was dumbfounded. I said, 'How?' She then called one of the mullas in the shrine and asked him to perform the ceremony for us. We decided on a five *tuman* brideprice [merely symbolic], which I was to give her at the end of our contract."

"She took me to her hotel," continued Muhsin, "and introduced me to her mother as her brother's friend. They had a one-bedroom suite in the hotel. At nights when her mother was sound asleep, she would come to me where I was sleeping on a couch in the living room. To make sure her mother was asleep, she would shake her. I was curious to know how frequently she makes *sigheh* contracts. When I asked her, she swore that this was her first time, that since her divorce from her opium-smoking husband several years ago our *sigheh* was her first intimate contact with a man. She told me that for the past few days she had been feeling the need to have sex, and because of that she was afraid she might commit a sin. She said she was so frustrated that she even thought of propositioning the hotel's busboy. We parted after three days, and she gave me her telephone number in Tehran. When I called her, however, she said that she would see me only if I would marry her permanently. I told her that I couldn't do that, and that was the end of our relationship."

Early in his life, Muhsin claimed, he learned about women. When he was thirteen years old, two teenage sisters in his neighborhood initiated him into the nuances of male-female relations. In a rhetorical and almost formulaic sense he narrated a few of his half-secret affairs with several young women in his neighborhood.

With the collaboration of his wife, Muhsin finally described one of his latest, longest, and most complicated *sigheh* marriages to a woman whom I call Turan. She was a lower-middle-class divorced woman working as a teller in a bank in Tehran. Muhsin happened to meet Turan in the police station to which he was assigned. Her house was robbed, and she needed police assistance. Her subsequent and frequent trips to the police station, under the pretext of identifying her belongings, culminated in a budding friendship with the young and handsome Muhsin. After several intimate meetings, Turan asked Muhsin to *sigheh* her in order to justify their relationship to her sixteen-year-old daughter. "I married her," said Muhsin, "and used to go there for lunch. But by the time Razi found out about it, I was staying there overnight too." Razi, however, did not discover her husband's *sigheh* marriage for quite some time. Muhsin became more and more involved with Turan, taking her to his villa in northern Iran. "I had to lie to Razi, and tell her I was going on official trips."

At this point, Razi who was intermittently present in this interview, joined in and described how the increasing inattentiveness of her husband toward her and their children led her to discover her husband's affair. By putting bits and pieces of information together, she eventually was able to solve the puzzle. Not only did she learn of her husband's serious involvement with Turan, she also found out Turan's whereabouts. With the help of a friend, one day Razi mustered enough courage to go to Turan's house. "I was there when Razi came in," Muhsin resumed. "I hid, but she knew I was there. It was no use." In that tense face-to-face confrontation, and in the presence of their husband, Razi warned her rival: "Stay away from my husband. He would never leave his children for the sake of another woman." Muhsin nodded his head in approval. Apparently, Razi knows Muhsin's Achilles' heel. He truly loves his children; one could not miss the tenderness and affection in his behavior toward them.

"I don't know what was with her," mused Muhsin. "Turan had bewitched me. She would use witchcraft to keep me attached to her. She could make me want her so much that at ten o'clock at night I would get into my car and drive straight to her place still in my pajamas. She had a magic charm, a talisman, which she would use any time she wanted me. It was really effective." Muhsin and Razi concurred on the effectiveness of Turan's charm. Describing the talisman to me, Razi said, "It was made of a piece of bronze. On one side of it was a drawing of a dragon with flames bellowing out of its open mouth, its tail winding upward. In front of the dragon's mouth the names of Turan and Muhsin, the Prophets, famous lovers such as Majnun,[20] and all kinds of symbolism of love and affection were etched. This was all for the purpose of keeping Muhsin attracted to Turan." Razi explained. "On the other side of the talisman my name was printed upside-down, and next to it was the Satan's name, along with a few other such evil names, all for the purpose of diminishing Muhsin's love for me. That woman could pull Muhsin toward her any time she wanted to!" Razi concluded.

Muhsin's discovery of the magic charm was accidental, but Razi's deciphering of the charm's symbolism required some ingenuity. On one of his visits to Turan's home, he felt it under the cushions on which he was sitting. He took it home to show it to Razi. Fascinated by its intricate design, Razi took it to an amulet reader, who deciphered it for her. To neutralize its bewitching effects, he recommended that she should take the charm and throw it into running water. Razi then took it outside of Tehran's city limits and buried it in a stream. "Four or five days after that," said Muhsin, "our *sigheh* relationship was completely over." "And," Razi concluded, "from then on he didn't set foot there."

Turan was Muhsin's *sigheh* for two years, during which time he claimed to "control her activities": he demanded to know with whom she socialized, what time she would get home, where she went, and so on. He was so possessive of her that even when a divorced friend of Turan came to stay with them for a while, Muhsin warned her, "If you want to stay in this house you should do as I tell you." However, when later on this very same friend of Turan asked Muhsin to *sigheh* her, Muhsin obeyed her. "She told me," said Muhsin, "to leave Turan and *sigheh* her instead. For a few months, unknown to Turan, I was with both of them at the same time. By the time Turan found out, our relationship [i.e., his with Turan] was almost over." Muhsin continued his new *sigheh* marriage for another year, and he believed that she, too, tried to use witchcraft on him but that "it didn't work." Muhsin also had a short-term affair with Turan's teenage daughter. He said, "Turan's daughter was paying too much attention to me, and so I took advantage of her. I took her to our villa at the Caspian Sea. Turan really trusted me, but her daughter caused it all to change."

Muhsin seemed to be totally unaware (or pretended to be) of his own role in these games of sexual politics. Abrogating all responsibility and displacing it onto women, even a sixteen-year-old child, he not only underscored his perception of his own desirability but his inability to restrain himself with women. Frequently Muhsin stressed—directly or indirectly—his physical appeal to women; he found it "natural" that women should want to be with him. He found it equally "natural" for him to follow his sexual instinct wherever it might take him.

Asked why he made *sigheh* contracts, he answered, "When one can do something right, why do it otherwise? Anyone who knows about *sigheh* and knows how easily it is done wouldn't forgo that for something forbidden. Why shouldn't I do it? I am a believer, and it is permitted. I don't want any doubts in my affairs. From among seventeen girls [virgins] and women friends of mine, only four or five of them were not *sigheh*. Some of these women wanted to know why I would suggest *sigheh* to them. I would say, because it is lawful, *halal*. Those who were experienced would immediately say okay. I *sigheh* because it makes me feel more comfortable, makes me feel better. Illicit intercourse makes me sick of myself. I would even wash myself [take a bath] afterward. When I do that, I don't use our own washcloth. But when it is *sigheh*, I don't have any worries. It is my own wife. One goes to her with greater peace of mind, and without any anxieties." I am not quite sure whether Muhsin projected backward the prevailing religious sentiments of the time to include all his sexual relations as a *sigheh*.

Muhsin's latest *sigheh* (still secret) is with the next-door neighbor, who is a friend of Razi. She is a young divorced woman in her mid-thirties who lives with her three children. This friendship, like his others, was apparently initiated by the woman. "My wife," said Muhsin casually, "must have told her how good I am as a lover." When this neighbor approached Muhsin, he welcomed it and immediately suggested to *sigheh* her (this being after the revolution, it made even greater sense to him). "My neighbor didn't know *sigheh* was so easy. She had no objections to it, except that she wanted to know why we should do it, and what would happen if we didn't do it. I reminded her that it was better because we would then be religiously pure, *pak*, for each other and sexually permitted. We made a *sigheh* agreement for five months. She is an expert. She has known other men too."

Muhsin showed me the narrow entrance to his room through which he would sneak out at night, creeping into his neighbor's room, which was located exactly opposite. The door opened up to a small balcony where his neighbor's door also opened. This small room is Muhsin's territory, so to speak. He would sit on a mattress and smoke opium throughout most of the day. His wife believes that, on the average, Muhsin smokes a thousand *tumans*' worth of opium per day. (Considering that he was unemployed and that his wife was not working, this amount was clearly excessive. Those who knew him suspected that he might be working for the Islamic regime's secret police.) Muhsin, according to his wife, has gained weight and hardly ever moves. There is a twin bed in one corner of the room where he sleeps. "My wife and I do not sleep together. She shows no interest in what I could teach her." He said ruefully, "Other women go crazy over me, but my own wife isn't interested."

At one point, when Razi came into the room, he started teasing her. Addressing me in a tone of voice that conveyed disbelief and annoyance, she

said, "He is out of his mind. At our age [thirty-nine] and after five kids, he
expects me to do all those naughty things." I could see that it was not difficult
for him to slip out of that room in the middle of the night and sneak into his
neighbor's little room without arousing any suspicion. The two rooms were
hardly three feet apart, and his wife usually slept in their children's room.

"Most men," said Muhsin, "look for expert women. These women
perform what one's own wife does reluctantly, or refuses to do altogether."
He attributed the reason for most marital problems and breakups to "man's
sexual dissatisfaction. The same is almost true for working women. These
women have enough money and aren't after financial settlements. They look
for a man who can satisfy them. Most women who make *sigheh* contracts
have their own homes, although they usually do not associate with their own,
or the man's relatives. Some women," he went on, "*sigheh* because they want
a protector, or they might be mindful of their neighbors' gossip. Poor women
and married men, in any case," he concluded, "*sigheh* more frequently."

Men who contract *sigheh* marriage, in Muhsin's view, "are from all
classes," but mostly those who are already married or are nouveau riche. "As
soon as men come into some money," he said, "they go after *sigheh*. Women
can't accept their husband's affairs and make one's life miserable, forcing the
husband to do it secretly. Women, on the other hand, hide their *sigheh* less.
They may hide it from their sons or their fathers."[21] In Muhsin's opinion,
some of the women who *sigheh* "exhibit some neurotic behavior, but I don't
know whether it is because of what they are doing [i.e., becoming a *sigheh*],
or their deprivation" — of sex, or love?

Muhsin said that he did not register any of his *sigheh* marriages. Beyond knowing that women should keep '*idda*, he did not know much about
the legal aspects of *sigheh*. Even regarding '*idda* he was misinformed,
thinking that the period of waiting is the same in both forms of marriages. I
asked him whether any of his *sigheh* marriages resulted in pregnancy. He
replied, "It happened three or four times, but I have a Jewish doctor friend
who would perform abortions."

He had contracted many more *sigheh* marriages and conducted
more affairs than I have noted here. He claimed that in most of these cases
he was approached by the women. From his descriptions, however, one
could infer that he usually set the stage, as when he would offer to give rides
to veiled or unveiled hitchhiking women. Significantly, most of the negotiations leading up to propositions for temporary marriage were made in his car.
In such instances, a car's function is analogous to that of a veil. Just as a veil
is a woman's "portable shield," legitimizing her presence in the public domain, metaphorically speaking, a private car is also a couple's "veil," or
shield, enabling them to enjoy a degree of privacy while legitimizing their
association in public.

Muhsin's expression for such encounters was: "So and so got caught in my net." Once he gave a ride to a veiled hitchhiking woman who happened to be from Qom. He expressed an interest in her, and they made a *sigheh* contract. He then visited her in Qom, and in some of his one-day visits he claimed to have had sexual relations with the woman's mother and a maternal cousin as well. Muhsin frequently bragged about his "excessive concupiscence," describing how he used to have seven or eight *sighehs* at the same time. Although on the one hand he lamented the loss of his prowess, on the other he attributed these "deviations" to his early marriage. "Because I married very young," he reflected, "I was full of complexes." Drawing a moral conclusion from a parable he had told me earlier, he said, "One thinks other people's wives are better than one's own. There is really no difference."

A few of his *sigheh* wives were introduced to him by a matchmaker whom he had known. He would approach Muhsin and say, in his words: "She is pretty and has a house, and if you pay a few hundred *tuman* a month you can be with her." Muhsin categorized matchmakers into two types: "The first type operates within big cities, are well organized, and influential. The other type operates individually." In religious centers, in his opinion, matchmakers are of the second type. "Previously, under the Pahlavi regime, most matchmakers were mullas, but not any more. They are afraid that now their actions might be misinterpreted by the Islamic regime. Now they arrange *sigheh* more for themselves rather than arranging them for others."

When asked what precautionary steps he would take regarding hygiene and birth control, Muhsin responded: "I am a specialist in women. I can recognize a virgin from a nonvirgin by looking at the corner of her eyes." He admitted that hygiene is a serious problem, and that it has gotten worse since the revolution. During the *Taghut* regime [a reference to the Pahlavis], he said, "The prostitutes had special health cards, and had to be inspected every week, or month. There were inspectors who would check them and their houses regularly. If their health cards hadn't been renewed, they would be fined or even arrested. But now there is no control. It is zero." It is illuminating to note how readily, but perhaps unconsciously, Muhsin associated *sigheh* with prostitution. And, just as before, he perceived hygiene as a female responsibility. As far as he was concerned, Muhsin said that he controlled the situation by his "sensory and olfactory perceptions." Whether he would be a health hazard to women never crossed his mind.

Asked whether or not he had frequented the "New City" (the prostitutes' quarter) in Tehran, he said he did not usually go there. But the few times he had gone there, he "bought a virgin and paid four thousand *tuman*. Every now and then we would go there for entertainment. Even there," he said, "people *sigheh*."

He believed that after the revolution the arena for male-female relationships has been shifted to within the extended family. "It is now more difficult to establish sexual relations outside of it. For the same reason, homosexuality and incest have increased. Corruption, *fisad*, and fornication, *zina*, are rampant nowadays" (see *Zan-i Ruz* 1987, 1104:14–15).

Dr. Hujjat al-Islam Anvari

Dr. Anvari was introduced to me by a friend of the family. He agreed to come to our house for an interview. Two days before our meeting, however, he telephoned back and said that for security reasons he did not find it advisable to leave his house. He invited me to go there, and my father and I went to his house in south Tehran. Dr. Anvari was a university professor in religious philosophy, as well as a religious leader, a hujjat al-Islam. By the time of our interview he had fallen out of favor, however, and was dismissed from the university. He was a friendly yet very forceful person and, like many other high-ranking mullas, he was straightforward. He was tall, dark-eyed, and imposing. He appeared to be in his late forties, was married, and had three children. One of his sons was in jail at the time of our interview.

Before starting our interview, he gave me a long and opinionated talk on the difficulty of research in the social sciences and the impossibility of being objective. He raised some methodological objections to the field of social sciences, which he viewed to be tainted by Western hegemony. But, above all, he questioned my motives for wanting to study the custom of *mut'a* in Islam. Acknowledging some of his concerns, I stressed the fact that his objections to methodology have occupied the minds of other thinkers as well, and that there were ways of overcoming some of these problems. I assured him that I was interested in understanding one of our customs that was least understood, if not misunderstood, by many Iranians as well as by outsiders.

Before I could get a chance to ask him any questions on the subject, however, he ventured his opinion. "One of the greatest accusations against Shi'a concerns *mut'a*. Many have told all sorts of lies about Shi'a and this practice." Distinguishing between compulsory acts, such as daily prayer, and recommended acts, "those acts whose virtues society has recognized and accepted" in Muhammad's Tradition, Dr. Anvari argued that *mut'a* was of the latter category; that it was mentioned in the Qur'an and was recommended by the Prophet. "Whatever the Prophet has recommended you must obey, and whatever he has prohibited you must avoid. The Shi'ites, the people of the Prophet's household, have unveiled some of these virtues and proceeded to implement and practice them. *Mut'a* is one of them." He concurred with the view that *mut'a* was prevalent in pre-Islamic Arabia but argued, "After the Muslim Prophet, the Shi'ites wanted to implement it according to the Islamic law."

Dr. Anvari began describing different types of marriages according to the Shi'a tenets and the logic behind them. "If you are wealthy, you marry permanently. If you aren't satisfied with one woman, or with two or three or four, you can go and *mut'a* other women." Making a comparison between women and capital, he said, "Women are like capital, *sarmayih*. Sometimes your capital is little, but sometimes it is a lot, and so you can have several wives. But," he continued, "if you don't have any capital to arrange a permanent marriage, go and contract *mut'a*, so that people's descent may not get lost."

He objected to 'Umar's prohibition of *mut'a* in the seventh century and viewed his action as unbinding, because "in the face of explicit Qur'anic permission, 'Umar's interpretation is worthless." He explained that *mut'a* was permitted because "death and destruction due to war were at their height, and therefore His Holiness Muhammad ordered men to marry widows of those martyrs, in order to preserve the stability of families. Just like now [a reference to the Iran-Iraq war]. A woman whose husband is dead wants to have someone who would supervise her sons." He made no mention of daughters. In order to prove 'Umar's prohibition of *mut'a* legally unbinding and humanly ineffective, he recounted the names of several Sunni religious leaders and the Prophet's companions who had contracted *mut'a* marriages frequently. "Ahmad-i Nasa'i, the author of 'Sunan,' who was murdered in A.H. 303," said Dr. Anvari, "had four permanent wives and was making *mut'a* contracts all the time. Or, 'Abdullah ibn-i Zubair had seventy *mut'a* wives in Medina and instructed his sons not to let these women marry after his death." He then referred me to Amini's *Al-Ghadir* (1924, 6:223) for a list of Sunnis who have performed *mut'a*. Dr. Anvari argued that "*mut'a* was prevalent during the reign of Abu Bakr and 'Umar," the first and second caliphs, and only toward the end of his life did 'Umar prohibit it. "Why should he have waited that long?" asked Dr. Anvari rhetorically. "Because he was jealous of his Holiness 'Ali [the Shi'ites' first imam]. Had 'Umar not banned *mut'a*," Dr. Anvari quoted Imam 'Ali, "no fornicator would be found on earth." He then described in detail how 'Umar was prompted to outlaw *mut'a* because of a personal vendetta against Imam 'Ali, who had allegedly made a short-term contract of *mut'a* marriage with 'Umar's sister.

This same "historical" anecdote had been described to me by Amin Aqa in Mashhad, but when I repeated it to my father, he became very indignant. However, when Dr. Anvari with such ease and pride graphically repeated the story, my heart sank. Anxiously, I awaited my father's reaction, but he, keeping his poise about him, said, "But how do we know it is true?" "Of course it is true," the hujjat al-Islam Anvari retorted. "What is so wrong about it? Of course 'Ali contracted *mut'a*. He was a man like any other man, if not more man. Everybody does *mut'a*. I do it too. There was 'Umar who was the caliph, the king, and there was 'Ali, who was only a farmer, *ra'yat*.

Who would dare to *mut'a* the king's sister? Therefore, 'Umar banned *mut'a*." He paused briefly and then continued. "Even many Sunnis themselves were skeptical of 'Umar's injunction. People of Mecca and Medina view *mut'a* as legitimate and don't like 'Umar's order, but because it is the king's command, they follow it."

A Meccan woman with whom he had apparently made contracts of temporary marriage on his trips to Mecca had complained to him, said Dr. Anvari, that only during the pilgrimage did they (i.e., women) have an opportunity to contract temporary marriages. She confided to him, in the hujjat al-Islam's words, "If 'Umar hadn't banned *mut'a*, we would be making a lot of money." He continued, "Now I have friends in Mecca and Medina who do it secretly. Women do it because it is economically very profitable, especially during the pilgrimage." While admitting to *sigheh* himself occasionally, he, however, refused to divulge any details.

Asked how he would establish a *sigheh* relationship and whether or not there were any matchmakers involved, he became indignant, raising his voice: "There are no matchmakers, no institutions, and no committees to arrange *mut'a* marriages. The Orientalists, *mustashriqin*, have started these rumors." The hujjat al-Islam then vehemently accused the Orientalists of misrepresenting the institution of *mut'a* by writing false accounts of the role and activities of matchmakers in motels, inns, and the like. "But," he asked, "if people do it legitimately, what is so wrong about it? What do people do when they need something?" Addressing me, he continued rhetorically, "If you want some fabrics, you go to the drapery. If you want chickpeas, you go to the grocery. If you want permanent marriage and want to live together forever, you must meet certain requirements. But it is different for *mut'a*," he stressed. "Permanent marriage is not called *mut'a*. *Mut'a* means merchandise, goods, *mata'*. For a permanent marriage you pay brideprice, *mahr*, whereas for *mut'a* you pay consideration, *ajr*. Why is this called *mut'a*? Simple! I rent a car and give something in exchange. It is called *mut'a* because I don't want to be bothered with establishing a family, or to pay daily expenses. Marriage, on the other hand," he continued, "is like a hamlet or a sown field, for which you pay a price."

His conceptual distinction between the form, the objective, and the meanings of permanent and temporary marriage underlies the very foundation of the Shi'i doctrinal assumption and supports my contention that not only do the two forms of marriage belong to two separate categories of contracts, but they point to two different categories of thought and rationalization concerning the nature of man, woman, and their sexual and material needs, as well as to how the society should be organized and controlled. His recognition of these gender-differentiated legal, erotic, and social models and his articulation of the problem, however, stand in sharp contrast to that of the Ayatollah Mutahhari and the majority of the contemporary ulama's views.

In Dr. Anvari's opinion, terrible things would happen to men should they be forced to abstain from sexual intercourse: "He who doesn't do this will develop a tumor at the bottom of his spinal cord."[22] He was adamant about the physiological and psychological harm of sexual abstinence for men, and he launched into a long and opinionated monologue on the "natural" differences between men and women. "Instincts and materials, *mavvad*, that exist in men are lacking in women." Referring to man's primordial wife/mother, Eve, he attributed the following anecdote to Shaikh Tusi: "Adam once asked Eve to go to him. Eve said, 'You want me, you come to me' " (see also Mutahhari 1974, 15). "That's why," leaping from this socioreligious lore to a predetermined biological programming, he concluded, "men have to proposition women, and women ought to be obedient to their husbands." If this were true of Adam and Eve, he seemed to be reasoning, then it must have some biological basis and, therefore, must be true for all humans at all times. Note that in this anecdote Eve actually disobeys Adam.

Asked about the channels through which people learn about *mut'a*, he said, "Learning about *mut'a* doesn't require any particular place. If I see a modest woman, I present my case." However, in his view, "People know little about *mut'a* because nobody tells them about it, and under the Pahlavi regime people were discouraged from making contracts of *mut'a*." Asked who usually initiates a *sigheh* union, he said tersely, "If I want to *mut'a*, I propose it to a woman who is passing by. If she wants it she will say yes, and if not she will say no. And that's that." He paused briefly and went on: "Or you might have known her already, and so you go to her directly and express your desire."

At this point, a learned guest, who had just happened to drop by while we were there and was present for part of our discussion, joined in. "*Sigheh* occurs mostly in marked and popularly known areas within a shrine. In Qom, it is the Atabaki Yard in the northeast part of the shrine where during certain hours women who want to *sigheh* loiter." Indignantly, the hujjat al-Islam interrupted, "These might be just rumors. Of course it does happen in the holy places, *'atabat*, but it occurs in other places, too." As if realizing how unwarranted his outburst was, he changed his tone of voice and continued: "Though it might be more frequent in the holy places." His guest resumed again, also undaunted. "It also happens more frequently when people are on pilgrimage." Dr. Anvari interrupted him again. "That is because there are many pilgrims who go there to seek help from these holy shrines. There might be menopausal women who offer themselves to you as you read a prayer. Some women pass you by and offer themselves. It is the same way in Mecca. It is due to sexual drives." Continuing the dialogue, his guest launched into a long talk about religion, morality, law, and custom. He was beginning to sound disrespectful of the tradition when Dr. Anvari, obviously annoyed with him, cut him short and said, "Colonialism has tried to equate *mut'a* with prostitution and say 'what is the difference between this or that?' " He emphasized: "Yes. *Mut'a* is like prostitution, but because it has the name of God, it is permissible. Any type of pleasure that does not have the name of God, you mustn't enjoy."

I asked him why, if *mut'a* is legally permitted and religiously blessed, is it culturally stigmatized? Dr. Anvari responded: "When we interpret *mut'a* as temporary pleasure, then it assumes certain meanings and certain connotations. One may have one's own car. But if you rent a car, you pay for it every time you use it. One may have one's own cup; only you drink from it. But in the streets and religious public drinking places, *saqqa khunih*, there are cups from which everyone drinks. You may not drink water in a coffee house because everyone uses the same glass. You look down upon it. Likewise, because *mut'a* has similar meanings and connotations, the society looks down upon it. That's why the Prophet has recommended *mut'a* for its religious reward. That's why the public drinking places have religious significance and are named after the Prophet or the Imams.[23] That is to encourage people to go there and drink the water.[24] Now," he continued, "I may want to *mut'a*, and from the viewpoint of religion and law it is considered good too. So I go and do it secretly! You do not announce it to the public [because it is a good deed]. At the same time it is a matter of male potency, *qudrat*, too!" He then gave the example of the Shi'i second imam, Hassan, who is famous for his beauty and his numerous marriages.[25] "Most women wanted to be with him, and so he made them his *mut'a*," he said. "A lot of women want it themselves."

As to what motivates people to *mut'a*, Dr. Anvari also subscribed to the male majority view: "Men are motivated by their sexual needs and do it so as not to get sick; women do it because of financial need." Asked if he thought women were also erotically motivated, he responded, "Possibly, but they lie," apparently not remembering his earlier comments on women's sexual attraction to the second imam and others. Dr. Anvari and his guest, individually and jointly, took turns to stress how women often mask their true feelings. Paradoxically, although they viewed women's marital motivations as transparent (being financial), they expressed bewilderment as to what women are really up to! Both men articulated the common Iranian attitude, presuming honesty to be a male virtue and deceit a feminine trait. After a lengthy and at times animated discussion among all of us, Dr. Anvari modified his ambivalent view of feminine opacity and transparency. This time, however, he displaced transparency onto social class, suggesting: "Lower-class women do it because of financial needs, and there are a lot of them; whereas higher-class women do it because of sexual needs."

As for a place of residence for the consummation of a *mut'a* marriage, Dr. Anvari said that it depended on the nature of the agreement between the partners, their financial ability, the length of their *mut'a* marriage, and other such conditions. Contradicting some earlier statements, he said, "Many people go to the religious centers both to find a *sigheh* as well as to reside there after signing the contract. There are identified locations and quarters in the shrines in Iran, Iraq, Syria, and Egypt. Women who know about these marked areas will go there and are ready to receive guests." Dr. Anvari went on. "The length of *mut'a* marriage is usually one or two hours, or one night. If it is more than that, it might lead to a permanent marriage." Subscribing to the currently prevalent idea of temporary marriage as a trial marriage, he said, "*Mut'a* is a gate for permanent marriage. It allows for some mutual familiarity. This is a cultural way for getting to know one's future spouse. In fact," he stressed, "the engagement period *is* like a *sigheh*. Most marriages that end in divorce occur because the partners didn't know each other at first, because it is done blindly. Islam says you must know each other." I asked him if this was the case, then why did more women not do it? He replied, "Because men take advantage of it. They may *mut'a* one woman, and later on claim that their temperaments didn't agree, and so let go of her, and so on!"

The hujjat al-Islam Dr. Anvari led our long interview to a humorous end by telling us the following anecdote, underscoring once again the necessity of the institution of temporary marriage in society: "Once a group of worshipers surprised a couple under the pulpit in a mosque. Feeling indignant, they shouted at the man: 'Aren't you ashamed of yourself? Don't you have any religion?' The man answered 'I have a religion; I don't have a place!' "

Mulla Ifshagar

I came upon Mulla Ifshagar's name accidentally.[26] A librarian at the Mar'ashi Najafi library in Qom, where I was doing research, gave me his name and address, vouching for his scholarship. I telephoned him and briefly described my research, asking whether he would be willing to grant me an interview. His initial comments came back as a shock to me. He said that I should first understand and accept the premise that in Islam, "women are regarded as half men, if not less," and that I should start my research from there. I was astounded! This was the first mulla ever who with such clarity admitted women's unfavorable position in Islam. He agreed to see me that day.

Mulla Ifshagar turned out to be one of the most critical minded, well-read, and up-to-date mullas with whom I have ever talked. He expressed his opinions openly and freely. He was critical of the Islamic regime and was not apologetic about his views regarding Islam in general and the regime of the Ayatollah Khomeini in particular. He was thirty-five years old, married, and had one child. He had traveled to Europe and was particularly impressed with Swedish society. I interviewed him three times.

Mulla Ifshagar started by giving me a detailed critique of the institution of slavery in Islam, emphasizing the fact that slavery has never been abolished in Islam. Although he saw some functional similarities between slavery and *sigheh* marriage, he said that rather than writing on *sigheh*, I should devote my time and energy to researching slavery in Islam. From his point of view this institution has escaped critical thinking and writing. Only much later did he make some comments on the institution of temporary marriage. He likened sexual drives to hunger and thirst, arguing, "If you have enough food at your disposal you don't have to worry about it. Similarly, when sexuality is not an issue, you don't have to worry much about it. Any time you want it you can have it. You can devote your attention and energy elsewhere." He said, "In Muslim countries, because of all sorts of sexual taboos, one's time and energy are consumed by efforts to find ways of gratifying one's needs." He believed that the Prophet had realized the importance of sexual needs and that "he allowed people to satisfy these desires as long as they did not infringe upon other people's rights." Infringement, from his point of view, meant that "a married woman can't have sexual relations outside of marriage because she belongs to her husband."

Like Mulla X, he maintained a perspective of geographic determinism on the intensity of sexual desire. "In colder climates," he opined, "people are frigid, while Easterners, who live in hotter climates, are obsessed with sex." Asked what he perceived to be the motivating factors for a *sigheh* marriage, he replied, "Lack of affection and not having a protector for women, and sexual satisfaction for men." Because of his busy schedule and because we had spent so much of our time discussing slavery in Islam, we had to end our interview, but he promised to contact me later.

Two days later as I was recording some of my observations, the doorbell rang. A loud masculine voice asked for a certain Khanum Haeri! My host looked at me perplexed, and I became alarmed.[27] The man's voice came in again, announcing that there was a phone call for me in the small office of an old inn adjacent to our house! My host and I put on our veils quickly and rushed to the innkeeper's office. I picked up the receiver hesitantly and immediately recognized Mulla Ifshagar's voice. I was puzzled, as I had given him the telephone number of my host's in-laws. Apologizing for having inconvenienced me, he said that the reason for not calling me there was because he was afraid of being identified. (He was a well-known mulla and was regularly performing religious rituals for many Qomi families.) But because

he had something important to tell me, he had finally decided to risk tele-
phoning me at the inn. I suggested a meeting at his house; he declined. I
suggested the shrine yard; he rejected that too, arguing that many people
knew him, and besides, it was not proper for us to be seen whispering into
each other's ears in public. Given the overzealous mood of the country, I
fully appreciated his objections. He then offered to come to our house, and I
accepted an appointment for two o'clock that afternoon. This invitation,
however, made my host unhappy. She was constantly worried about what
others may say behind her back. Apologizing for the inconvenience, I promised to keep our interview short.

At two o'clock sharp Mulla Ifshagar was at the door. I led him to the
guest room and, as is the custom in Qom, left ajar the door to the room. This
is to dispel any suspicions of wrongdoing between a man and women who are
left alone in a room. My host served us tea, and to please her, much to my
own regret, I told Mulla Ifshagar that we could meet for only two hours. He
did not object to this time restriction and said he appreciated my host's concern. When he left, however, I discovered that my host and her mother, taking a precautionary step, had left the house, leaving me and the mulla alone.
This was to signal to those neighbors who might have seen Mulla Ifshagar
coming to her house that she had nothing to do with him. It was then that I
panicked as I thought about what might have happened if the revolutionary
guards had seen Mulla Ifshagar walking in and my host going out!

The first thing he asked me was to promise him not ever to reveal
his identity to anyone. Mulla Ifshagar had a tendency to interrupt himself and
to free-associate. It was a little uncomfortable, if not embarrassing, to constantly try to bring him back to his main points. For that matter, it was at
times difficult to follow his narrative, though in writing up his interview I
have tried — as much as I am able — to give it some order. Despite all that,
he shared with me his thoughts, making a devastating exposé of the activities
of some of his fellow mullas, who, in his view, comprise the largest group of
people who indulge in *mut'a* marriages.

Mulla Ifshagar began: "In a closed society like ours there are two
types of *mut'a* marriages. One that is similar to prostitution, and women
who do it are either in financial need or are emotionally deprived. But this
constitutes only ten percent of the total *mut'a* population." Addressing me,
he said, "That's why you have not been successful in finding many *sigheh*
women. You are looking at the wrong place [the shrine]. The second form of
mut'a," Mulla Ifshagar continued, "the real thing, goes on among high
school students, even between some teachers and their students. Ninety
percent of the *mut'a* population is from among those who use *mut'a* as a solution to their sexual problems. In a closed society like ours, sexuality is sup-
pressed and repressed. So when people find a way of satisfying it, they be-

come greedy. Their time and energy are spent in finding ways and means of gratifying their desires."

He made a distinction between the rate of maturity between boys and girls. Arguing that "girls mature faster than boys in Iran, emotionally and physically," Mulla Ifshagar attributed much of a girl's precocity to a mother's obsession with a daughter's marriage almost from the moment of her birth. "That's why these young girls," he concluded, "are eager to meet men and to get to know them. Two ways are open to them. One is to become a lesbian, which is prevalent in Iranian high schools.[28] The second is to have a heterosexual relationship. The latter are those who contract *sigheh* as a solution to their sexual problems."

Asked to be more specific, Mulla Ifshagar stated, "Most families in Qom have weekly or monthly religious gatherings and prayers. They usually have at least one or two regular mullas who perform these rituals for them. From early on, these mullas get to know different members of a family, including the young girls. They establish special relationships with these impressionable young girls." How some mullas find their way into the hearts and minds of these girls, according to Mulla Ifshagar, is "by looking intensely and suggestively into their eyes; saying a few words relevant to their situation; showing understanding for their problems; and projecting their ideas into these little girls' minds, making them believe in what they say." In short, he continued, "These mullas exert a sort of 'hypnotic influence' over these girls.[29] By showing sympathy and understanding, such mullas eventually become the girls' mentor, or benefactor, *bani*. The basic trust that develops as a result remains the most significant relationship in the lives of these girls." Throughout their lives, Mulla Ifshagar said, women refer to these mullas time and again, seeking their help and guidance in matters of concern to them. The greatest proponents of the benefactor system, according to Mulla Ifshagar, are a group of sayyids, known as Sadat-i Shirazi, who actually "buy and sell" a right to their privileged positions.[30] He did not tell me just exactly how they do this, but other informants told me that by recommending each other to families whom they know, these mullas come to know a much wider network of families, women, and particularly young girls.

In his view, the roots of women's impressionability and gullibility are to be sought in their strict religious and educational upbringing. "Because they are religiously inclined," he reasoned, "they seek refuge in religious figures, who from the point of view of their families are nonthreatening and legitimate. It is even considered a socially proper relationship. It is here that these household mullas become matchmaking mullas. Soon they suggest *sighehs* to these girls as solutions to their personal problems [conflicts with parents, desire to have a relation with a member of the opposite sex, and the like]. Being from a religious background, these young girls easily fall into their trap. First, the mullas make *sigheh* contracts between such girls and their own friends or sons; and from then on they become more and more expert, knowing precisely what to do. Most significantly," he concluded, "a divine, unspoken, and secretive relationship is established between these mullas and the girls. They become women's benefactors."

From the perspective of Mulla Ifshagar, the objective of these *sigheh* relationships is twofold: "One is that *sigheh* is legal and is religiously approved of; and second is that it creates some sort of shield around the relationship with the girls, at least for the time being [no one else can approach them]." As for the mullas themselves, "They also have relations with everyone. It doesn't matter to them whether or not these women are married. And the women themselves are gullible enough to follow their instructions and eventually keep on making contracts of *sigheh* marriage."[31] He concluded, "The more a particular ideology devalues women, the easier it is to reach them. The easier they are reached, the less respect they receive."

Mulla Ifshagar, like the rest of my informants, believed that *sigheh* contracts have increased since the revolution. To substantiate his claim, he described the following event. After the revolution, he said, the establishment of religious boarding schools became fashionable in Qom. One such boarding school was instituted by a highly educated man who was exiled during the reign of the shah but who returned to Iran after the revolution. This man put on his religious robe once again and became a Friday prayer leader in a mosque outside of Qom. Some sixty-seven girls from ages ten to twenty registered in his boarding school. They came from all over Iran in order to study in his new institution.

Gradually, the headmaster's wife became suspicious of her husband's activities and of the nature of his relationships with his students. Putting together bits and pieces of information, she eventually realized that he was having illicit relations with some of them. She brought the matter to the attention of the authorities, demanding that her husband be questioned. "Religious leaders," said Mulla Ifshagar, "are tried in a separate court, so that religious scandals may not reach the public" (see also *Iran Times* 1987, 801:1). In this case, all that the court did was to sentence the headmaster to *sigheh* all eleven girls. The court's verdict was based on the premise that he could not legally marry them permanently all at once. He was, however, ordered to relinquish his religious position as the Friday prayer leader, but he ignored this prohibition and continued to perform the Friday prayers. The headmaster's wife, who had appealed to the court expecting justice, found herself a temporary cowife to eleven teenagers! Mulla Ifshagar was not quite clear of the details of these agreements, that is, the lengths of these *sigheh* marriages, the amount of the brideprices paid to each student, or whether or not the headmaster maintained them all at once.

Asked of the reaction of the girls' families, Mulla Ifshagar said that they all kept the matter quiet. "The families did not want anybody to know anything about it."[32] In my view, the shame of rape or other sexual relations outside of marriage is so strongly felt in Iran that many families, particularly the middle classes, prefer to suffer privately rather than to pursue the matter publicly through judicial channels. Mulla Ifshagar maintained that the situation in other schools is not much different. "Those from religious backgrounds know what they want, what to do, and they do it frequently."

"During the Qajar dynasty," the mulla said, "*mut'a* marriages were openly made, but then its practice went underground during the Pahlavi regime. It was then that it became secretive, and the society came to take a negative attitude toward it. Now, after the revolution, it is more open." Though not dismissing the institution of temporary marriage categorically, he continued, "*Mut'a* is like an underground Mafia organization. Everyone knows about it, but nobody talks about it. It is like a termite nest. Nobody sees the termites, but all hear them chewing the foundations. Nowadays," he concluded, "mullas *sigheh* much more frequently than was intended by the Prophet, but it is less frequently used by nonreligious people. Anywhere there are mullas, there are more sexual activities."

"Our society is a society of maintaining public façades," observed the astute mulla. Criticizing the distinction Iranians make between the "outer" and the "inner" aspects of self, *zahir va batin*, he narrated the following anecdote: "Shah 'Abbas Safavid [sixteenth century; famous for his incognito ventures into the city to observe the life and activities of his subjects] in one of his anonymous inspections visited a village, and because of bad weather was forced to stay there overnight. It was cold, and the shah asked for a blanket. He was told that, alas, there were no more blankets, but that they had a saddle bag that could do the job. The shah said, 'All right, bring me the thing but don't mention its name.' Our society," concluded Mulla Ifshagar, "operates on the same maxim. Bad in our society is not the act itself, but its publicity. The more we hide our problems, the more room is left for deception and corruption."

Because of the unusual form of this particular interview, and its nearly conspiratorial and controversial content, I was often not certain how to respond to his attacks on the Islamic regime or to his criticism of the institution of temporary marriage and the role of the mullas. Why was he telling me all these things? I wondered. Was it because he thought I was an outsider, and so, safe? Or, was it because he was trying to test my national allegiance, and to see whether or not I was a spy? Because of such worries, our conversation was not as lively as it could have been, and I did not feel as free in asking him questions as I would have liked to do. In this interview, it was hard to overcome barriers of self-censorship.

DISCUSSION

In this chapter I presented the views of some Iranian men, most of whom
happened to be mullas of one rank or another. Perhaps because of this, general patterns of agreement in their thinking and perception of *mut'a* marriage are readily discernible. Their motives in making a contract of temporary marriage are less complex than the women's, but their objective reflects
more the officially formulated Shi'i position. With the exception of Muhsin,
my male informants tended to refrain from divulging much about their personal lives, and their narratives were less elaborate and intimate than those
of the women. Men's narratives tended to remain primarily on an impersonal
level, and their descriptions of the institution were more pedagogical,
global, principle-oriented, formulaic, and public. The male informants
tended to stress the more public aspects of *mut'a* "to wear the cloak of legitimacy and law," as it were, but their female counterparts tended "to take off
their mask" and to unveil a portrait that was more intimate and private. The
women's narratives were more inward looking and reflective. Whereas men
on the whole defended the institution (even Mulla Ifshagar did not call for
abolishing it), women exhibited ambivalence toward it and questioned its
implications for their personal and married life.

From the interviews of these men, too, emerge pictures different
from, though overlapping, the traditionally valorized ideal images of the genders and their relations. Three interconnected themes recur in men's case
histories, namely, the centrality of eroticism, the desirability of self versus
ambivalence toward the other, and marital security.

The Centrality of Eroticism

Men are favored by the ideological and legal superstructure, and
they are aware of this. Almost unanimously they emphasized eroticism as
their principal motivating factor in making a contract of *mut'a* marriage, justifying this with assumptions regarding (male) human nature, fear of getting
sick, prevention of a "sinful act" (fornication), and the climate. In addition, a
few also included other motives such as a desire for progeny, needing a wife-
servant, and contempt for, or revenge upon, the first wife. Above all, they
perceived the function of temporary marriage in terms of its necessity for
men's sense of health and well-being. For that matter, they reiterated the
Shi'i official view of the necessity of satisfying male libidinal drive and supported the thesis of the advantages of temporary marriage for psychological
development of a healthy individual and for preserving social order. In addition, my male informants justified the legitimacy of *mut'a* on the basis of

the belief that Islam is a religion of compassion and simplicity, having as its main objective solving human problems. *Mut'a* marriage, they argued, is a case in point. Whether explicitly or implicitly, these men argued that men cannot, and should not, limit themselves to one woman, because of their "nature."

That these men's motivation for making a contract of temporary marriage should be primarily erotic, or that their justification for its legitimacy is consistent with that of the Shi'i doctrine, is not really a revelation. Their objective and behavior are consistent and in keeping with the social and legal role models envisioned for men historically. What is surprising is the image of the negotiating, active, and erotically motivated women that emerges from men's narratives. Men's portrayal of women, and of their own interaction with them, differs not only from the ideal of the feminine role, of women's behavior forged socially and legally for them, but also from the ideal of the men's own role as well. Men portrayed themselves, unconsciously perhaps, as being passive and at the receiving end of the relationship, at least initially. Not only that, ironically, in relation to these men, women seemed to have the upper hand. The veil that cloaks women and conceals them behind it denies a recognition of their individuality and forbids sparks of distinction of one woman from another. Simultaneously, their anonymity enables women to see men, to target them, and to approach them as they please without being indiscreet and conspicuous. Unprotected by a prophylactic veil symbolically, men are paradoxically vulnerable to the desiring gaze of veiled women.[33] Contrary to the societal image of female passivity, women of the stories of my male informants all emerged as determined subjects who initiated their *sigheh* relationship primarily because they felt physically attracted to the men. Far from being rendered impotent by this apparently unconventional behavior of women, these men in fact welcomed their approach, for the most part; they allowed themselves to become objects of women's desire, and they obeyed their demand.[34]

Although my male informants had no trouble identifying their own erotic motive as the primary reason for making a contract of temporary marriage, they expressed uncertainty regarding women's true motive. The ubiquitousness of the logic of contract, and its manifestations in men's perceptions of themselves and of women, looms large here again. An Islamic marriage contract obliges men to pay women, whether in the form of brideprice or consideration, for a permanent or temporary right over the object of desire that is in the woman's possession. By the same logic, women cannot be simultaneously in possession of the object of desire and desire it, too. Rather, women get paid for relinquishing it. Therefore, from a male point of view, if men's motive for making a contract of *sigheh* is fundamentally erotic, it then follows that women's motive cannot be anything but financial: if half of the equation is true, logically then the other half must also be true. In their everyday interactions, however, as we learned, these men came to know women who turned the assumptions of feminine ideals, female motives, and normative gender relations inside out.

I have argued that divorced and widowed women have greater legal autonomy than married women, and that at this stage of their life cycle women's capacities of execution and obligation merge more closely than at other stages. The autonomy exercised by women in their relations to men I interviewed—corroborated also by the stories of my female informants—underscores my contention. Not only do divorced women in theory have greater legal capacity to execute their will, they actually do put it to use. Almost unanimously, my male informants said that they were propositioned by women, or that they believed women to be the ones who initiate an invitation to a *sigheh* marriage contract.

Desirability of Self versus Ambivalence toward the Other

A mature Muslim man's legal status remains stable and constant throughout his entire life cycle, regardless of whether he is married, divorced, or widowed. Ideologically, a Muslim man is perceived to be a complete individual legally, physically, psychologically, and socially. Women, on the other hand, are perceived to be defective; their legal and social statuses undergo several changes and shifts during their lifetime. Within the framework of marriage a woman's legal status changes to that of an object whereas the man's remains the same. A man's relation to his wife, thus, is symbolically mediated through the object of exchange, the woman's sexual and reproductive capacity. So long as the behavior of the husband and the wife coincides with the sociolegally structured boundaries of dominance and subordination, each gender's perception of the self and the other remains relatively congruent with the ideal marital model. Men's perception of "fullness" of the self, however, may be challenged when this ideal model is upset and the genders' actual behavior diverge significantly from that of the ideal.

Unequivocally, men approved of the objective of the institution of temporary marriage for themselves, but they expressed doubts about its implications for the women who actually use it. The symbolic association of woman with that of an object confronts men (and women) with conflicting images of women, and necessarily of themselves. Despite the fact that my male informants were propositioned by actively negotiating women, and despite the fact that they almost automatically obeyed the demands of these women, they sometimes perceived *mut'a* women as being like a "rented car," for which you pay, or other times as "a drinking cup," from which you drink,

and still other times as "medicine," which cures men's ills. In all these categories, women are seen as objects whose raison d'être is understood only in
relation to men, and whose primary function is believed to be the maintenance of men's physical well-being and possibly their spiritual balance.

Men expressed their moral ambivalence regarding the propriety of
sigheh marriage for women within the two extremes of prostitution and
piety. Sometimes they categorized a *sigheh* woman as a "downright prostitute" (presumably because she approaches men directly, or because she does
not keep herself chaste during her waiting period; she is "public"), and at
other times as a "pious" woman who makes a contract of *sigheh* only to please
God (performing a meritorious act, quenching men's thirst, or disobeying
'Umar). On the other hand, that women may also perform *sigheh* because
they are motivated erotically seems to fit no predetermined and culturally
known social or legal framework, or not one the men wish to acknowledge
publicly. In any case, not only did men have a hard time believing women's
real motive, but because of the perception of the "public" nature of *mut'a*
women, they were ambivalent about the implications of *mut'a* for practicing
women. They stated reservations about women's moral character and the
public's perception of their role.

My male informants, however, were as articulate about their ambivalence toward *sigheh* women as they were silent about their own ambivalence toward themselves. While these men apparently welcomed women's
initiation, and the respite it afforded them from their expected role of being
the ever-determined, decisive, and dominant male, they were not comfortable with the implications of this role reversal for themselves, either. Like
sigheh women, men perceived, though perhaps not clearly, the tension between the ideal masculine behavior and their actual obedience to and depen-
dence on women. Realizing this incongruity between the actual and the ideal
for both themselves and the women, yet unable or unwilling to turn down a
feminine invitation to a sexual union, some of my male informants were bewildered about women's desires, and others felt vulnerable. Men, however,
did not articulate their sense of vincibility the way the women did. They displaced the doubt regarding their own action onto women, abrogating any
sense of personal responsibility and self-control in their erotic encounters.
They accused women of dishonesty, or of using witchcraft, or of sexual control and manipulation. These men viewed the autonomy exhibited by *sigheh*
women as peculiar to this category of women only, as exceptional rather than
the rule and, as such, in conflict with the expected, normative, natural, and
ideal role of women. What was left unexpressed in the men's narratives was
their reflections on their own presumably unconventional behavior of passivity and obedience. Although, on the one hand, men felt good about their own
popularity with women, on the other hand they did not see the *sigheh*

woman as a positive role model to be emulated by their own daughters, for example.

Despite this initial role reversal and exercise of a degree of feminine autonomy, however, once the contract was agreed upon, the status of the temporary wife shifted once again: from that of a relatively autonomous, negotiating, and active subject to that of an object of desire. Because of the contractual form of marriage and the nature of the exchange in this contract, often the temporary spouses' roles revert to the traditional and dominant patterns of subordination and domination.

Marital Security

We may finally note the relative absence of divorce among men who chose to have temporary wives. Not surprisingly, many of them seemed to make a distinction between their married life and their erotic life (see also Adamiyyat 1977, 22–23). Except for Mulla X, who was divorced, all my male informants were living with their families. Some had a *sigheh* who was unknown to their wives (Mulla Hashim), some had a *sigheh* despite their wives' objections (Amin Aqa), and others, like Muhsin, had frequent liaisons with the tacit knowledge of their wives. Having had the support of the law, religion, and custom, not only do these men have greater control over their own lives, they do not have to suffer the trauma of separation from their children or the anxiety over public moral indignation of divorce. If men are not happy with one wife, or even if they want "a change of taste" (as a Persian expression would have it), they can simply make another contract of marriage. Despite some women's initiation, for the most part men have the ultimate control over the outcome of their relationship. Many men use the threat of a remarriage as a way of manipulating their wives, playing one woman against another.

Such arrangements, though giving the institution of marriage in Iran an appearance of stability, are misleading indicators of such stability or of the intimacy of marital relations. Because of the structural dynamics of the institution, undercurrents of animosity and antagonism are likely to develop between husband and wife, which often get displaced to other women, particularly to divorced women. Such tensions and tendencies, though often muted and unacknowledged, potentially militate against the formation of a trusting and meaningful relationship between husband and wife, driving them apart and to the opposing poles of the relational spectrum. The case histories of Tuba, Furugh, Iran's *sigheh* cowife, as well as that of Amin Aqa, Mulla Hashim, and Muhsin are but a few examples.

CONCLUSION

B Y ANALYZING THE CONCEPT OF CONTRACT and the marriage exchange, I have sought to provide insight into the way the Shi'i ideology perceives social order and social control in general and male-female relationships in particular. I have argued that the root of the legal and ideological ambivalence toward women is to be sought in the contractual structure of the permanent and temporary forms of marriage. I have also demonstrated that the tension between the religious acceptance of temporary marriage and its cultural disapproval (because of its close association with prostitution) translates into a widespread moral ambivalence toward the institution and the women, but seldom toward the men. Consequently, those who practice it tend to keep their activities secret. Several pertinent themes recurring throughout my analysis merit further examination, to bring into better focus our understanding of the institution of temporary marriage, of the women and men in Iran.

AMBIVALENCE TOWARD WOMEN

The Shi'a doctrine projects a double image of women through the contractual laws of temporary and permanent marriages. We may ask here, What is a woman from a Shi'i perspective? Is she a precious commodity that may be owned, bought, or leased? Is she a person created like a man who can be in charge of her own life, negotiate contracts, control their outcome, and exchange gifts? Is she a decision-making adult or a minor? Looking at the women's status developmentally, and through a discussion of the different forms of Shi'i marriage contracts, I have shown that at any given point in her life cycle a Shi'i Muslim woman may be perceived to be all or some of the above simultaneously.

Such legal ambivalence is reflected in a variety of vastly popular binary images of women. Images of women as controller/controlled, seducer/seduced, cunning/gullible, and pious/adulterous, all have wide currency in the Perso-Islamic literature. In one of the most fascinating literary treasures of the Middle East, the tales of *A Thousand and One Nights*, the superimposition of many of these binary images is elegantly portrayed. Indeed, the whole story is based on one such dominant binary opposition: that of order/disorder. Through the cunning of an adulterous queen, society is brought to the brink of disorder. But the mediation of another woman, Shahrzad, restores order to society and sense to the king.

The underlying ambivalence toward women is not reflected just in literature and folklore. The Qur'an itself conveys this ambivalence toward women as well. In the Holy Book women are sometimes depicted as objects to be treated kindly or harshly, and at other times as persons created of the same material as men (compare suras of Women 34 and the Cow 223 with the Private Apartment 13). Many *hadiths* and sayings of the Prophet, the imams, and other Muslim leaders further underscore this ambivalence. For example, the Prophet Muhammad is frequently quoted as having said: "Women are the trappings of Satan" (cited in *Burhan-i Qat'* 1951–63, 2:681; Razi 1963–68, 350). In another context, however, he is alleged to have stated: "From your world I do not like anything but women and perfume" (quoted by Ayatollah Mishkini 1974, 118). Such ambivalence finds its resonance in the following popular adage in Iran: "Women are a pain, *bala*. May no house be without it."

A *sigheh* woman especially is a target of cultural and legal ambivalence. Personally, she might be more mature and experienced than other women (because she has married at least once and divorced), and legally, she is freer than married and virgin women to negotiate on her own behalf, choose her male partner(s), and exercise her own decision-making power. She is her own person, as it were. A divorced woman's status is the closest that a Shi'i Muslim woman can come to having legal autonomy. Autonomy, however, is not a trait socially approved of for women in Iran. Although some men may welcome it, and even be fascinated by the alluring autonomy of women, as is apparent in the "*sigheh* myth," they are at the same time fearful of the arbitrariness implied in it: just as they may be selected for a treat, they may be let go unceremoniously.

Because temporary marriage is a contract of lease and its objective is sexual enjoyment, *sigheh* women are seen not only as objects of exchange (indeed, they are referred to as the object of lease, *musta'jirih*) but also as temporary sexual partners. There is thus a close structural association with prostitution. Consequently, the custom of temporary marriage and its propriety involve cultural questioning and conflicting feelings, and women who make use of it are also perceived with moral ambivalence. Much to women's disappointment, temporary marriage often bestows them neither with the masculine protection nor with the social prestige they so earnestly seek.

AMBIVALENCE TOWARD *MUT'A* MARRIAGE

Tuba, one of my women informants, said, "First I thought only bad women *sigheh*. Now I regret why I did it in the first place. Both times I thought they were going to marry me. Both swore to the Qur'an that they would live with me, and both tricked me." The structural similarities between temporary marriage and prostitution escape no one but confuse many. The moral tension between the two institutions was time and again stressed not only by people who do not contract temporary marriage but by many whom I interviewed, including some of my female informants. Tuba's statement is a telling example. Some people associated temporary marriage with prostitution and therefore perceived it to be a potential threat to a woman's honor and reputation. Others, though approving of the institution on principle, doubted its implications for women who actually make use of it. Confused by the official rhetoric, many divorced and widowed women, including some of my informants, made a contract of temporary marriage thinking that it would be similar to a permanent marriage and hoping that it would be lasting and secure. For example, Iran was perfectly willing to be Amir's lover, in which case she would have not become pregnant and would have been spared the ambiguities of status and personal confusion that were a result of her temporary marriage. Her disillusionment with her *sigheh* marriage had left her bitter. "It is an absurd thing," she said, "because no one makes a commitment."

The popular ambivalence also leaves young virgin women in a sort of cultural double bind. If they do marry on a temporary basis, or even make a nonsexual arrangement as a trial marriage, they may risk their reputation and their chances for a proper permanent marriage and a desirable marriage settlement. If they do not do it, it is also likely that they may end up in an unsatisfactory marriage. In a culture where virginity is treasured, no woman can afford to gamble with her "symbolic capital" without running the risk of tarnishing her reputation and greatly diminishing her chances for a desirable permanent marriage.

It is important to contemplate the issues of male obligation, responsibility, and commitment in a temporary marriage. Here is where ambiguities abound in the marriage contract. On the one hand, the contemporary ulama recommend temporary marriage because of its minimal reciprocal responsibilities, emphasizing the easy condition for contracting it and recommending its use for the young generation. On the other hand, they ignore implications of the lack of responsibility in this form of marriage — for example, the relative ease with which paternity can be denied. Viewed in relation to each other, and in practice, the incompatibility of these injunctions becomes clear. In other words, although there is a legal framework for temporary marriage—and this is emphasized by the ulama—legal loopholes and stratagems also abound. That the contract is private, requiring no witnesses or registration (despite some efforts to change this), that men can leave their temporary wives any time they want to, and that legally men can deny their children without being put through an oath-taking procedure (required in a contract of permanent marriage), all are evidence of the ambiguity of the law and its blurred boundaries.

The ulama insist that because of the contractual form of *mut'a*, conditions agreeable to both partners may be negotiated initially. In the Ayatollah Najaf'i Mar'shi's reasoning, "Nobody forces women to agree to a contract of temporary marriage" (personal communication, summer 1978). What is lacking in such masculine Shi'i reasoning is the fact that men and women negotiate from a position of inequality: legally, economically, psychologically, or socially. It is true that some women initiate a relation leading into a contract of temporary marriage, but beyond their immediate needs, many men are not interested in committing themselves, and they do not have to. The extreme temporariness of a contract of *mut'a* marriage, its stated objective of male erotic enjoyment, and the contemporary ulama's emphasis on its minimal responsibility are some of the factors contributing to difficulties in making a mutually beneficial contract of temporary marriage (see note 3, below).

Save for a few shrewd ones (Mahvash and Fati), *sigheh* women, whether through their own confusion about the objective of temporary marriage, their fear of losing a prospective husband, their desire to love and to be loved, or other sociocultural pressures, are in a vulnerable position to begin with. They can hardly afford to demand any commitment or concessions from men who would be marrying them for only two hours, two nights, two months, or even two years. Iran, Tuba, and Shahin assumed — or, rather, were misled into thinking—that there is some security in this relationship, and that they would be provided for by the men who confessed "love" for them. Not being familiar with the law, they learned about its specifics from the men who persuaded them to turn a vague idea into practice. Some were genuinely surprised and hurt to find out that they were "tricked," in Tuba's words, and simply let go once they fell out of favor, or when they no longer fulfilled what their temporary husbands had married them for. Furugh and Nanih, being a bit older, were somewhat resigned to their destinies. Apparently, they had realized that as long as they did not make any demands on their temporary husbands, their relationships would hold.

AMBIVALENCE TOWARD FEMALE SEXUALITY

We may finally ask, What is female sexuality from a Shi'i legal perspective, and how is it being represented ideologically? How is it being perceived by women and men who make use of a contract of temporary marriage? Having its roots in the contractual structure of marriage, the ideological ambivalence toward women is inevitably and inextricably intertwined with ambivalence toward female sexuality. In the Shi'i ideology the man is assumed to be driven by his sexual drives, to have "animal" energy. The woman, on the other hand, is perceived to be the source of energy, to be the nature itself, something like water, so self-evident that it does not need representation or explanation; something that is life giving and life threatening, frightful and fascinating, necessary and superfluous at the same time. Unlike male sexuality, for which there are several sociolegal frameworks from a Shi'i perspective, not only has female sexuality escaped representation — being as self-evident as it presumably is — but because of its "nature" it is necessarily reactive to male sexuality. If men are not present, women have presumably no need of sex (they are in possession of it, or are *it*), but in the presence of men, women are perceived to become sexually insatiable. In other words, in each other's presence a man cannot help but want to have sex, while a woman cannot help but yield. This may partly explain the obsession with veiling and covering women: to disguise, veil, disfigure, and cover this simultaneously fascinating and frightful being before whom men are presumably reduced to their bare instincts.

According to such masculine understanding of the nature of female sexuality, women are perceived either to be "free" from or "enslaved" by their own sexuality. They are free from it because as objects of desire they cannot desire that which they already possess. Even within permanent marriage where one can legitimately assume that recreation and procreation converge, the Shi'i official view of female sexuality is foggy. Except for the woman's every-four-month right of intercourse, a right that has more to do with allowing women a chance to conceive, no provision is made for female sexuality.

Women are perceived to be "enslaved" by their sexuality because by "nature" they cannot refuse to yield; it is in their nature to want to be taken. Female sexuality thus escapes representation because it is not recognized as a phenomenon in and of itself. For that matter, it is perceived as neither positive nor negative, neither passive nor active. It becomes associated with these adjectives only in *relation* to male sexuality. The erotic passivity and activity of women make sense only within the context of women's life cycle, and in relation to male sexuality. Fear of female sexuality, from the Shi'i vantage point, becomes meaningful therefore not so much within the context of marriage (where women are presumably controlled), but outside of it, when women are divorced and least subject to male control (legally or actually), but more susceptible to giving in to the forces of "nature" that propel them to action.

The ethnographic data presented here challenge such an understanding of male-female relations and sexuality. The diversity of women's experiences with *sigheh* marriage and their articulation of their sexual desire and personal needs bring out not only the differences in the perceptions of the women and the lawmakers, but among women themselves. All my female informants, with the possible exception of Ma'sumih, were aware of their sex appeal to men who married them temporarily, and they communicated a clear sense of their own desires and needs. Not only that, having gone through one or more marriages, they learned to choose, to take initiative, and to turn men into their object of desire. Men, too, contrary to the ideal masculine model, welcomed the women's approaches and allowed themselves to be objects of women's desire and fancy.

Further, the accounts given by male informants dispel the myth of female sexual passivity and throw doubts on the popular misconception of the class backgrounds of women who contract a *sigheh* marriage. Frequently, these men were approached by women who not only were attracted to them physically but who were financially secure enough to offer to pay them some money.[1]

MALE-FEMALE PERCEPTIONS OF *MUT'A* MARRIAGE

Rosen has commented, "One of the most intriguing problems raised for anthropologists is how the members of a single society, though sharing in a broad set of cultural assumptions, may nevertheless possess diverse interpretations of reality" (1978, 561). Not surprisingly, as members of the same culture, Iranian men and women share a general understanding of law and ideology. When we compare the accounts of my male informants with those of the women, however, it becomes apparent that the structure of sex segregation and the patterns of the genders' access to public knowledge and other resources have contributed to Iranian men's and women's different interpretations, perceptions, and expectations regarding the institution of temporary marriage, themselves, and the other. The inherent masculine bias in the Islamic concept of contract is self-evident and appears natural to Iranian men. Most of my male informants concurred with the dominant Shi'i official view, appearing not to have any confusion about the legal objective of the temporary marriage for themselves, or about their own role in it.

Women's understanding of the law and of their role vis-à-vis men is more complex, covering a broad spectrum of views. At one end of the continuum there are women who manifest piety in their behavior and claim to be religiously motivated. They articulate essentially the existing dominant, male-biased ideologies, which are internalized as their own. Whether or not they are aware of the dual conception of women in the law, they pay lip service to the law and view it as enhancing the women's cause. Some may object to the institution of temporary marriage on a personal ground, but not on principle. Others claim to approve of the institution on both grounds. Some of the female supporters of the Islamic regime whom I interviewed (see note 16, Introduction) fall in this category.

On the other hand, there are women such as Mahvash and Fati who also pay tribute to the law but do so for a different reason. They are aware of the legal conceptualization of sex-as-an-object, and its irresistible power to men. Unlike the first category of women, however, they appropriate the religious ideology, subverting it to achieve their own objectives. They have no illusions as to the purpose of temporary marriage, though they may feel uncertain about their own role within it. Nor do they express any feelings of regret, disillusionment, or guilt. Whether or not they feign obedience to law, or "masquerade" it, or are really pious, they indulge in religious glorification of the institution of temporary marriage, emphasizing its religious reward. Like the women in the first category, Mahvash and Fati project public images of themselves that are skillfully constructed in the image of the dominant "other" of women. Time and again these two informants stressed their piety in terms of their obedience to law, which in their view upholds men's need for multiple sexual partners. Like their male counterparts, these two informants perceived temporary marriage as a positive and necessary social institution.

Fati and Mahvash suffered unhappy childhoods and marriages, and both felt abused by their family of orientation. However, forced to rely on their own resources so early in life, and being from religious backgrounds and semiliterate, they discovered the underlying assumption of sex-as-an-object in the marriage law and manipulated it for their own benefit. Evidently, these two women clearly perceived the nature of the exchange in a *mut'a* marriage. They seemed to know exactly what they wanted — as far as their marital life was concerned — and how to go about obtaining it. They viewed their activities as legally appropriate and religiously rewarding. They learned how to "market," *kasibi,* in Fati's words, a commodity that is much sought after in their society. However, although their portrayals of their self-images were closely modeled after the Shi'i image of the ideal Muslim woman (obedient, veiled, and passive), the picture that emerged from their descriptions of their activities clearly reflected the tension between the ideal and the real. While paying tribute to the religious law, these women acted autonomously, chose their own partners, and almost fatalistically accepted the implications of their behavior.

At the opposite end of the spectrum are those women who are also aware of the objectification of women through marriage but, unlike those who manipulated it, objected to such a conceptualization and were disappointed to discover themselves victims of it. Not only did Iran, for example, object to the image of woman as an object, she rejected the ideal of the passive woman and acted autonomously. She, however, assumed that she could have more control over the outcome of her relationship. Being educated, with a secular worldview, Iran emphasized mutual love as an object of exchange. She found the whole idea of brideprice ridiculous and found it meaningless in reality (she was not able to collect it in her first marriage). Awakened to the ambiguous legal structure of temporary marriage, despite all vows of reciprocal commitments and love, she cried foul, rejected *mut'a* marriage, and perceived it to be demeaning to and abusive of women.

Between these two perspectives rest the views of other *sigheh* women. These women had little knowledge of the law before their temporary marriages, and because of this, perhaps, they neither completely accept the institution on purely ideological grounds nor do they totally reject it on personal and experiential grounds. Some, like Shahin and Tuba, exhibited a confused perception of *mut'a* and an ambivalence toward their own role in it. Others, such as Furugh, Nanih, and Ma'sumih, maintained an attitude of unquestioning resignation toward *mut'a* and their own fates.

Women in the last two categories do not share the underlying Shi'i assumptions that women are the contractual objects of pleasure in a *mut'a* marriage. Rather, they view themselves as individuals interested in establishing meaningful and mutual interpersonal relationships, which they had apparently not enjoyed in their failed permanent marriages. Awakened to the second-class status of temporary marriage in Iran, its close public association with prostitution, and the stigmatized role of a *sigheh* woman, they philosophized about their decision for choosing the less culturally valued temporary marriage. With the exception of Furugh and Nanih, and perhaps Iran, they suffered uncertainty in their status and felt insecure about not being married permanently.

Iranian men and women, in other words, expressed different perceptions of reality, construed on the basis of their different positions on the social structure and based on their own particular needs. Whereas my women informants expected or hoped for a meaningful and perhaps lasting relationship, men viewed a *sigheh* marriage as primarily a pleasurable sport — one necessary for their health or religious merit-making. Whereas the women here expected their temporary husbands to facilitate their transition from their liminal states (as divorced women), the men viewed women as provisional objects who would satisfy repressed needs and would take them away from their daily routines and structured life. Whereas *sigheh* women often perceived their temporary husbands as their main sustenance, the men viewed women as supplementing their lives. Whereas women articulated a sense of self-doubt, a gullible self, men appeared to project strong self-concepts, a desirable self.

True to the logic of marriage contract, men and women, however, shared the popular perception of the "other's" motivation for contracting a *sigheh* marriage. This is to say, men generally assumed a financial motivation behind women's temporary marriages, despite the fact that some of them had been approached by women for other reasons. And women, likewise, believed that men *sigheh* primarily because of sexual reasons, despite the fact that some were disappointed to find their temporary husbands interested in their domestic services, rather than their sexual companionship.

CHOICE AND AUTONOMY

Men and women also concurred on the excitement and novelty of choosing one's own sexual partner(s), something they apparently missed in their segregated lives and arranged marriages. As in the tales of *A Thousand and One Nights*, physical barriers of walls and veils, as well as cultural ones of modesty and prudishness, seemed to mean little when a man or a woman wanted to communicate a message of desire to the opposite sex. The institution of temporary marriage, as we learned, greatly facilitates various forms of communication and relationships between men and women.

I was surprised to discover that in spite of all the rules and etiquette of modesty, veiling, and segregation, many men and women who desire to approach each other do so directly and unceremoniously. Shrines are particularly conducive places for such erotic meetings. In addition, there are mutually understood verbal and nonverbal signals and techniques for communicating with a member of the opposite sex. Frequently, men told me that if they wanted to *sigheh* a woman—who would signal her availability through subtle cues—they would simply walk over to her and express their intention to her. Women, though a bit more discreet, conveyed their intentions to men in coded but relatively transparent verbal comments or mutually understood nonverbal gestures.

Observers of the Middle East have commented on the nature of social control of women and the rigidity of the social structure (e.g., Vieille 1978). From the material presented here, it is evident that such control and segregation may appear to an outside observer to be more immutable, uniform, and static than they really are. Viewed developmentally, as I have pointed out, such control and rigidity are more applicable to the two categories of young virgins and married women. Divorced (and widowed) women, though subject to cultural stigmatization, do legally and actually have greater autonomy and control over their own lives than do women in the other two categories.

MARRIAGE: THE DRAMA OF GENDER RELATIONS

In chapter 4 I argued that the most significant and culturally meaningful role of the institution of temporary marriage, in both its sexual and nonsexual forms, is to legitimize as "marriage" the ever improvisational variations of gender relations. It enables the sexes to cross boundaries of sex segregation and to associate unencumbered by moral dilemmas, guilt, and the physical and symbolic barriers of a veil. In a marriage contract is contained the drama of gender relations in Iran.

The life stories of men and women presented here bring into focus the fundamental and focal value of marriage in society and the overwhelming desire of Iranian men and women to be married. It is the most significant rite of passage in Iran, and not only does it confer status and prestige on men and women, it also establishes the only legitimate channel for association between the sexes, erotic or nonerotic. The absence of alternative male-female relations, on the one hand, and the structure of sex segregation in Iran, on the other hand, culminate in the investment of *all* the genders' expectations, hopes, and desires in the institution of marriage. Men and women, with little familiarity with each other's worlds, bring into the relationship socially upheld and idealized images of the other, reified as a result of their long-segregated lives. The climax of all these emotions in the institution of marriage, however, renders the institution brittle, and the drama inevitable. It makes the marital relation tense, insecure, and potentially — and, as we learned, actually — a disappointing one, especially in the case of temporary marriage.

Given the legal and economic structure of the marriage contract and its social significance, a woman's realization of her proper place in society is possible only through her association with a man, most particularly with her husband. She finds personal validation and public recognition through marriage. It is through a culturally appropriate permanent marriage that a woman's cultural value and social status are established, because her husband has paid a brideprice for her and acknowledged her desirability by choosing her to become his wife. He has given her the opportunity to reach the next stage of her life cycle — motherhood. In marriage, the point of a woman's life is resolved, at least momentarily.

Almost all my female informants, those whose stories have been presented in detail, as well as others, expressed a desire to be married permanently, even those who had apparently no problem in frequently manipulating *sigheh* marriage contracts to their own advantage. After going through two disappointing temporary marriages, Tuba believed that she would prefer to marry a "blind man" than to be a *sigheh*, and Mahvash wished she could marry permanently, but that in its absence she was willing to *sigheh* for "at least three to four months" (i.e., to achieve a longer and more secure marriage). Confused by the rhetoric of the contemporary Shi'i ulama as to the absence of any fundamental difference between temporary and permanent marriage, many women contract a temporary marriage to escape the liminality and the stigma of their status as divorced women, only to realize that just as much ambivalence is associated with temporary marriage, if not in fact more.

For men, too, marriage is the only legitimate channel for establishing a sexual relation with a woman. However, they are not restricted to one woman at a time. Economic security through marriage is most often not an objective for men, nor is their status enhanced significantly by marriage, though a socioeconomically advantageous marriage may help. Men do not suffer the stigma of divorce and escape the marginality that is so often the fate of divorced women. Through marriage, men confirm and validate the social structure and ensure its continuity without sacrificing their personal autonomy or desires.

CONTINUITY AND CHANGE IN THE INTERPRETATION OF *MUT'A* MARRIAGE

Throughout my discussion I have attempted to bring to light continuities and changes in the interpretation of the institution of temporary marriage in contemporary Iran. I have argued that so long as the Shi'ites' significant other remained the Sunnis, the ulama endeavored to justify *mut'a* as a form of marriage. Challenged by secularly educated urban Iranian women and men and by the West, the contemporary ulama have been called upon to address themselves to the implications of this custom for modern Iranian society, to respond to the charges that *mut'a* is legally equivalent to hire or lease, that it is abusive of women, and that it is in fact legalized prostitution.

A 1974 editorial critical of *mut'a* marriage, which appeared in an Iranian women's journal, asserted that *mut'a* was a form of hire and was demeaning to women. This drew the following response (reprinted several times since) from the Ayatollah Mutahhari:

What does it [*mut'a*] have to do with hire and a fee? Is the time limit in this marriage the cause of its being excluded from the definition of marriage and acquiring for itself a form in which "fee" and "hire" are appropriate terms? And is it only because it is explicitly ordained that the *mahr* (dower) must be "fixed" and "definite" that this *mahr* is being depicted as the rental charge? We ask whether, if there were no dower and the man did not place anything before the woman, she would then regain her human dignity. (1981, 54; original translation)[2]

Responding to the same charges, Makarim Shirazi writes: "Is not temporary marriage but a reciprocal marriage contract, but for a specified period, and with the observance of all the other conditions? Does this reciprocal contract, *payman-i du janibih,* differ legally from any other agreements and contracts?" (1968, 376).

Acknowledging the popular ambivalence toward temporary marriage, the contemporary ulama have used various innovative strategies to defend the institution. They have used a language that is less indicative of its objective, using a term that closely resembles that of permanent marriage, that is, *izdivaj-i muvaqqat,* "temporary marriage," instead of *mut'a* or *sigheh,* and *mahr,* "brideprice," instead of *ajr,* "consideration." This, in addition to confusing many about the objective of *mut'a* marriage, is aimed at "purifying" it from some of its negative connotations. After the revolution of 1979 and the coming to power of the Islamic regime, the ulama's tactics have shifted from the defensive to the offensive. While criticizing the "decadent" Western-style "free" male-female relationship, they propose temporary marriage as its equivalent, with the difference that because the latter is legitimate, it is morally superior. Islamic law (many Shi'i commentators refer to Islamic law when they mean Shi'i law), the Ayatollah Mutahhari argues, had the foresight some fourteen centuries ago to provide a legal and moral solution for its youth without forcing them into a period of "asceticism" or abandoning them into the chaos of "sexual communism" (1981, 54). Improvising on the nonsexual provision in a contract of temporary marriage, the ulama have offered a radical interpretation of the custom in the form of trial marriage: one that in their view is appropriate for, and applicable to, the requirements of a modern society, and one that theoretically allows a young man and woman to marry temporarily while preserving the woman's virginity.

Unwittingly, however, while the ulama vehemently object to referring to *mut'a* as a contract of lease, to the money exchanged as consideration, and to the thesis of "objectification" of women through marriage contract, they have laid their stress squarely on the contractual aspect of *mut'a* marriage in order to provide supporting arguments in defense of the custom and its implications for women. At the same time that the ulama continue to emphasize the legitimacy of the form, they have shifted their arguments from the negative and rigid connotations of the contract to its positive and negotiable aspects. Their argument, though not new, is much more focused and forceful than that of their predecessors. They say, since *mut'a is* a contract, women can therefore insert favorable provisions into it to safeguard their own rights.[3] What they neglect, however, is that precisely because marriage is a contract, men have to agree to its terms, too. Should they find some clause undesirable, they can simply refuse to sign the contract and call off the agreement altogether. The ability to marry more than one woman at a time gives men the upper hand; if one contract is not agreeable, if a woman is too demanding, there is always another one. Unless there are real incentives, or a man really very badly wants a marriage contract, he can decide to sign or not to sign; it is his prerogative. As far as men are concerned, it is not very difficult to refuse to sign a marriage contract; neither their reputation nor their chances are jeopardized the way a woman's is by calling off a marriage contract. *Sigheh* women are already in a precarious situation, socially, psychologically, and often economically. Although initially they are a partner to the contract, and sometimes they instigate one, ultimately they are abused by the same structure, a structure that conceptually and legally relegates them to the status of an object of lease. As such, they cannot afford to rock the boat, as it were. Besides, as we learned, the ulama's argument makes little sense in light of the prevalent misinformation regarding temporary marriage and women's general ignorance of even the most rudimentary aspects of the law.

The continuities and changes in the official interpretations of *mut'a* imply not only a basic ideological ambivalence toward *mut'a*, they also indicate the fluidity of the current events, the permeability of sexual boundaries, and the dynamics of the situation. At the level of ideology Islamic law is believed to be ahistorical and unchanging, but at the level of practice, as I have demonstrated, it interacts with other sociohistorical phenomena, and it changes in response.

notes
glossary
bibliography
index

NOTES

INTRODUCTION

1. The term *mut'a* is Arabic in origin, and it has been translated as "conditional" marriage, "usufruct" marriage, "temporary" marriage, and "fixed-term" marriage. Although its correct translation is "marriage of pleasure," the term "temporary marriage" has been adopted here, for it is a more accurate translation of the Persian term for *mut'a* marriage, which is *izdi-vaj-i muvaqqat*.

2. Schacht, however, argues, "There is no reason for singling out the tradition on 'Umar's prohibition of *mut'a* and considering it any more authentic than other counter-traditions" (1950, 267). However, since the question of who actually banned *mut'a* is not relevant to the discussion here, I shall accept the popular Shi'i belief that holds 'Umar responsible for the ban.

3. Some Sunnis have been quite inventive in circumventing the law by agreeing to a timetable privately but not inserting it in the marriage contract. At the end of the specified period the husband utters the divorce formula and thereby ends the marriage contract. See "Mut'a" 1927, 775; Levy 1933, 2:149; Snouck Hurgronje 1931, 12–13.

4. The Shi'ites trace the origin of Shi'i jurisprudence to the Imam Ja'far-i Sadiq (d. 765 A.D.), one of the Prophet Muhammad's descendants and the Shi'ites' sixth imam. As with the other Shi'i twelve imams, Imam Sadiq is believed to be infallible (Nasr 1977, 14), hence the divine authority vested in his sayings. Although his views and pronouncements constitute one of the most definitive sources of Shi'i jurisprudence, it was not until late tenth century that the Shi'i law was organized and systematically coded by three Shi'i scholars. One of them was the well-known early eleventh-century scholar Shaikh Abu Ja'far Muhammad-i Tusi (955–1067), whose book of *An-Nahayih* (1964) I have consulted extensively. From other historical periods, and in chronological order, I have selected one or two of the most noted books of that era. These include: Rashid al-Din al-Maybudi's (twelfth-century) edition of *Tafsir* of Khajah ʿAbdullah-i Ansari (1006–1089) known as *Kashf al-Asrar va ʾUddat al-Abrar* (1952–61); Shaikh Abu al-Futuh Husayn Ibn ʿAli Razi's (twelfth-century) *Tafsir* (1963–68); Muhaqqiq Najm al-Din Abu al-Qasim Ja'far Hilli's (1205–77) *Sharay' al-Islam* (1968) and *Mukhtasar-i Nafi'* (1964). As Hilli's systematic works are used more extensively in religious and legal teachings, I have followed his stylistic approach more closely than that of the others. See *Khudamuz-i Luma'ih* by Mihdi Gha-zanfari (1957). The author acknowledges that his version of *Luma'ih* is a commentary on *Luma'ih-i Damishqiah* by Muhammad ibn-i Makki-i ʿAmili-yi Jazini (1333–84), also known as Shahid-i Awwal (the First Martyr), and that it is primarily taken from *Rauzat al-Bahiyya* by

Zainuddin ibn-i Àmiliy al-Jubaì (1506–58), also known as Shahid-i Sani (the Second Martyr). The monumental works of these authors are currently used as textbooks in the religious centers of Qom and Mashhad. Because of the popularity of this source, I shall follow custom by using the subject for the citation rather than the name of its author; *Kitab-i al-Naqz* (1952) by Abu al-Jalil Razi Qazvini (fifteenth century); *Hulyat al-Muttaqin* (n.d.), by 'Allamih Muhammad Baqir Majlisi (1628–1700). From the works of contemporary ulama I have chosen *A'in-i Ma* (Our custom) (1968) by Muhammad Husayn Kashif al-Ghita' (1877–1954); the books of exegesis *Tauzih al-Masa'il* by the Ayatollahs Ruhallah Khomeini (b. 1902), and another by Haj Sayyid Abulqasim Khu'i (b. 1899); *Shi'ite Islam* (1977) by the Ayatollah Allamih Sayyid Muhammad Husayn Tabataba'i (1903–82); and *Nizam-i Huquq-i Zan dar Islam* (Legal rights of women in Islam) (1974) by the Ayatollah Murtiza Mutahhari (d. 1979). The latter author has written extensively on the status of women, marriage, and sexuality in Islam.

5. The sign "P#" refers to a particular answer or explanation given by the ayatollahs in their books of exegesis, *Tauzih al-Masa'il*. Two versions of the Ayatollah Khomeini's *Tauzih al-Masa`il* are used in this book; one has no date and the other is dated 1977. Therefore, where the letter "p" is specified, the reference is to that particular page number.

6. Unless otherwise specified, all translations from Persian to English are mine.

7. Although, legally, children of both forms of marriage have equal rights, in reality children born of temporary unions are perceived to have a somewhat stigmatized social status. The perceived differences between the two relationships is reflected in the following idiomatic phrase, said in situations when one has been neglected: "am I a *sigheh*-born child?"

8. By "ideology" I mean "that part of culture which is actively concerned with the establishment and defense of patterns of belief and value" (Fallers, cited by Geertz 1973, 231).

9. The looseness of ties of temporary marriage may be underlined by comments made by Hujjat al-Islam Mahdavi-Kirmani in his conversation with reporters from *Zan-i Ruz* (a weekly magazine), who asked him to clarify the status of women and children in this form of marriage: "I have frequently reminded our sisters that the right to marry is with them. As much as possible do not marry temporarily without a document. If you are willing to do so [marry without documenting it], a man would be more than happy to marry temporarily for one month or two, and then go about his own business, particularly if he happened to be an irresponsible and good-for-nothing person. Now, because it is temporary marriage, the courts do not vigorously enforce the law. Therefore, a child who is born of such union does not know his father. Then when they [women] refer to the court we cannot establish the paternity. Just because one has a hypothetical name of 'Hasanali' we cannot issue a birth certificate" (*Zan-i Ruz* 1986, 1060:16).

10. The procedure of *li'an* is as follows: a man who has accused his wife of adultery has to swear four times before a judge that he is not lying. The fifth time he is required to take the oath of damnation and say: "May God's curse be on me if I am lying." The judge then asks the wife to respond to her husband's accusations. If she admits to his charges, she will be stoned. If she insists that he is lying, she has to swear four times that he has lied. The fifth time the judge asks her to take the oath and say: "May God's wrath be on me if he is honest." The judge then severs the marriage for good. The husband will receive lashes if he is proven a liar. The wife will be stoned to death if he is right. (Tusi 1964, 532–37; Hilli SI, 939–55 and MN, 265–67; "Nikah" 1953, 569; Katuzian 1978, 107; Langarudi 1977, 123; Shafa'i 1973, 211).

11. In 1978 as my research progressed, an interesting phenomenon began to emerge. Despite their initial disclaimers, most people, upon further probing, identified a relative, a friend, or an acquaintance who had contracted a temporary marriage. I believe that temporary marriage was then, and is now, much more prevalent than many Iranians realize or would like to admit.

12. For a contemporary view on both subjects, see the Ayatollah Mutahhari's *Legal Rights of Women in Islam* (1974) and *Sexual Ethics in Islam and in the West* (n.d.), as well as Tabataba'i et al., *Temporary Marriage in Islam* (ca. 1985).

13. Likewise, whereas *mut'a* marriage is considered shameful in most rural areas and villages in Iran, its practice is more tolerated in urban areas. As rural villages are small "face-to-face" communities, people avoid making a contract of temporary marriage in their own villages, for it would be very difficult to make such relationships secret. Those who wish to contract a temporary marriage often do so by visiting one of the numerous pilgrimage centers in Iran.

14. *Savab,* literally meaning reward, can be conceived as a system of direct communication between God and human beings, a "divine contract," as it were, between the supreme deity and his subjects. Good deeds are reciprocated, or expected to be reciprocated, with favorable rewards.

15. Although on the whole the contemporary ulama argue that the existence of temporary marriage contributes to (or even maintains) public health, their notion of public health is ideologically a hypothetical one. They make a causal association between male sexual satisfaction and public health; i.e., if men are sexually satisifed, then public health is maintained. Temporary marriage, the ulama believe, not only keeps men sexually satisfied, it prevents them from visiting prostitutes; hence, public health is guaranteed and morality is upheld. The ulama reject any association between temporary marriage and a possibility of health hazards like venereal disease (see Mutahhari 1974; Tabataba'i et al. ca. 1985; Bihishti ca. 1980; and Bahunar et al. 1981). To my knowledge, nothing has been said on the sexually transmitted AIDS in connection with temporary marriage.

16. Lectures given on the subject at Hussainyih Irshad, a well-known mosque and educational center in north Tehran, 1980. In 1978, just as the revolt against the shah was gaining momentum, I attended an all-female religious gathering in which a young teenage woman was the key preacher. She spoke on the role of women in Islam and concluded by agreeing with Imam Ali (the Shi'ites' first imam and the Prophet's son-in-law) that vis-à-vis men, women are deficient in intelligence, religion, and inheritance. Later on, I interviewed her privately at the home of a well-known pious woman who is the director of an all-female boarding school in Qom. Like Mrs. Bihruzi, this young articulate preacher said that she would have no objections to her husband's *mut'a* marriage(s), should he desire them. So thoroughly did she seem to have internalized the dominant ideology that her rationale, besides reiterating men's sexual need, was that because *mut'a* was religiously and legally prescribed, she could not have any objections to it. She was not married at the time of our interview. Our host, however, who was separated from her husband and had two young daughters, was adamantly against *mut'a* marriage for married men, but because of her religious convictions she did not condemn the institution of temporary marriage itself.

17. Registration of all marriage contracts became a legal requirement in 1931. This law, however, had little if any effect on the registration of temporary marriages. Even some contracts of permanent marriage went unregistered, perhaps because of a host of factors: lack of legal representatives in many small villages, distance to local registration offices, lack of knowledge of the law, unwillingness to report child marriages, and the like.

18. This new and presumably prophylactic arrangement, however, has proved to be virtually a health hazard. Worshipers and pilgrims who try to approach the inner sanctum often get caught in the middle of the shoving and pushing enthusiasts with no outlet to retreat. I observed several women who had fainted as a result of pressure and who had to be rescued after much screaming and warning by other women, and the cursing of the shrine's male workers, who were trying to get them out to fresh air.

19. In December of 1981 I interviewed a young unmarried woman who happened to be an Iran-Iraq war refugee in Qom. She said that once, when she was walking in the shrine yard, a mulla whispered to her, asking her to become his *sigheh*. She said she looked around, trying hard to determine what had given the mulla the impression that she might want to become a *sigheh*. Noticing that she had worn her veil inside out, she quickly took it off and before the bewildered eyes of the mulla put it on correctly, walking away contemptuously.

20. The Steel Latticed Window not only makes the wishes of the *sigheh* men and women come true, according to folk beliefs, it performs other miracles, such as returning sight to the blind, strength to the crippled, and health to the diseased.

21. In 1986 I learned of a fascinating legal dispute involving a contract of temporary marriage that took place in the western United States. Apparently, a highly educated Iranian woman and an American professor agreed on a short-term contract of *mut'a* marriage privately. The idea of temporary marriage was suggested by the Iranian woman to her American suitor, who did not really take it very seriously but accepted it only to please her. For her, however, as she later claimed in the court, it was a binding moral and legal contract. They renewed their "contract" several times for two years. When, however, the American man left his "temporary wife" in order to marry another woman, she took him to court and demanded a proper marriage settlement. The case is pending.

22. In 1978 the Ayatollah Khomeini was still living in exile, and therefore the Ayatollah Shari'atmadari was the highest-ranking religious leader in Iran. The latter, however, was later alleged to have participated in subversive activities against the Islamic regime and so was stripped of his title and leadership — an act unprecedented in the history of Shi'i Islam. The Ayatollah Shari'atmadari died in 1986.

23. After spending some time in the shrines, I realized that the areas that are at the crossroad of pilgrims' traffic have a strategic value. The thousands of pilgrims who pass through these areas give money to mullas who happen to be sitting there to perform some desirable religious rituals on their behalf. In Qom and Mashhad I observed mullas taking turns to sit in these evidently lucrative corners.

24. I interviewed two young women in the shrine in Qom, one of whom was very angry about the implications of the Iran-Iraq war for women and the fact that she had not been able to marry and to settle down. When I asked her whether she would consider a *sigheh* marriage, she became annoyed at my question, saying, "I'd rather die than marry those filthy mullas." Apparently, she assumed that only mullas contract *sigheh* marriage. I did not find it prudent to pursue the conversation.

25. The Zoroastrian form of temporary marriage, however, seems to be a hybrid between *mut'a* marriage and another pre-Islamic marriage of Arabia known as *nikah al-istibza'* (lit., "marriage of seeking intercourse"). In this latter form of marriage a husband, despairing of virility, would seek another man's assistance to impregnate his wife. When assured of his wife's pregnancy, the temporary husband would be released from further obligations, and the permanent husband would resume his marital duties. He would be known as the child's pater. The Zoroastrian temporary marriage was regarded as an act of "solidarity with a member of one's community," but the Arabian "marriage of seeking intercourse" was regarded as an act of seeking progeny (Perikhanian 1983, 650; Mernissi 1975, 35–36).

26. Such attitudes of negligence or disdain are still prevalent in Iran. I was frequently challenged by people who felt that in the face of pressing economic needs, the ongoing war between Iran and Iraq, and the sociopolitical chaos, a study of temporary marriage was indeed trivial.

27. See, for instance, the socially conscious poems of Iraj Mirza (n.d.), Farrukhi Yazdi (1941), 'Ishqi (n.d.), and Bahar (1965).

28. The Unveiling Act was passed in December of 1936.

29. See *Zan-i Ruz* from 1966 through 1967 for a series of articles and exchanges between the Ayatollah Mutahhari and the magazine's writers.

30. See note 4, above.

1. MARRIAGE AS CONTRACT

1. I am not setting the two concepts of elevation and objectification as structural opposites, for the elevation of women, or placing them on a pedestal, is simply a variant form of objectification. Further, the emergence of a third perspective by Muslim feminists should be noted here. Inspired by the new wave of Islamic fundamentalism, these scholars are also returning to the Qur'an, aiming to revive the original spirit of the religion. In their view, the Qur'anic precepts are much more sympathetic to women than the later traditions, elaborated and relayed exclusively by men, made them to be. See Hassan 1985, 1987; Ahmed 1986.

2. Pesonal interviews with some of the high-ranking Shi-i ulama including the late Ayatollah Shari'atmadari and Ayatollah Najafi Mar'ashi, summer 1978, Qom.

3. For a definition of *hukm* and its variations, see Sangalaji n.d., 7–8; Imami uses the terms *ahliyyat-i tamattu'* (lit., "capacity of enjoyment [of one's rights]"), and *ahliyyat-i is-tifa'* ("capacity of obligations"). 1971, 4:151–59.

4. The Shi'i literature is saturated with assumptions of women's biological, religious, and legal "incompleteness" or "defect." See, for instance, *Nahj ul-Balaghih* by Imam Àli 1949, 1–4:170–71; Razi 1963–68, 313; and Majlisi n.d., 79–82. For contemporary interpretations, see the Islamic regime's *Layihih-i Qisas* ca. 1980; Tabataba'i 1959, 7–30; Mutahhari 1974; Fahim-Kirmani 1975, 300–306.

5. In her memoir, Taj al-Saltanih, daughter of Nasir al-Din Shah Qajar (1831–96), writes that her father had eighty wives, including many *sighehs*, and some Turkman and Kurdish slave girls, who were captured in a war with the Turkmans (1983, 14–15).

6. An irrevocable, *lazim*, contract is that type of contract in which "neither party has the right to cancel the contract unilaterally, unless under special circumstances" (Sangalaji n.d., 13).

7. Langarudi is among a few contemporary lawyers who argue that a contract of lease differs from a contract of *mut'a* because the use of the object of lease may be postponed in the former but not in the latter; consummation of *mut'a* ought to follow the conclusion of the contract (1976, 147).

2. PERMANENT MARRIAGE: *NIKAH*

1. Citing Ibn al-Subki, a Sunni scholar, Mahmasani, a Shi'i himself (1960, 182), defines ownership, *milkiyyat*, in Islamic law as "a legal interest vested in a thing itself or in its usufruct, giving its beneficiary the right to profit from it or receive compensation for it according to the attribution which he possesses."

2. Marriage legitimizes intercourse, but since a Muslim man is legally permitted to have sexual intercourse with his slave girl, the act of marrying one's own slave girl is considered redundant.

3. Hilli specifies that although one can recite the formula for a marriage contract in any language, the contract is void if one uses terms such as "sale," "gift," or "ownership," regardless of whether the amount of brideprice has been specified in the contract (SI, 443). That one may not legally use these terms in the marriage contract does not change the fact that structurally a marriage contract does establish ownership, as I have discussed in the text.

4. *Vaty* literally means to "stampede," as in the case of being trampled under the hooves of horses (see Dihkhuda 1974 and Wehr 1976, 1078).

5. *Khanivadih* is a generic term in Persian meaning both household and family. Here, it means a nuclear family.

6. In my discussion of the rules and procedures of permanent and temporary marriages I have primarily, though not exclusively, followed Hilli's format and organizational approach, for he is the most widely read and consulted in the religious centers in Iran.

7. According to Schacht, the "essential form of a contract in Islamic law consists of offer and acceptance . . . where offer and acceptance are taken not in their common and everyday meaning but as essential formal elements which for the juridical analysis constitute a contract" (1964, 22).

8. Marriage payments in Islamic societies are highly ritualized and symbolic, associated directly with family pedigree, class, and geographical locations, i.e., city, village, and tribe. At its core, however, an Islamic marriage payment is an economic transaction, notwithstanding its symbolic dimension (see Hilli SI, 517; Tusi 1964, 476–83; *Luma'ih*, 143). Given the etymological meaning of *mahr* as "price" and the role of the wife as a party to the marriage contract, as well as being the beneficiary of the brideprice, I think the term "brideprice" is more appropriate in the case of an Islamic marriage than "bridewealth" or "dowry." By "brideprice" I do not mean the price that is exchanged for a bride, but the price that the wife herself receives in exchange for relinquishing a right to her own body. (For a full discussion of the debate over the proper use of terminologies, see Goody and Tambiah 1973; also Gary 1962.)

9. Cited by Noel Coulson in lectures given at the Law School, Harvard University, October 1984.

10. "Intercourse on the account of a mistake" may occur, for example, when a man marries a woman during her waiting period, thinking that she is cleared of her period of sexual abstinence (see the chapter on *'idda*).

11. On coitus interruptus, see Ghazali Tusi, 1975, 320–21. For a complete discussion of birth control methods, including coitus interruptus, see Musallam 1986. See also Ayatollah Khomeini's opinion on the use of the IUD and whether men can administer the fitting of this device, *Zan-i Ruz*, no. 1103 (1986):11.

12. On the concept of abortion and the different amount of blood money payable at various stages of conception, see Validi, 1986.

13. Unless otherwise specified, all translations from the Qur'an are taken from *The Meaning of Glorious Qur'an* by Mohammed Marmaduke Pickthall.

14. The Family Protection Law that was passed in 1967, and amended later on in 1975, did try to limit the unilateral right of the husband to divorce. After the revolution of 1979, however, the law was scrapped and replaced by the traditional *shari'a* precepts, colored by the Islamic regime's own interpretation of these precepts. See note 3, Conclusion.

15. "It is related," writes Ghazali Tusi, "if prostration was permitted to any one but God, women were required to prostrate before their husbands" (1975, 322).

16. Men are strongly advised not to initiate sexual intercourse with girls under the age of nine, even though they are permitted to marry them. Some of the legal scholars have even considered it forbidden, *haram* (Hilli SI, 437).

17. The ulama's uncertainty regarding the permissibility of sodomy in the case of women may be underlined here by their definition of sexual intercourse: "Intercourse, *vaty,* is penetration either in the vagina, *qubul,* or anus, *dubur"* (Hilli MN, 241; see also *Luma'ih,* 140; Khomeini n.d., 450–53).

18. Since child marriage is permissible in Islam, conditions may exist under which a girl may be divorced before having reached the age of puberty. In such a case, the divorced child is not bound to maintain a period of sexual abstinence before contracting another marriage, for presumably no possibility of pregnancy exists.

19. For a discussion of "legal options," *khiyarat,* see Imami 1971; Langarudi 1976, 215–23; and Katuzian 1978, 246–70.

20. In a rebuttal to Dr. Mihrangiz Manuchihrian (a woman senator during the Pahlavi regime), who objected to lack of financial provisions for a wife during the *'idda* of her husband's death, the Ayatollah Mutahhari argued, "The criterion for giving *nafaqih* is not the wife's financial need. If, from the point of view of Islam, women had not been given the right to own their own property while they are married, then this objection would be justified. But the law *has* given ownership right to women; and they can always keep their own property intact because they are also supported by their husbands. So, why should women be paid *nafaqih* after their nest is destroyed [i.e., the husband's death]? *Nafaqih* is for ornamenting, *zinat bakhshidan,* the man's nest. After the destruction of this nest, why should it be necessary to continue paying the wife?" (1974, 227–28). Implicit in this astonishing statement are two assumptions: of the congruency of theory and fact and of the universal application of law—that because women are given the right to own property it must necessarily mean that all women at all times have some property, and that they can keep it, too.

21. In 1981 in Kashan, I had the opportunity to talk to two women lawyers who were still working for the office of the public prosecutor, though they had been demoted after the revolution. I sat in their office for hours and talked with them extensively. I talked privately to several women who came to this office and discussed their problems with them. From these discussions and further talks with the women lawyers, I understood that the underlying reason for some men's refusal to support their wives was their preference for sodomy. Even when some of these women did take their case to court, many shied away from telling the judge the real reason behind their husband's refusal of support. They were left unprotected, unsupported, and vulnerable. See also *Zan-i Ruz* ca. 1975, 503:12, 81.

3. TEMPORARY MARRIAGE: *MUT'A*

1. Haqqani Zanjani writes, "in the beginning of Islam when decadence and promiscuity were rampant," the Prophet would remind people that Islam has permitted *mut'a,* and that they should use this 'healthy method' rather than using unlawful means" (1969b; 31–33). See also Yusif Makki 1963, 10–12.

2. Patai argues that the first reports about temporary marriage in the Middle East are recorded in the Talmudic and Roman sources. Citing the Talmud, Patai writes that this form of marriage was legal "among the Jews of Babylonia in the third century," and that "even sages and rabbis when visiting in another town used to practice this custom" (1976, 127; see also Pomerai 1930, 160; "Mut'a" 1927, 774).

3. Fayzee argues that this was a form of "legalized prostitution" tolerated by the Prophet in the earlier days of Islam, but that he prohibited it later on (1974, 8–9).

4. "The world is like a commodity, *mata',* and its best commodity is a pious woman" (Sani'i 1967, 173).

5. For a complete description of *mut'a* marriage see: Tusi 1964, 497–502; Hilli SI, 515–28; *Luma'ih* 2:126–34; Kashif al-Ghita' 1968, 372–92; Khomeini 1977, P#2421–31; Khu'i 1977, P#2421–31; Mutahhari 1974, 21–52; Bihishti ca. 1980:329–35; Yusif Makki 1963; Shafa'i 1973; Imami 1971–74; Murata 1974; Langarudi 1976; Katuzian 1978. For English sources refer to Levy 1931, 1:131–90; Fayzee 1974, 117–21).

6. Although in the Qur'an the exchange of this money is referred to as *ajr* (literally, wage or reward) in order to set it apart from brideprice, *mahr*, in a contract of permanent marriage, many of the contemporary Shi'i scholars have used the term *mahr* to refer to both forms of marriage payments. Popular usage also follows the same tendency.

7. In this context it is significant to note the legal terminology used to identify women's marital status. Because marriage is a form of contract of exchange, reciprocal obligations are accrued on the basis of whether or not the object of sale or exchange has been used. On the basis of this premise, legally a woman who has had intercourse with her husband is referred to as "penetrated," *madkhulih*, and the one who has not consummated the marriage is referred to as "unpenetrated," *ghayr-i madkhulih*.

8. Referring to *Kashf al-Lisam* of Fazil-i Hindi, Shafa'i writes, "Payment of half of consideration in case of dismissing a temporary wife [before consummation] is analogous to that of brideprice payment in the case of a contract of permanent marriage. Since analogy, *qias*, is forbidden in Shi'ism, therefore, in a contract of temporary marriage the wife is entitled to all of her consideration regardless of whether or not consummation has taken place" (1973, 189).

9. The fact that a condition for nonsexual relations may be inserted in a contract of temporary marriage does not necessarily render its pleasure principle useless. It assumes, rather, a broader base for pleasure, one that is not limited to sexual intercourse.

10. See note 10 to the Introduction.

11. Apparently, some resourceful men and women have used a legal stratagem regarding this injunction. This stratagem calls for the temporary husband to make a gift of the remaining time of the existing contract and release his *mut'a* wife from her obligations. He can then make a fresh contract for another temporary marriage with the same woman. He should dismiss her again immediately, and without consummating the marriage (Browne 1893, 462–63). Because in the last contract sexual intercourse has not taken place, the temporary wife is not bound to observe the waiting period and can therefore remarry with another man immediately. Although I was told that some women do use this stratagem as a way of getting around the requirement of the waiting period, many mullas to whom I spoke objected to this legal maneuvering, finding it strongly reprehensible, if not forbidden.

12. The extreme Islamic anxiety over the purity of paternity is the rationale, in my view, for accepting a denial of paternity at face value in the case of a temporary marriage. Apparently, a man is never sure of his temporary wife's whereabouts, and hence of his own role as a genitor.

13. Kashif al-Ghit'a 1968, 271; Qazvini n.d., 59–60; "Mut'a" 1953, 419; Yusif Makki 1963, 27. Kashif al-Ghita' argues that *mut'a* was prevalent among the Quraysh nobles (the Prophet's tribe), the Prophet's companions, and the elite, and that many of their children were products of *mut'a* unions. 'Abdullah-i ibn-i Zubair, whose father was one of the Prophet's companions, is a case in point. His mother, Asima, was the daughter of Abu Bakr, the first caliph and the Prophet's father-in-law (1968, 272; see also Tabataba'i 1977, 227). Stern also argues that at least one of the Prophet's numerous marriages must have been a *mut'a* marriage (1939, 155). Her reasoning is that this particular wife was not categorized as the "Mother of Believers," as were Muhammad's other wives, nor did she remain a widow after Muhammad's death, as did his other wives.

14. Translated by A. J. Arberry. Some of the Shi'i ulama even claim that the early Qur'anic passage on *mut'a* contained a reference to a time limit that was omitted later on (Razi 1963–68, 358; Kashif al-Ghita' 1968, 225; Yusif Makki 1963, 21).

15. See note 10 to the Introduction.

16. In a conversation I had with one of my informants, Dr. Hujjat al-Islam Anvari, he stressed his approval of temporary marriage by stating flatly: *"Mut'a* is like prostitution except that one has the name of God and the other doesn't." See his interview in chapter 6.

17. It is significant to point to a similar attitude of some of the contemporary Shi'i ulama. A Friday prayer leader and prosecutor in Qom, Usif Sani'i, argues: "Marriage of a Muslim man with an American woman is not only void, *batil*, but it is forbidden, *haram*. Not only has Islam forbidden such marriages, it does not want Muslims to be in contact with strangers" (quoted in *Iran Times*, no. 788 [1986]:5).

18. 'Allamih Muhammad Baqir Majlisi, the most renowned seventeenth-century Shi'i scholar, describes the reason for 'Umar's prohibition of *mut'a* marriage in the following anecdote: "One day 'Umar entered the house of his sister 'Afza; behold, he saw a baby in her arms, and she was giving it milk . . . he became so angry that he trembled with violence of his wrath and broke into a sweat. He seized the child from his sister's bosom and rushed out from the house. He kept straight on his course until he reached the masjid, where he went to the top step of the pulpit (*minbar*), and cried out: 'Call the people that they assemble for prayers.' . . . Accordingly they all came to the masjid. Then 'Umar said: ' . . . Who is there of you who would be pleased to have his household see that one who has no husband has given birth to the like of this (holding forth the child), — to see the mother in the very act of giving him milk?' Under these circumstances they readily answered, 'We would not like it.' . . . Then he went on to say, 'This very hour I went to her house and saw this boy in her arms, and I put her to the oath as to how this child came to her. She said that she had been temporarily married. Therefore, O multitude of people, I pray you to make known also to those who are not here that this temporary marriage (*nikah-i mut'a*), which was allowed to Moslims in the time of the Apostle of God, this have I now declared to be forbidden. And from now on, whoever is guilty of it I will most certainly scourge" (quoted by Donaldson 1936, 361–62, from *Bahar ul-Anvar*, v. 13).

19. The Shi'i and Sunni ulama have argued at length as to what exactly is the intention of the Holy Book in making this analogy between women and a "tilth," and how to interpret the meaning of this Qur'anic verse. Many of the Shi'i contemporary ulama have argued that this should not be taken as a permission of sodomy. The classic scholars, however, seemed to have been more inclined to interpret this passage literally, supporting their reasoning by another saying by the Prophet: "A woman belongs to her husband; he can treat her however he pleases" (see "Zan dar Islam" 1977, 50–51; Munzavi ca. 1975, 194–96).

20. That marriage of *shighar* is prohibited in Islam supports my contention here. In pre-Islamic Arabia this was a form of marriage in which two men would exchange their daughters or sisters: each woman would be presented as a "gift" or "brideprice" in exchange for the other. Islamic law prohibits this form of marriage because "one woman's sexuality, *buz'*, is given as the other woman's brideprice." From the viewpoint of law this is considered a "sharing" of a particular woman's sexuality (see Hilli SI, 512–14; Levy 1931–33, 2:150; Jabiri-Arablu 1983, 175–76).

21. Despite his vehement objection to the conceptualization of woman as an object, in an unguarded moment the Ayatollah Mutahhari writes, "Islam recognizes the man as the buyer, *kharidar*, and the woman as the owner of the object, *sahab-i kala*" (1974, 323).

22. See Ayatollah Khomeini's recent opinions, *fatwa*, in *Zan-i Ruz* 1986, 1069:15, and 1071:11.

23. Freud writes, "It is hardly astonishing that the need was felt to isolate dangerous persons like chiefs/priests, by building a wall around them which made them inaccessible to others" (1918, 58). One may ask here, Why is there such an extreme preoccupation in the Islamic societies with veiling women, particularly with covering women's hair, with building a wall around them? Abulhasan Banisadr, the first Iranian president after the revolution of 1979, appealed to "science," rationalizing that women's hair is dangerous because "it has been proven that the hair of a woman radiates a kind of ray that affects a man, exciting him out of the normal state" (quoted in Tabari and Yeganeh 1982, 110). It remains to be seen just exactly how the sight of women's hair can throw men out of the normal state. It is not the radiation, however, that presumably causes men's metamorphosis. It is, rather, the symbolic association made between the hair on the woman's head and her pubic hair. When the woman as a person is merged with woman as an object, as I have argued, the woman comes to stand for sexuality; she is "it," the embodiment of sex itself. So long as women use the "prophylactic" veil, both sexes are presumably protected; the "dangerous" gender is isolated beneath her veil, and the endangered species is safe and saved, at least momentarily! But once the wall of the veil is removed, men have no choice but to gravitate to these bundles of sexuality, these ambiguous objects of desire.

4. THE POWER OF AMBIGUITY
Cultural Improvisations on the Theme of Temporary Marriage

1. The so-called "milk sibling," is another legal and cultural means of creating *mahram/namahram* relationships. Its discussion, however, is beyond the scope of this chapter. See Hilli SI, 458–72; Khomeini 1977, P#2464–97.

2. See note 20 in chapter 3.

3. Although not specified in the *hadith*, it is implied that these women were not married.

4. These two Qajar kings are particularly famous—or infamous—for the number of permanent and temporary wives in their harems. In a partial list of Fath 'Ali's and Nasir al-Din's wives, Azad has recorded 160 and 34 names, respectively (1983, 393–400). Taj al-Saltanih, Nasir al-Din's daughter, however, claims that her father had some 80 wives, permanent, temporary, and slaves (1983:14).

5. Morier's description of Haji Baba, though perhaps a caricature of a professional matchmaker, is apropos here. Approaching a newcomer, he states, "The hakim's widow was the fattest of the three, and therefore I [Haji Baba] made no scruples in proposing her to Osman who at once acceded to my offer. Softening down the asperities of her temper, making much of her two eyebrows in one, and giving a general description of her person, suited to the Ottoman taste, I succeeded in giving a favorable opinion to the bridegroom of his intended" (1855, 303).

6. Sir Arnold Wilson does not specify the religious background of the said woman. Legally, Shi'i Muslim women are not permitted to marry non-Muslim men, be it temporarily or permanently.

7. Reporting on temporary marriage in "Love and Marriage in Persia" (1862), an anonymous writer claims that "the proceeding of taking a lady on a short lease, is common even among Christians residing in Persia," and that "the average price of an Arminian lady is from ten to fifteen tomauns [*sic*]," whereas that of Persian women is approximately forty *tuman* (p. 489). He does not specify why there was such a discrepancy.

8. Arranging a marriage on behalf of another person without his or her knowledge is known as '*aqd-i fuzuli*. Notwithstanding the differences of opinion among the ulama, some

argue that in such a case, although the contract is valid, its consummation depends on the consent of the man and woman (see Hilli SI, 451; *Luma'ih*, 96–97; Khomeini 1977, P#2373–74).

9. *Haji* (feminine, *hajiah*) is an honorific title afforded to those who have completed their pilgrimage to the holy city of Mecca. In Iran it may also be used casually to refer to an old or middle-aged man of some wealth. The Anglicized term is "hajji."

10. This incident took place during the Pahlavi regime when the Family Protection Law of 1967 was in effect. The law stipulated that if a man married his second wife without a court permission and his first wife's consent, he and the notary public who performed the ceremony would be jailed for up to two years.

11. According to the United Nations 1986 census report, the average age of first marriage for rural and urban Iranian women is 16.4 and 16.8, respectively. The national average age is 16.3 for illiterate women, and 17.5 for literate ones. Women with a college degree, however, averaged at 22.3 (*Kayhan* 1987, 141:12).

12. For a dramatic presentation on this theme, see Kupper 1970.

13. For a case of brother-sister incest, see *Zan-i Ruz* 1987, 1104:14–15, 45.

14. According to the Shi'i law of inheritance, children born of a temporary marriage have equal rights with the children of a permanent marriage.

15. Khatib-Shahidi (1981) has translated this term as "marriage of convenience." Although the institution does indeed imply such an arrangement, I think the term "lawful association" is closer to the intention of the agreement. In an essay published in *Iranian Studies* 19 (1986):23–54, I translated this term as "permissible familiarity." Since then, however, I have revised my interpretation and think that "lawful association" is a better translation than the two mentioned.

16. I have not been able to verify whether a woman who is observing the *'idda* of death (of her husband) is legally permitted to make a nonsexual *sigheh*. What is certain here is the fact that Zarrin did arrange a nonsexual *sigheh*, and that it was not perceived to be improper by any of her associates. The point I wish to emphasize here is the way this custom readily lends itself to widely different, yet culturally meaningful, situations.

17. It is highly unlikely that child abuse was on anyone's mind when this law was formulated.

18. As early as the time of Shaikh-i Tusi (eleventh century) it has been maintained that one glance at one's intended bride is all right. See also Hilli SI, 434–35. But apparently many contemporary religious men and women find this practice objectionable.

19. For another variation of the state-sponsored, arranged temporary marriages between Iranian war widows and Syrian Shi'i men, see *New York Times*, July 5, 1985, pp. 1–2.

20. Many of these women did not wear the long black traditional robe. Rather, they used what has come to be known as an "Islamic veil," meaning a long overcoat and a big, dark or dull scarf.

21. Apparently, the extent of these *sigheh* marriages became so alarming that the Ayatollah Khomeini had to be consulted. Subsequently, he issued a new religious edict, declaring the necessity of a father's permission for all forms of *sigheh* marriage (n.d., 300–301).

22. Youth, *javan*, is a generic term including both genders. In popular Persian usage, however, it has come to imply primarily young men.

23. See interviews with Hujjat al-Islam Hashimi Rafsanjani, the speaker of the parliament, in *Zan-i Ruz*, November 1985, 1045:4–5, 52–53, 58.

24. Perhaps this variation of *sigheh* should not be classified as a "type" per se. This informant was the only one who told me of its possibility. However, I include it here to underline the extent to which the boundaries of the institution may be stretched to include newly arising situations.

5. WOMEN'S LIFE STORIES

1. *Khanum* means "lady" or "Mrs." in Persian.

2. Upon entering a shrine in Iran, as a form of respect, people must take off their shoes and proceed barefooted.

3. In retrospect, in the view of the events that led to the revolution of 1979, her comments become significant. In Qom in the summer of 1978 the one most important topic of conversation was the political activities of the Ayatollah Khomeini, directed at that time against the Pahlavi regime from Paris.

4. My host, like many other women in Iran, arranges a monthly religious gathering, *rawzih.* On this particular day, the 5th of Ramazan, A.H. 1398 (July 1978), none of the three religious preachers whom she had invited showed up. When certain that they were not likely to come, I asked her to let me be the "speaker" instead of her absent mullas. I started my tape recorder and explained my research to the ten to fifteen women present and asked them to tell me of their thoughts and feelings on the subject of *mut'a* marriage. This turned out to be one of the most exciting and unique group interviews I had in Iran. Mahvash, who apparently did not have a good reputation among many of these women, was present in this gathering. She took advantage of the situation to preach to us on the religious reward of *sigheh* and on men's concupiscence, and she admonished women to be aware of the "natural" differences between the sexes.

5. The belief in the sexual potency of the sayyids is so strong that a woman sayyid is believed to start her menopause some ten years later than other females (Khomeini 1977, P#2504; Imami 1972, 5:75).

6. I neglected to ask Mahvash how these men gained this knowledge.

7. For a series of similar charges leveled against wives, sisters, and daughters, and the "appropriate" decisions made by their related men, see *Kayhan-i Sal* (Annual Kayhan), section on women and family, 1972, 2:30–31.

8. Until the summer of 1978 many pilgrims, and some local men and women, would use the labyrinthine yards of shrines and their open chambers as a place for their sojourn. I met several pilgrims who actually lived in the shrine for the duration of their pilgrimage. Mahvash and Ma'sumih, like the bag ladies familiar in the United States, would use the shrine as their place of residence, carrying their belongings during their waking hours in a plastic handbag.

9. This she could boast to do in 1974, but not at the present time. In fact, the trend seems to have been reversed. Nowadays, fear of persecution at the hands of the puritanical revolutionary guards leads many to claim to be *sigheh* even if they are just friends.

10. The term *khul* literally means half-witted but is specifically reserved for the eccentrics! Women are particularly at a high risk of being labeled eccentrics, even if their behavior and manners are just slightly off-beat.

11. According to Islamic law, ablution, *ghusl*, must be performed after sexual intercourse. Since ablutions are usually done in public baths (many homes lack private baths, particularly the homes of the lower classes), such private rituals become public knowledge. Amin Aqa's wife, Zainab, discovered her husband's secret *sigheh* contracts because of his frequent trips to the public bath-house.

12. Many Iranians use the phrase "taking a bath" as a euphemism for sexual intercourse.

13. I believe Fati Khanum made these last comments, hoping that I, in turn, would pass them on to her in-laws. This way, presumably, she could let them know that in fact it was Isma'il who wanted to save the marriage, and not she.

14. Fati's expression was *kaftar paruni kardan*, which literally means "flying pigeons." She used this expression in a derogatory sense, pointing out a behavior unbecoming to a decent woman. I find this expression to be culturally very loaded, symbolically and visually capturing the double-edged sense of autonomy for women. Autonomy is, metaphorically speaking, having the ability to "fly." But if it is exercised by women, like flying pigeons, it is bound to attract attention, leading subsequently to their "capture." Hence, Fati's ability to identify this particular woman among many others present in the shrine.

15. Interested couples can perform the ceremony themselves.

16. In this connection, it is interesting to note that some men use the term *manzil*, meaning "house" or "home," to refer to their wives. The implicit assumption is one of permanency and ownership. The idiomatic phrase in English "a man's house is his castle" may be transplanted and interpreted in Persian as "a man's wife is his castle."

17. Fati Khanum was indeed correct, for according to the ulama, intercourse includes both variations. Accordingly, "Intercourse, *vaty*, is the disappearance of penis, *hashafih*, in vagina or anus" (*Luma'ih*, 140; see also Hilli MN, 241; Khomeini n.d., pp. 450–53).

18. Prior to the revolution of 1979, the Iranian civil law adopted the classic Shi'i interpretation by according an adult virgin Shi'i woman, eighteen or older, some degree of autonomy. Under certain circumstances she could arrange her own marriage, provided that the legislators were assured of the unreasonableness of her father or paternal grandfather in objecting to her marriage (Article 1043, cited in Langarudi 1976, 24).

19. When I was recording Shahin's case history, I noticed that some dates do not match.

20. See Al-i Ahmad's short story "Zan-i Ziyadi" in *Zan-i Ziyadi* (The superfluous woman) (1963).

21. Whether this particular mulla actually suggested the elimination of the brideprice, or that this is Shahin's understanding of the transaction, I am not sure. According to Shi'i law, brideprice must be specified in a contract of temporary marriage, otherwise, the contract is invalid.

22. *Nanih*, meaning "nanny," in the popular Persian vernacular also implies a middle-aged domestic female servant.

23. If a *sigheh* contract is renewed with the same man, and before the expiration of the time of the contract, the woman is not obliged to keep *'idda*. See chapter 3, section on *'idda*.

24. Although customarily in Iran a woman's brideprice is stated in the marriage contract, its payment is usually deferred. It may be claimed during the divorce. Not all women are lucky enough to receive all or some portion of their brideprice, however. Thus, by saying that "I let him keep my brideprice," what Tuba really means is that she did not claim it. See also the section on *khul'* divorce, chapter 2.

25. During the late 1960s and 1970s blond hair became almost a universal fetishism in Iran, replacing rapidly the once prevalent herbal hennah. Evidently, the ex-queen Farah became the women's role model when she dyed her hair blond. Another informant, Fati Khanum, described her attractiveness to men in virtually the same terms.

26. A promissory note, *suftih*, is a written promise of payment in lieu of brideprice, payable at a later date.

27. Tuba's mother was a part-time domestic at the house of a wealthy Kashi family. This family advised Tuba and helped her to go to court and seek justice.

28. Perhaps such comments should not be interpreted literally. In some cultural contexts they imply strong desire and the seriousness of the situation.

29. "Iran" is a popular female name. This informant's name was changed to Mahin by the editor of the *Women and Revolution in Iran* (Boulder, Colo.: Westview Press, 1983), pp. 231–52.

30. The term *bivih* refers to either a divorcée or a widowed woman but colloquially refers usually to the latter.

31. We must note here a significant shift in the public representation of an ideal female role model. Prior to the revolution of 1979, the more traditionalist elements in the society upheld Fatimah, the Prophet's daughter and wife of the Shi'ites' first imam, as a symbol of feminine virtue. She has been depicted as an obedient, passive, content, and frugal woman. This ideal image, however, is presently accompanied with that of the active, politically combative, and outspoken Zainab, the Prophet's grand-daughter. Although for political expediency the Zainab model is publicly supported, in the privacy of marital relations and in relation to men, the Fatimah model is still the preferred one. The extreme opposition of these two "ideal" models has left many women—and men, too—confused as to exactly what is expected of them.

32. Although apparently Iran gave up her infant son voluntarily at the time of her divorce, her reasoning was that she would have to relinquish his custody anyway, because of the Islamic law requiring the paternal custody of boys two years and older. Iran thought that if she were to be separated from her son when he was two years old, her separation from him would be most unbearable.

33. On the insecurity of women within marriage, refer to an editorial in *Zan-i Ruz*, addressed to Hujjat al-Islam Ali Akbar Hashimi Rafsanjani, the Speaker of the Parliament (1985, 1048:3). See also Rosen 1978, 565.

6. MEN'S INTERVIEWS

1. Ironically, the Ayatollah Shari'atmadari, who was religiously and politically active under the secular regime of the shah, was tried, incarcerated, and kept under house arrest by the present Islamic regime. He died in 1986 in isolation, and after a relatively long period of house arrest.

2. The procedure for a Qur'anic divination is as follows: After making a wish, a mulla or a person well familiar with the Qur'an opens the Holy Book, reading the first line of that particular sura and interpreting it.

3. I do not know why I expected the mullas to be prudish in expressing their views on sexuality. I had never talked to them before on this subject and had no way of knowing how they would behave.

4. There are ten *rials* to every *tuman*.

5. Buzurgi's belief that "free" relationships are equivalent to prostitution is a telling indication of how deeply the idea of exchange and contract is etched in the Iranian mind. The concept of contract precludes any assumption of free exchange, even if that exchange is of love.

6. Unfortunately, I was unable to interview this woman because she had gone on pilgrimage to Mecca.

7. *Pak* is an adjective, literally meaning "pure" or "clean."

8. One of my friends who was in Tehran during the summer of 1983 told me that her brother-in-law also had a good supply of these signed *sigheh* documents. He, in turn, told her of the widespread use of these documents by men of all ages and backgrounds. Significantly,

however, not all men who keep these signed documents do actually contract *sigheh*. Rather, they use it as a way of minimizing confrontation with revolutionary guards, in case they happen to be in the company of an unrelated woman.

9. Mulla Pak was referring to the Family Protection Law, which was passed in 1967 and amended in 1975. According to the law, men wishing to marry for the second time were obliged to obtain a court permission. The court would in turn inform the first wife of her husband's intention. The husband was required to satisfy the court of his ability to maintain two wives equitably and justly. Upon considering his financial ability and his wife's sentiments, the court would then pass a judgment (see Haeri 1981, 220–28). Although the law was sidestepped by the Islamic regime when it came to power, it was not officially abolished until 1981.

10. This had become almost a stock response. Many knowledgeable men whom I interviewed, whether accepting the institution in theory or in practice, were genuinely surprised—some were offended—to find me interested in talking to others about it, particularly to women. They seemed to believe that once the rules and procedure of *mut'a* are known, or its history has been studied, there is no point in gathering more information.

11. For a report on the opening of a modern educational and dormitory complex for women in Qom, see *Kayhan International* 1986, 697:19.

12. In this regard, see the tragic fate of a *sigheh* woman who was hanged in Tehran on a Monday morning in the winter of 1984. This woman had been left a widow with three small children to support. She became a *sigheh* to a married man who had two young children from his first marriage. When after a year her secret *sigheh* marriage became public knowledge, she strangled her cowife's two little children. She accused her cowife of revealing the fact of her temporary marriage (see *Kayhan* 1984, 12094, 23).

13. I neglected to ask him whether these women were divorced, married, or virgins.

14. The term "prostitute" or "harlot" has been historically used in Iran as an opprobrious epithet for women who behave differently from the ideal, or exert some degree of personal will in opposition to their fathers, husbands, or political leaders. Ironically, women who opposed the shah's regime and those who opposed the Islamic regime were both labeled "prostitutes." For an interesting historical account of such name-calling at the time of the Prophet's death, see Beeston 1952.

15. It is of course not possible to verify such claims easily. But reports from other informants corroborate these patterns of behavior.

16. I have not been able to locate this tradition in the Persian translation of *Luma'ih*. It might be that it is cited in the original Arabic version. However, my informant, Dr. Hujjat al-Islam Anvari, described the same story, and Razi Qazvini in his *Kitab-i al-Naqz* relates this story but without mentioning Imam 'Ali's name (1952, 601–602). Allamih Majlisi in *Bahar al-Anvar* describes this anecdote in great detail (see chapter 3, note 18) but without mentioning the name of the man who made the temporary contract with 'Umar's sister (cited by Donaldson 1936, 361–62). See also Shafa'i 1973, 119.

17. It is most interesting to contemplate what this anecdote reveals about the Shi'i concepts of polity and virility, and the relationship between the two—both of which are prized virtues of a patriarchal system. Magnifying his unsurpassed virility, the anecdote expresses the symbolic revenge the Shi'ites level against the Sunnis for their political "emasculation" of 'Ali, whom they believe is the rightful heir to the Prophet.

18. It was not altogether out of respect that Amin Aqa insisted on obtaining his wife's permission. He needed Zainab's consent for a second marriage because of the requirement of the Family Protection Law of 1967, then in force.

19. Amin Aqa's daughter obtained her divorce before the Islamic revolution of 1979, when the Family Protection Law made it easier for women to sue for divorce.

20. *Majnun*, which literally means "crazy," is the name of one of the most famous legendary Arabo-Persian lovers.

21. Why some middle-class Iranian women prefer to hide their *sigheh* marriages from their fathers, brothers, or even sons is perhaps a complex and complicated cultural phenomenon, requiring further research. Part of the explanation may lie in an explicit legal assumption, though perhaps tacit culturally, that women do not enjoy sex, presumably because they get paid for it; or that it is shameful for women to make expressions of their erotic likes or dislikes. Since a *sigheh* marriage is directly identified with male eroticism, middle-class women who contract it, not apparently having any financial needs, are perceived to be making their sexual desire public, thus exhibiting a behavior contrary to the ideal.

22. Such beliefs are not exclusive to Shi'i Muslim men. The Greeks' belief closely resembles the Persians'. In Burgel's words, a "man's abstinence from sexual intercourse as a rule results in his becoming melancholic, as soon as the putrid matter of the retained semen reaches his head" (1979. 89).

23. Providing water to the thirsty is religiously meritorious because of its symbolic association with the martyrdom of the Shi'ites' third imam, Husayn, who was denied access to water and was later martyred in A.D. 640.

24. The connection in his analogy between public drinking places and women who *mut'a* was perhaps unconscious but is reflective of the way some segments of society view *sigheh* women: as a means of quenching men's "thirst" momentarily, when men have no access to their own drinking cups.

25. According to *Nasikh at-Tavarikh* n.d., 7:284, the number of Imam Hassan's wives has been recorded to be between 250 and 300.

26. *Ifshagar* is a nomen agentis, literally meaning "he who reveals." This term became particularly popular during the first couple of years after the revolution of 1979. It refers to agents who "reveal" political or religious wrongdoings of those presumably conspiring against the Islamic regime.

27. My anxiety can be appreciated once understood in the context of the highly tense and politically unstable situation prevailing in Iran in 1981.

28. What is exactly the form and the frequency of lesbianism in Iran, I do not know. Notwithstanding Mulla Ifshagar's comments, I have yet to meet an Iranian woman who would tell me of any lesbian experiences. I had a chance, however, to discuss this issue with a high school teacher from Shiraz who had taught for many years in an all-girls' school there. He confirmed Mulla Ifshagar's assertion, explaining to me that his knowledge came from his frequent conversations with his student advisees. He was a counselor in this high school, but he was fired after the revolution of 1979.

29. Mulla Ifshagar frequently emphasized this notion of "hypnotic influence" of mullas, implying the nature of the unequal power relations between young maturing girls and the mullas.

30. Sayyids can also be mullas.

31. This was probably more prevalent during the previous regime, for during the time I was in Qom, local newspapers frequently reported the execution of alleged adulterers.

32. Among the students was a fourteen-year-old girl from Kerman whose family, upon learning of the situation, had taken her back to Kerman. The informant who told me about this case knew the girl and her family, and said that the family had created a "wall of silence" around the issue, and that the girl was being tightly controlled.

33. It is interesting to note here the Qur'anic cautions regarding the danger of "gaze." Sura of Nur (24:30–31) reads: "Tell the believing men to lower their gaze and be modest. That is purer for them. . . . And tell the believing women to lower their gaze and be modest, and to display of their adornment only that which is apparent, and to draw their veils over their bosoms, and not to reveal their adornment save to their own husbands or fathers." Al-Zamakhshari (d. 1144), in his exegesis of this verse is reported to have said: "A look, then a smile, then a greeting / Then talk, then a date, then a meeting" [intercourse] (cited by Swanson 1984, 193). The causal and inevitable progression of events from a look to the "meeting" of the sexes is repeatedly noted by Muslim commentators of different eras and is a popular cultural belief. Despite the fact that men are also told to avert their gaze, the belief is that it is the woman who is responsible for blocking the male gaze; hence, women are the ones to be veiled. Ironically, however, not only does the veil deny the penetrating male gaze, it enables women to use their own judiciously. Because men and women are forbidden to socialize with each other, or to come into contact, their gazes find new dimensions in Muslim Iran. Not easily controllable, or subject to religious curfew, glances become one of the most intricate and locally meaningful means of communication between the genders. As we learned, many Persian men and women who want to *sigheh* convey their intentions primarily by looking at each other.

34. Although from the life stories of some of my female informants one would also get the picture of the active, if not always initiating woman, the image is particularly striking in the stories of men. The reason for this difference lies perhaps in the tension women felt between the ideal image of the passive woman who is sought out by men and their own actual behavior. Realizing this, women tended to emphasize their more conventional, "private" role, portraying a picture closer to the ideal one. Men, on the other hand, tended to emphasize women's unconventional behavior, stressing their more "public" action.

CONCLUSION

1. We may never know how frequent and prevalent temporary marriage is among virgin women, middle- or upper-class women, or among the merchant families, who because of their greater religious affiliation seem more likely to approve of the institution of *mut'a*—at least in principle—than the more secularly oriented upper-income Iranians. Among these socioeconomic classes, family disapproval is greater and reprisal—direct or subtle—is more severe. Although some divorced women of the middle class may accept a risk of a partial or total rejection by their families, I believe many others save themselves the trouble—and their families embarrassment—by simply taking a trip to a pilgrimage center, where they can discreetly make a contract of temporary marriage for the period of their sojourn.

2. It is significant to note here the complete turnaround of the interpretation of marriage payment, consideration, *ajr*, to brideprice, *mahr*, in the Ayatollah Mutahhari's argument. When the Sunni scholar Imam Fakhr-i Razi argued that the meaning of *ajr* in the Qur'an should be interpreted to mean the same as *mahr*, the Shi'i ulama argued against it and maintained that the two were meant to refer to the two different forms of marriage payments representative of the two types of marriage in the Qur'an. The Ayatollah Mutahhari's interpretation challenges the opinion of his Shi'i predecessors (see Fakhr-i Razi 1938, 10:48–54).

3. On the basis of the idea of contract, the Islamic regime is trying to formulate its own version of family law—known as "the conditions at the time of the contract," *sharayt-i zimn-i 'aqd*. It consists of twelve provisions, which are to be *read* to a marrying couple at the time of signing their contracts. Every single clause must be separately agreed to and signed by both parties for the law to take effect. These conditions are generally very tame, with the pos-

sible exception of the clause related to divorce, which is apparently the most controversial one. Clause one requires that "if a request for divorce is submitted to the court by the *husband*, and if the court recognizes that such request has not been due to the wife's disobedience of her wifely duty, or her bad temperament and behavior, the husband is required to give her *up to* half of his income earned *during the time they have been married* together, or something equivalent to it as decided by the court" (*Iran Times* 1986, 760:11, emphasis added). This law is obviously flawed, not only in terms of its content but in terms of its procedure—not to mention its intention. First, it does not grant women a right to sue for divorce—that being the unilateral right of the husband. The new law simply excludes women. Should a woman sue for divorce, however, she must channel her request through the age-old system of divorce of the *khul'* kind (see chapter 2, marriage cancellation). But in this case, not only do women not receive any compensation, they have to satisfy their husbands financially in order to secure their freedom. Second, the law is intended to be vague, leaving much to either the man's or the court's discretion in deciding whether a wife has been obedient, good, bad, or temperamental. Third, the amount to be given to a divorced woman, assuming that she emerges successfully from the first two ordeals, is only up to half of his earnings, or its equivalent, as established by the court. Above all, this provision would be totally null and meaningless should a man refuse to sign the contract to begin with! According to *Iran Times*, in just the month leading to Ramazan (1986) more than one hundred marriages were canceled at the last minute when the parties became aware of the implications of these conditions. Apparently, the women's families requested these conditions to be included in the contract, and the men's families refused to agree. Although this is potentially a step in the right direction, unless these conditions are formulated clearly and unless they are routinely taught to the public the old problems will persist, and more agony and heartbreaks are to be expected.

GLOSSARY

āb	water	*bā'in*	irrevocable
āb-i taubih rīkhtan	absolved (washed) through penance	*balā*	pain
		bānī	founder, benefactor
aḥkām	commandments	*bārvar*	fruitful
ahlīyyat	capacity (legal)	*bāṭil*	void
ā'in-i fiṭrat	law of nature	*bay'*	sale, purchase
ajal	date, appointed time	*bazl*	to give, bestow
ajīr	wage earner, captive	*bazl-i muddat*	a gift of the remaining time
ajr	reward, payment		
ākhūnd	religious preacher	*bī insāfī*	unfair
amā'	slave girl	*bī māni'*	unmarried, unprotected
āqā	sir, mister, master		
'aqd	to knot, to coagulate; a contract	*bih khudī khud*	intrinsically
		bīrūnī	outside, public quarter
'aqd-i fuzūlī	to make a marriage contract on behalf of someone without his or her permission		
		bīvih	a divorced or widowed woman
		buẓ	vulva, vagina
'āqilih zan	wise woman		
'aql	intelligence, wisdom		
arkān	pillars, fundamentals	*chadur*	a long all-covering veil
ashkhās	people		
aṣl	foundation, basis		
'atabāt	holy places, shrines	*dā'im*	permanent
'avaz	compensation, recompense, something exchanged for something else	*dard-i dil*	stories (lit. "pain") of the heart
		dast-i duvvum	second hand
'azl	coitus interruptus, discharge	*davā*	medicine
		dīn	religion

231

dīyih	compensation, blood money	*hashafih*	penis
		havū	cowife
dubur	rump, buttocks	*hayvānī*	animalistic
dukhūl	penetration	*hibbih*	bestow, gift
dushman	enemy	*hurr*	freeborn

fahshā	prostitution	*idārī*	office worker, employee
faskh	annulment		
fatwa	religious edict, a legal opinion issued by an ayatollah (in Iran)	*'idda*	the period of waiting after divorce or death of the husband
fisād	corruption	*ifshāgar*	he who reveals, a term that came to vogue after the Islamic revolution, implying he who reveals (or reports) wrongdoers
fitrat	nature, disposition, temperament		
gharīzī	instinctive	*ijāb*	offer
gharīzih	instinct	*ijārih*	hire, lease
ghayr-i madkhūlih	unpenetrated	*ijtihād*	independent judgment in legal/theological question
ghusl	ablution	*ilāhī*	divine
gunāhkār	sinner	*imām*	prayer leader, for Shi'ites the *imam* is an infallible and divinely inspired religious and political leader
hadīth	"Tradition," sayings of the Prophet Muhammad and his companions, one of the four sources of Islamic law		
		iqā'at [sing., *iqa'*]	unilateral acts
hājī	he who has made his pilgrimage to Mecca	*irs*	inheritance
		istifādih-i buz	use of the vagina
halāl	lawful		
ham khābigī	sleeping together	*istikhārih*	divination
hammām	bath	*istimnā'*	masturbation
haqq	right, truth	*istimtā'*	enjoyment, sexual enjoyment
		izdivāj	marriage
haqq-i hamkhābigī	right of sleeping arrangement	*izdivāj āzmāyishī*	trial marriage
haqq-i musallam	inalienable right	*izdivāj-i muvaqqat*	Persian term for *mut'a*, temporary marriage
haqq-i vatye	right of intercourse	*izdivāj-i sīgheh*	temporary marriage
harām	unlawful or forbidden, particularly by the religious law		

jabr	compulsion	*mahr*	brideprice
jāhilīyah	era of ignorance, a reference to pre-Islamic Arabia	*maḥram*	lawful, permitted (in Persian); rules of veiling and gender avoidance do not apply
jamā'	intercourse		
javān	youth	*majnūn*	crazy
jāyiz	permissible	*makr*	cunning
jins	object, gender	*makrūh*	reprehensible, blameworthy
jinsī	sexual		
		mard sālār	chauvinist
		matā'	merchandise, goods
kabābī	kabab seller, also a place where *kabab* is sold	*mavvād*	materials
		milk-i yamīn	that which your right hand possesses (Qur'an), slave ownership
kāsibī	business; to earn, to make a living		
khadamih	shrine workers, servants	*milkīyyat*	ownership
		mu'āvizih	exchange
khām	raw, young	*mubāḥ*	permissible
khānivādih	family, household, nuclear family	*mubārāt*	divorce by mutual consent, separation
khānum	lady, Mrs.	*munqaṭa'*	interrupted, temporary
kharīdār	buyer		
khilt-i nasab	mixing of parentage	*musta'jirih*	object of lease
khīyārāt	legal options	*mustashriqīn*	Orientalists
khul	crazy		
khul'	"divorce" initiated by woman; to take off, e.g., one's clothes	*nafaqih*	financial support of permanent wife
		nāmahram	unlawful (in Persian); rules of veiling and gender avoidance apply
lavāṭ	homosexuality		
lāzim	indissoluble, irrevocable, necessary	*nanih*	nanny, middle-aged female servant
li'ān	oath of damnation, cursing		
		nāqiṣ	incomplete, defective
mabī'	object of sale	*nāshizih*	disobedient
madkhūlih	penetrated	*naskh*	cancellation
maḥal	lit. "place," location; in the case of marriage, the determination of circumstances surrounding the marriage of two Muslims, i.e., whether they are both Muslims	*naẕr*	vow
		nikāh al-amā'	slave marriage
		nikāh al-istibẕa'	lit., "marriage of seeking intercourse"
		nushūz	disobedience
		nutfih	embryo

pāk	clean, pure	*savāb*	religious reward
pāksāzī	purification, cleansing	*SĀVĀK*	Iranian security police under Muhammad Riza Pahlavi's regime
panjirih	window		
panjirih-i fūlād	Steel Latticed Window		
paymān-i dū jānibih	reciprocal contract	*sayyid*	lit. "master," an honorific title for the Prophet Muhammad's descendants
pūshīyih	that which covers, facial veil		
		shahīd	martyr
		shahr-i nū	lit. "new city," red-light district
qabūl	acceptance	*shaikh*	lit. "old man," used as a term of respect
qiās	analogy		
qismat	fate, destiny	*shari'a*	religious (Islamic) law
qubh	shamefulness	*Shi'ite*	a partisan, a follower of Iman `Ali and his descendants, those who believe that after the Prophet's death leadership should have gone to `Ali, the Prophet's son-in-law. The Shi'ites split from the larger Islamic community and are further branched into groups, including the Twelvers (also known as the Ithna `Ashri'ites) and the Isma'ilies
qubul	front, front part (euphemism for vagina)		
qudrat	power, potency, virility		
rahim	womb		
rashīdih-i bākirih	an adult virgin woman		
rawzih	a religious ceremony		
rawzih khūn	religious preacher		
ra'yat	farmer		
rij'ī	returnable	*shubhih*	dubiousness, uncertainty
rūhānīyun	the "clergy," religious figures		
		sīgheh mahramīyyat	nonsexual *sigheh*
		sīgheh-rū	a woman who frequently contracts temporary marriage
sa'ādat	salvation, good fortune		
sabūr	patient (adj.)	*sīgheh `umrī*	*sigheh* for life
sādih	simple, naïve, gullible	*suftih*	promissory note
sāhab-i kālā	owner of the object	*sunnat*	tradition of the Prophet Muhammad
sahl	easy		
saman	price	*Sunnī*	one who follows the way of the Prophet Muhammad; "the orthodoxy" as opposed to the Shi'i sect; those who chose the Prophet's father-in-law, Abu Bakr, to succeed him after his death
saqqā khūnih	religious public drinking places		
sar	head, top		
sarguzasht	life story		
sarmāyih	capital		
sarparast	protector, supervisor		

sūra	a chapter in the Qur'an	*ulamā* (sing., *`ālim*)	Islamic religious scholars
tafsīr	commentary on the Qur'an	*vālī*	guardian, governor
taghābun	mutual deception	*vaty*	intercourse, to stampede
ṭaghūt	an idol, a false god; a term coined by the Ayatollah Khomeini to refer to Shah Muhammad Riza Pahlavi (r. 1941–79)	*vilāyat*	guardianship
tajāvuz	aggression	*yā'isih*	despairing of pregnancy, menopausal
ṭalabih	religious student		
ṭalāq	divorce, repudiation		
tamattu'	enjoyment	*ẓahir va bāṭin*	outer and inner self
tamkīn	obedience		
tamlīk	to become owner of	*zan*	woman
taqīyyih	dissimulation	*zawjih*	permanent wife (in the Shi'i legal discourse)
taslīm	submission		
taṭhir-i raḥim	purification of the womb	*zinā*	fornication
taubih	penance	*zir-i panjirih-i fūlād*	under the Steel Latticed Window
tulīd-i nasl	regeneration, reproduction		
tūmān	Iranian monetary unit		
Twelver Shi'ite	*see* Shi'ite, above		

BIBLIOGRAPHY

Abbott, Nadia. 1942. "Women and the State in Early Islam." *Journal of Near Eastern Studies* 1(1):106–26.

Abdul-Rauf, Muhammad. 1972. *Marriage in Islam*. New York: Exposition Press.

Adamiyat, F. 1356/1977. *Afkar-i Ijtima'i va Siyasi va Iqtisadi dar Asar-i Muntashir Nashudih-i Dauran-i Qajar* (Social, political, and economic thoughts in the unpublished documents of the Qajar era). Tehran: Agah Press.

Ahmed, Leila. 1986. "Women and the Advent of Islam," *Signs* 2(4):665–91.

'Alavi, Sayyid E. 1353/1974. *Hall-i Mushkil-i Jinsi-i Javanan: Az Russell ya Islam* (Solving youth's sexual problems: Of Russell or Islam). Tehran: Ghadir Press.

Al-i Ahmad, Jalal. 1348/1969. "Jashn-i Farkhundih" (The auspicious celebration), in *Panj Dastan* (Five stories). Tehran: Ravaq Press. 2nd ed., 1976.

———. 1342/1963. *Zan-i Ziyadi* (Superfluous woman). 2nd ed. Tehran: Javid Press.

'Ali Ibn Abi Talib (Imam). 1328/1949. *Nahj al-Balaghih* (Collected speeches and sayings), ed. Haj Sayyid `Ali Naqi Fayz al-Islam. 6 vols. in 2. Tehran: Sipihr Press.

Amini, Ayatollah Ahmad A. A.H. 1372/1952. *Al-Ghadir*. vols. 5–6. 2nd ed. Tehran: Haydari Press.

Aminuddin, B. 1938. "Woman's Status in Islam: A Muslim View." *Muslim World* 28(2):153–63.

Amnesty International Report. 1986. *Iran*. N.p., n.p.

Arberry, Arthur J. 1955. *The Qur'an Interpreted*, trans. from Arabic. New York: Macmillan.

Ardihali, Muhammad H. n.d. *Yik Silsilih Danistaniha-yi Zanashu'i az Nazar-i Islam* (A series of marital issues from the viewpoint of Islam). Tehran: Iqbal Press.

Ardistani, Sadiq. n.d. *Islam va Masa'il-i Jinsi va Zanashu'i* (Islam and sexual and marital problems). Tehran: Khizir Press.

Azad, Hasan. 1362/1983. *Pusht-i Pardiha-yi Haramsara* (Behind the walls of the harems). Urumih (Azerbaijan): Anzali Press.

Badawi, Gamal A. 1972. "Polygamy in Islam." *Al-Ittihad* 9(1):19–23.

Bahar, Muhammad Taqi (Malik al-Shu'ara). ca. 1344/1965. *Divan-i Ash'ar* (Collection of poetry). Tehran: Amir Kabir Press.

Bahunar, Hujjat al-Islam Muhammad Ja'far, et al. 1360/1981. *Ta'limat-i Dini* (Religious education). Tehran: Davarpanah Press for the Ministry of Education.

Bateson, Gregory. 1972. *Steps to an Ecology of Mind.* New York: Ballantine Books.

"Bay' " (Bai'). 1953. *Shorter Encyclopaedia of Islam.* Leiden: E. J. Brill.

Beeston, A. F. L. 1952. "The So-Called Harlots of Hadramaut." *Oriens* 5:16–22.

Benjamin, S. G. W. 1887. *Persia and the Persians.* Boston: Ticknor.

Berque, Jacques. 1964. "Women's Intercession." In *The Arabs: Their History and Future,* 172–89. New York: Praeger Press.

Betteridge, Ann. 1980. "The Controversial Vows of Urban Muslim Women in Iran." In *Unspoken World,* ed. by Nancy A. Falk, 141–55. San Francisco: Harper and Row.

Bihishti, Ayatollah Muhammad H. ca. 1980. *Shinakht-i Islam* (Knowing Islam). Tehran: Daftar-i Farhangi-yi Islam (A publication of the Office of Islamic Culture).

Binning, R. B. M. 1857. *A Journal of Two Years' Travel in Persia, Ceylon, etc.* London: W. H. Allen.

Bourdieu, Pierre. 1977. *Outline of a Theory of Practice.* Cambridge: Cambridge University Press.

Browne, Edward G. 1893. *A Year Amongst the Persians.* London: Adam and Charles Black.

Bullough, Vern L. 1973. *The Subordinate Sex.* Urbana, Ill.: University of Illinois Press.

Burgel, J. C. 1979. "Love, Lust, and Longing: Eroticism in Early Islam as Reflected in Literary Sources." In *Society and the Sexes in Medieval Islam,* ed. by Afaf L. S. Marsot. Malibu, Calif.: UNDENA Publications.

Burhan-i Qat'. 1330–42/1951–63. Ed. by Muhammad Mu'in. 5 vols. Tehran: Zavvar Press.

Burman, S., and B. E. Harrell-Bond, eds. 1979. *The Imposition of Law.* New York: Academic Press.

Chardin, J. 1927. *Travels in Persia.* London: The Argonaut Press.

Chubak, Sadiq. 1346/1967. *Sang-i Sabur* (The patient stone). Tehran: Javidan-i 'Ilmi Press.

Collier, Jane F. 1975. "Legal Processes." *Annual Review of Anthropology* 4:121–44.

Coulson, Noel. 1959. "Muslim Custom and Case Law." *The World of Islam* 6(1–2):13–24.

——. 1964. *A History of Islamic Law.* Ilkley, Yorkshire: The Scholar Press.

——. 1969. *Conflict and Tensions in Islamic Jurisprudence.* Chicago: University of Chicago Press.

Crapanzano, Vincent. 1980. *Tuhami: Portrait of a Moroccan*. Chicago: University of Chicago Press.

Curzon, G. N. 1892. *Persia and the Persian Question*. 2 vols. London: Longman, Green.

Dashti, Ali. ca. 1975. *Bist va Sih Sal* (Twenty-three years). Tehran: n.p. (also published under the name of 'Ali Naqi Munzavi).

De Lorey, E., and D. Sladen. 1907. *Queer Things about Persia*, London: Nash.

Dihkhuda, `Ali Akbar. 1338/1959. "Sigheh." In *Lughatnamih-i Dihkhuda* (Dihkhuda dictionary), ed. by M. Mu'in, serial no. 44, p. 401. Tehran: University of Tehran Press.

———. 1353/1974. "Mut'a." In *Lughatnamih-i Dihkhuda* (Dihkhuda Dictionary), ed. by M. Mu'in and S. J. Shahidi, serial no. 204, p. 318. Tehran: University of Tehran Press.

Donaldson, D. M. 1936. "Temporary Marriage in Iran." *The Muslim World* 26(4):358 –64.

Dundes, Alan. 1976. "Myth." *Encyclopaedia of Anthropology*, ed. by D. E. Hunter and P. Whitten, 279–81. New York: Harper and Row.

Dwyer, Daisy H. 1979. "Law Actual and Perceived: The Sexual Politics of Law in Morocco." *Law and Society Review* 13(3):739–56.

Eickelman, Dale F. 1981. *The Middle East: An Anthropological Approach*. Englewood Cliffs, N.J.: Prentice-Hall.

Elwan, Shwikar. 1974. *The Status of Women in the Arab World*. New York: League of Arab States.

Encyclopaedia of Islam. 1927 (1st ed.). 4 vols. Leiden: E. J. Brill and Luzac.

Esposito, John. 1975. "Women's Rights in Islam." *Islamic Studies* 14(2):99–114.

———. 1982. *Women in Muslim Family Law*. Syracuse: Syracuse University Press.

Fahim Kirmani, Murtiza. 1975. *Chihrih Zan dar A'inah-i Tarikh-i Islam* (Images of women in Islamic history). Tehran: Farus Press.

Fakhr-i Razi (Imam). 1357/1938. *Al-Tafsir al-Kabir*, vol. 10. Egypt: al-Bahiyat al-Misriyah.

Family Protection Law. *See* Qanun-i Himayat.

Farah, Madelain. 1984. *Marriage and Sexuality in Islam*. Salt Lake City: Utah University Press.

Farrukhi Yazdi, Muhammad. 1320/1941. *Divan* (Collection of poetry). Tehran: Markazi Press.

"Fath 'Ali Shah va Zanha-yi Sigheh'i" (Fath 'Ali Shah and *sigheh* women). 1347/1968. *Armaghan* 37(3):121–25.

Fayzee, A. A. A. 1974. *Outlines of Muhammadan Law.* 4th ed. New Delhi: Oxford University Press.

Ferdows, Adele K., and Amir H. Ferdows. 1983. "Women in Shi'i Fiqh: Images through the Hadith." In *Women and Revolution in Iran,* ed. by Guity Nashat, 55–68. Boulder, Colo.: Westview Press.

Freud, Sigmund. 1918. "Taboo and the Ambivalence of Emotions." In *Totem and Taboo,* 26–97. New York: Vantage Books.

Gary, R. F. 1962. "Sonjo Bride-Price and the Question of African 'Wife Purchase.' " *American Anthropologist* 62(1):34–57.

Gazder, M. W. 1973. "Women in Islam and Christianity." *Muslim News International,* November, pp. 18–21.

Geertz, Clifford. 1973. "Religion as a Cultural System." In *The Interpretation of Cultures,* 87–125. New York: Basic Books (first published in 1966).

———. 1984. *Local Knowledge.* New York: Basic Books.

Ghazali Tusi, Imam Abu Hamid Muhammad. 1354/1975. *Kimiya-yi Sa'adat* (The alchemy of happiness), ed. by Husayn Khadivjam. 2 vols. Tehran: Franklin Press.

Ghazanfari, Mihdi. 1336/1957. *Khudamuz-i Luma'ih.* Tehran: Burhan Publishers.

Gibb, H. A. R. 1953. "Mut'a." In *Shorter Encyclopaedia of Islam,* 418–20. Leiden: E. J. Brill.

Giffen, L. 1971. *Theory of Profane Love among the Arabs.* New York: New York University Press.

Goody, Jack, and S. J. Tambiah. 1973. *Bridewealth and Dowry.* Cambridge Papers in Social Anthropology 7. Cambridge: Cambridge University Press.

Gough, Kathleen E. 1959. "The Nayars and the Definition of Marriage." *Journal of the Royal Anthropological Institute* 89:23–34.

Gulistan, Ibrahim. 1346/1967. "Safar-i 'Ismat" ('Ismat's journey). In *Juy va Divar va Tishnih* (The gutter and the wall and the thirsty). Tehran: Gulistan Studio.

Haeri, Shahla. 1981. "Women, Law, and Social Change in Iran." In *Women in Muslim Countries,* ed. by Jane I. Smith, 209–34. Lewisburg, Pa.: Bucknell University Press.

———. 1983. "The Institution of *Mut'a* Marriage in Iran: A Formal and Historical Perspective." In *Women and Revolution in Iran,* ed. by Guity Nashat, 231–52. Boulder, Colo.: Westview Press.

Hakim, M. T. 1350/1971. *Izdivaj-i Muvaqqat va Naqsh-i an dar Hall-i Mushkilat-i Jinsi* (Temporary marriage and its role in solving sexual problems), trans. from Arabic to Persian by Haydari Qazvini. Tehran: Burhan Press.

Haqqani Zanjani, Husayn. *See* Zanjani.

Hashimi-Rafsanjani. *See* Rafsanjani.

Hassan, Riffat. 1985. "Made from Adam's Rib? The Woman's Creation Question." *Al-Mushir* (Rawalpindi, Pakistan) 27(3):124–55.

———. 1987. "Equal before Allah: Woman-Man Equality in the Islamic Tradition." *Harvard Divinity Bulletin* 17(2):2–4.

Hidayat, Sadiq. 1328/1949. *Dard-i Dil-i Mirza Yadullah* (Mirza Yadullah's life history). Tehran: Muhsin Press.

———. 1342/1963. *'Alaviyih Khanum va Vilingari* (Mrs. `Alaviyih and Carelessness?). 4th ed. Tehran: Amir Kabir Press.

Hijazi, Qudsiyyih. 1345/1966. *Izdivaj dar Islam* (Marriage in Islam). A Publication of the Association of Guiding Women's Thought. Tehran: Haydari Press.

Hilli, Muhaqqiq Najm al-Din Abu al-Qasim Ja'far. 1343/1964. *Mukhtasar-i Nafi'* (Useful summations), trans. from Arabic to Persian by E. Yarshater and M. T. Danish Pazuh. Tehran: University of Tehran Press.

———. 1347/1968. *Sharay' al-Islam* (Islamic law), trans. from Arabic to Persian by A. Ahmad Yazdi and M. T. Danish Pazhuh, vol. 2. Tehran: University of Tehran Press.

Hinchcliffe, Doreen. 1968. "The Iranian Family Protection Act." *International and Comparative Law Quarterly* 17(2):516–21.

Howard, I. K. A. 1975. "Mut'a Marriage Reconsidered in the Context of the Formal Procedures for Islamic Marriage." *Journal of Semitic Studies* 20(1):82–92.

Hughes, T. P. 1964. "Mut'a." In *Dictionary of Islam*. Anarkali, Lahore: Premier Book House Publisher & Booksellers. (1st ed. published in 1885.)

Huquq-i Zan dar Dauran-i Izdivaj Chist? (What are women's rights during marriage?). 1362/1983. Tehran: Rahnama Press.

Imami, Sayyid Husayn. 1350–53/1971–74. *Huquq-i Madani* (Civil law). 5 vols. Tehran: Islamiyih Press.

Iraj Mirza, Jalal al-Mulk. n.d. *Kulliyat* (Collection of poetry). Tehran: Muzaffari Press.

Iran Times (an Iranian weekly paper). Washington, D.C.

`Ishqi, Mirzadih. n.d. *Kulliyat* (Collection of poetry). Tehran: Amir Kabir Press.

Ittila'at (an Iranian newspaper). Tehran.

Jabiri-Arablu, Muhsin. 1983. *Farhang-i Istilahat-i Fiqh-i Islami dar Bab-i Mu'amilat* (Encyclopedia of Islamic legal terms regarding transactions). Tehran: Amir Kabir Press.

Ja'fari Langarudi, M. J. *See* Langarudi.

Jamalzadih, Muhammad Ali. 1333/1954. *Ma'sumih Shirazi* (Ma'sumih from Shiraz). Tehran: Kanun-i Ma'rifat.

Kamali, Hashim. 1984. "Divorce and Women's Rights: Some Muslim Interpretations of Sura 2:228." *The Muslim World* 74(2):85–99.

Kashif al-Ghita', Muhammad Husayn. 1347/1968. *A'in-i Ma* (Our custom), trans. by Nasir Makarim Shirazi. Qom: Hadaf Press.

Katuzian, Nasir. 1357/1978. *Huquq-i Madani-i Khanivadih* (Family civil law). Tehran: University of Tehran Press.

Kayhan (London). Weekly newspaper.

Kayhan (Tehran). Daily newspaper.

Kayhan International (Tehran). Weekly newspaper.

Kayhan-i Sal (Annual Kayhan). 1351/1972. Tehran.

Keddie, Nikki, and Lois Beck. 1978. "Introduction." In *Women in the Muslim World,* 1–34. Cambridge, Mass.: Harvard University Press.

Ker Porter, Robert. 1821. *Travels in Georgia, Persia, Armenia, Ancient Babylonia, 1817–20.* 2 vols. London: Longman, Hurst.

Khakpur, Muhammad Mihdi. 1354/1975. *Jurm Shinasy-i Zanan* (Women criminology). Tehran: 'Ata'i Press.

Khan, Mazhar. 1972. *Purdah and Polygamy.* Lahore, Pakistan: Pakistan Imperial Press.

Khatib-Shahidi, Jane. 1981. "Sexual Prohibitions, Shared Space and Fictive Marriage in Shi'ite Iran." In *Women and Space: Ground Rules and Social Maps,* ed. by Shirley Ardner, 112–35. London: Croom Helm in association with the Oxford University Women's Studies Committee.

Khomeini, Ayatollah Ruhallah. n.d. *Tauzih al-Masa'il* (Book of exegesis). Tehran: n.p.

———. 1356/1977. *Tauzih al-Masa'il* (Book of exegesis). Mashhad(?): Kanun-i Nashr-i Kitan(?).

———. 1982a. "Non-Permanent Marriage." *Mahjubih* 2(5): 38–40.

———. 1361/1982b. *Zan* (Woman) [lectures and slogans, collected from 1341 to 1361]. Tehran: Amir Kabir Press.

———. 1983. *The Practical Laws of Islam,* trans. Tehran: Islamic Propagation Organization (an abridged version of *Tauzih al-Masa'il*).

Khu'i, Ayatollah S. A. 1356/1977. *Tauzih al-Masa'il* (Book of exegesis). Qom: n.p.

Kiafar, A. 1360/1981. *A'in-i Izdivaj-i Muvaqqat* (The procedures of temporary marriage). n.p., n.p.

Kidder, R. L. 1979. "Toward an Integrated Theory of Imposed Law." In *The Imposition of Law,* ed. by S. Burman and B. E. Harrell-Bond. New York: Academic Press.

Kirmani, M. H. Salihi. 1339/1960. "Zanan Bayad Azadi Dashtih Bashand, Vali Ma'ni-yi Azadi Chist?" (Women ought to have freedom, but what is the meaning of freedom?). In *Jahan-i Danish* (Qom: Dar al-Ílm Press) 1 (March):295–305.

Kressel, Friedrich, and Grant Gilmore. 1970. *Contracts: Cases and Materials.* 2nd ed. Boston: Little, Brown.

Kulaini, Abi Ja'far Muhammad. A.H. 1378/1958. *Al Furu' Min al-Kafi* (The Branches of the Law in *al-Kafi*). 6 vols. Tehran: Haydari Press.

Kupper, Hilda. 1970. *A Witch in My Heart*. London: Oxford University Press.

LaBarre, Weston. 1980. "Social Cynosure and Social Structure." In *Culture in Context*, 203–214. Durham, N.C.: Duke University Press.

Langarudi, Muhammad Ja'far Ja'fari. 1346/1967. *Tirminuluzhi-i Huquqi* (Legal terminology). Tehran: Ibn-i Sina Press.

———. 1355/1976. *Huquq-i Khanivadih* (Family law). Tehran: Haydari Press.

———. 1357/1978. *Irs* (Inheritance). 2 vols. Tehran: Amir Kabir Press.

Lapidus, Ira M. 1976. "Adulthood in Islam: Religious Maturity in the Islamic Tradition." *Daedalus* 105(2):93–108.

Layihih-i Qisas (The penal code of Islamic regime). ca. 1980. 2nd ed. Tehran: n.p.

Leacock, Eleanor B. 1981. *Myths of Male Dominance*. New York: Monthly Review Press.

Levine, N. E., and W. Sangree. 1980. *Women with Many Husbands: Polyandrous Alliance and Marital Flexibility in Africa and Asia*. A special issue of *Journal of Comparative Family Studies* 10(3).

Levi-Strauss, Claude. 1969. *The Elementary Structures of Kinship*. Boston: Beacon Press.

———. 1974. "Reciprocity, The Essence of Social Life." In *The Family*, ed. by R. Lewis Coser. 2nd ed. New York: St. Martin's Press.

Levy, Rubin. 1931, 1933. *Introduction to the Sociology of Islam*. 2 vols. London: Williams and Norgate.

———. 1957. *The Social Structure of Islam*. Cambridge: Cambridge University Press.

Lisan al-Mulk, Muhammad Taqi. n.d. *Nasikh al-Tavarikh* (Abrogator of the Histories). 8 vols. Tehran: Amir Kabir Press.

"Love and Marriage in Persia." 1862. *All the Year Around* 6(147):488–91.

Luma'ih. See Ghanzanfari.

Mahdavi, Shirin. 1985. "The Position of Women in Shi'a Iran: Views of the Ùlama." In *Women and Family in the Middle East*, ed. by Elizabeth W. Fernea, 255–72. Austin: University of Texas Press.

Mahjubeh. (An English-language journal for women, published by the Islamic Republic of Iran).

Mahmasani, Subhi. 1339/1960. *Qavanin-i Fiqh-i Islami* (Islamic law), trans. from Arabic to Persian by Jamal al-Din Jamali. Tehran: Musavi Press.

Mahmudi, 'Abdul'ali. 1359/1980. *Huquq-i Jaza'i-i Islam: Jara'im-i Nashi az Gharizih-i Jinsi* (Penal law of Islam: Crimes motivated by sexual instinct). n.p.: A Publication of Muslim Women's Movement.

Majlisi, 'Allamih Muhammad Baqir. n.d. *Hulyat al-Muttaqin* (Ornaments of the pious). Tehran: Qa'im Press.

Makarim Shirazi, Nasir. 1347/1968. "Izdivaj-i Muvaqqat Yik Zarurat-i Ijtinab Napazir-i Ijtima'i Ast" (Temporary marriage is an inevitable necessity in society), 372 – 90. Epilogue of *A'in-i Ma* by Kashif al-Ghita'. Qom: Hadaf Press.

Makdisi, George. 1979. "The Significance of the Sunni Schools of Law in Islamic Religious History." *International Journal of Middle East Studies* [Cambridge University Press] 10 (Fall):1 – 8.

Manuchihrian, Mihrangiz. 1357/1978. *Nabarabariha-yi Huquqi-i Zan va Mard dar Iran va Ruh-i Islah-i An* (Legal inequalities between men and women in Iran). Tehran: Penguin Press.

Mauss, M. 1967. *The Gift*, trans. by I. Cunnison. New York: W. W. Norton.

Maybudi, Rashid al-Din Ahmad ibn Muhammad. 1331–39/1952–61. *Kashf al-Asrar va 'Uddat al-Abrar* (Illucidating mysteries; also known as *Tafsir-i Ansari*). 10 vols. Tehran: Majlis Press.

Mazandarani Haeri, Ayatollah Muhammad Baqir. 1364/1985. *Izdivaj va Talaq dar Islam va Sayir-i Adyan* (Marriage and divorce in Islam and other religions). Tehran: 128 Press.

Mehdevi, A. S. 1953. *Persian Adventure*. New York: Alfred A. Knopf.

Mernissi, Fatimah. 1975. *Beyond the Veil: Male-Female Dynamics in a Modern Muslim Society*. New York: John Wiley and Sons.

Mihkail, Mona N. 1975. "Images of Women in North African Literature: Myth or Reality?" *American Journal of Arabic Studies* 3:37 – 47.

Mishkini, `Ali. 1353/1974. *Izdivaj dar Islam* (Marriage in Islam), trans. from Arabic to Persian by Ahmad Jannati. Tehran: Mihr Ustuvar.

Mohsen, Safia. 1974. "The Egyptian Woman: Between Modernity and Tradition." In *Many Sisters*, ed. by Carolyn J. Matthiasson, 37 – 58. New York: Free Press.

Moore, Sally Falk. 1978. *Law as Process*. London: Routledge and Kegan Paul.

Morier, James. 1855. *The Adventures of Haji Baba of Ispahan*. Philadelphia: Lippincott, Grambo.

Muhajir, A. A. 1345/1966. "Ta'addud-i Zujat va Mut'a" (Polygamy and *mut'a*). *Majalih-i Kanun-i Sar Daftaran* 10 (5 & 6):18 – 40.

Muhammad, Hasan. ca. 1364/1985. "Izdivaj-i Muvaqqat va Savab-i an" (Temporary marriage and its reward). In *Izdivaj-i Muvaqqat dar Islam*, ed. by Tabataba'i et al., 144 – 47.

Munzavi, Ali Naqi. *See* Dashti.

Murata, Sachico. 1353/1974. "Izdivaj-i Muvaqqat va Asar-i Ijtima'i-i An" (Temporary marriage and its social effects), M. A. thesis, Divinity School, University of Tehran.

Musallam, B. F. 1986. *Sex and Society in Islam*. Cambridge: Cambridge University Press.

Musavi-Isfahani, M. ca. 1985. *Inqilab-i Mihnatbar* (The wretched revolution). Encino, Calif.: Ketab Corporation.

Mushfiq-i Kazimi, M. 1340/1961. *Tehran-i Makhuf* (Horrid Tehran). Tehran: Ibn Sina Press.

Mustafavi, Sayyid Javad. 1351/1972 (reprinted 1356/1978). "Izdivaj dar Islam va Fitrat" (Marriage in Islam and nature). *Nashriyih-i Danishkadih-i Ilahiyat va Ma'arif-i Islami-i Danishgah-i Mashhad* (Journal of the Divinity School, University of Mashhad), Winter, pp. 150–88.

"Mut'a." 1927. *Encyclopaedia of Islam*, 3:773–76. Leiden: E. J. Brill and Luzac.

"Mut'a." 1953. *Shorter Encyclopaedia of Islam*. Leiden: E. J. Brill.

Mutahhari, Ayatollah Murtiza. 1353/1974. *Nizam-i Huquq-i Zan dar Islam* (Legal rights of women in Islam). 8th ed. Qom: Sadra Press.

———. ca. 1975. *Huquq-i Zan, Ta'addud-i Zujat, Izdivaj-i Muvaqqat* (Women's rights, polygamy, temporary marriage). Qom: Ahliyat Press.

———. 1981. "The Rights of Women in Islam: Fixed-Term Marriage," part 3. *Mahjubih*, October/November, pp. 52–56.

———. n.d. *Akhlaq-i Jinsi dar Islam va Jahan-i Gharb* (Sexual ethics in Islam and in the West). Qom: Sadra Press.

Nader, Laura. 1965. "The Ethnography of Law." *American Anthropologist* 67(2):3–32 (supplement).

Nasikh al-Tavarikh. *See* Lisan al-Mulk.

Nasr, Seyyed Hossain. 1977. "Preface," and "Appendix II." In *Shi'ite Islam*, by Allameh Sayyid Muhammad Husayn Tabataba'i, 3–28. Albany: State University of New York Press.

Natiq, Homa. 1356/1977. "Farang va Frangima'abi" (The west and imitating the west). *Alifba* (Tehran) 6:60–61.

Nelson, C. 1971. "Public and Private Politics: Women in the Middle Eastern World." *American Ethnologist* 1(3):551–62.

"Nikah." 1927. *Encyclopaedia of Islam*, 3:912–14. Leiden: E. J. Brill and Luzac.

"Nikah." 1953. *Shorter Encyclopaedia of Islam*, 447–49. Leiden: E. J. Brill.

Nuri, Allamih Yahya. 1347/1968. *Huquq-i Zan dar Islam va Jahan* (Legal rights of women in Islam and in the world). 4th ed. Tehran: Farahani Press.

Ortner, Sherry B., and Harriet Whitehead. 1981. *Sexual Meanings: The Cultural Construction of Gender and Sexuality.* Cambridge: Cambridge University Press.

Parsa, F. R. et al. 1346/1967. *Zan dar Iran-i Bastan* (Woman in ancient Iran). Tehran: Bistu Panjum-i Shahrivar Press.

Partington, David H. 1961. "The *Nisab al-Ihtisab:* An Arabic Religio-Legal Text."
Ph.D. diss., Princeton University.

Patai, Raphael. 1976. *The Arab Mind.* New York: Charles Scribner's Sons.

Perikhanian, A. 1983. "Iranian Society and Law." In *The Seleucid, Parthian and Sasanian Periods,* ed. by Ehsan Yarshater. *Cambridge History of Iran,* 3(2):627–76. Cambridge: Cambridge University Press.

Phillips, Wendell. 1968. "Women in Oman." In *Unspoken Oman,* 128–46. New York: David McKay.

Pickthall, Mohammed Marmaduke, trans. n.d. *The Meaning of the Glorious Qur'an.* New York: Mentor.

Pizhman Bakhtiari, H. 1344/1965. "Fath 'Ali Shah va Havashayash" (King Fath `Ali and his desires). *Yaghma* 18(3):154–57.

Pomerai, R. 1930. *Marriage: Past, Present, and Future.* New York: Richard R. Smith.

Porter. *See* Ker Porter.

Qa'imi, 'Ali 1353/1974. *Tashkil-i Khanivadih dar Islam* (History of the family in Islam). Qom: Dar al-Tabliqat-i Islami Press.

Qanun-i Himayat-i Khanivadih (Family protection law). 1351/1973. Tehran: Farukhi Publishing.

Qazvini, Akhund M. A. n.d. *Siyagh-i 'Uqud* (Forms of contracts). Tehran: 'Ilmiyih Islamiyih Press.

Qazvini Razi. *See* Razi Qazvini.

Qurbani, Z. 1344/1965. "Huquq-i Zan va Shawhar Nisbat bih Yik Digar" (The reciprocal rights of wife and husband). *Maktab-i Islam* 6(7):47–51.

Qutb, Muhammad. 1967. "Islam and Women." In *Islam, the Misunderstood Religion,* 173–243. Kuwait: Ministry of Awqaf and Islamic Affairs.

Rafsanjani, `Ali Akbar. ca. 1364/1985. "Pishguftar" (Introduction). In *Izdivaj Muvaqqat dar Islam* (Temporary marriage in Islam). Qom: Salih Press.

Razi, Shaikh Abu al-Futuh Husayn Ibn `Ali. 1382–88/1963–68. *Tafsir* (Commentary on the Qur'an), vol. 3. Tehran: Islamiyih Press.

Razi Qazvini, 'Abd al-Jalil. 1331/1952. *Kitab-i al-Naqz* (Book of Refutation). Tehran: Sipihr Press.

Robertson Smith, William. 1903. *Kinship and Marriage in Early Arabia.* Boston: Beacon Press.

Rosen, L. 1978. "The Negotiation of Reality: Male-Female Relations in Sefrou, Morocco." In *Women in the Muslim World,* ed. by L. Beck and N. Keddie, 561–84. Cambridge, Mass.: Harvard University Press.

Russell, Bertrand. 1929. *Marriage and Morals.* London: George Allen and Unwin.

Sabbah, Fetna A. 1983. *Women in the Muslim Unconscious*, trans. by Mary Jo Lakeland. New York: Pergamon Press.

Sadiqi Guldar, Ahmad. 1364/1986. "Shurut va Shurut-i Zimn-i 'Aqd" (Conditions and conditions at the time of contract). *Faslnamih-i Haqq*, December–March, pp. 704–10.

Safa-Isfahani, Kaveh. 1980. "Concepts of Feminine Sexuality and Female Centered World Views in Iran: Symbolic Representations and Dramatic Games." *Signs* 6(11):33–53.

Saleh, Sanya. 1977. "Women in Islam: Their Role in Religious and Traditional Culture." *International Journal of Sociology of the Family* 2 (September):193 –201.

Salihi-Kirmani. *See* Kirmani, M. H. Salihi.

Salnamih-i Amar-i Kishvar (Iranian census book). 1971. Tehran: Center for Iranian Census, Plan Organization.

Sangalaji, Aqa Muhammad. n.d. *Kulliyat-i `Uqud va Iqa'at va Qanun-i Riz`a dar Islam* (Contracts, unilateral acts, and milk kinship in Islam). Tehran: Firdawsi Press.

Sani'i, Safdar. 1346/1967. *Bihdasht-i Izdivaj az Nazar-i Islam* (The well-being of marriage from the viewpoint of Islam). Isfahan: Firdawsi Press.

Schacht, Joseph. 1950. *Origins of Muhammadan Jurisprudence*. Oxford: Clarendon Press.

———. 1964. *An Introduction to Islamic Law.* Oxford: Clarendon Press.

Shaban, M. A. 1976. *Islamic History: A New Interpretation* A.D. *600–750 (*A.H. *132)*, vol. 1. Cambridge: Cambridge University Press.

Shafa, Shujaiddin. 1362/1983. *Tauzih al-Masa'il: Az Kulaini ta Khomeini* (Book of exegesis: From Kulaini to Khomeini). Paris: n.p.

Shafa'i, Muhsin. 1352/1973. *Mut'a va Asar-i Huquqi va Ijtima'i-i An* (Mut'a and its legal and social effects). 6th ed. Tehran: Haydari Press.

Shahabi, M. 1329/1950. *Advar-i Fiqh* (Ages of jurisprudence), vol. 1. Tehran: University of Tehran Press.

Shaikh-i Baha'i Amili, Baha al-Din Muhammad Ibn Husayn. A.H. 1329/1911. *Jami'i `Abbasi* (The Abbasid compendium). Tehran: Mirza `Ali Asghar.

Sheil, M. L. 1856. *Glimpses of Life and Manners in Persia*. London: J. Murray.

Shirazi, S. R. n.d. *Bunbastha-yi Ijtima'i: Guftari Kutah dar Izdivaj-i Muvaqqat* (Social dead ends: A short essay on temporary marriage). Qom: Shafa Press, no. 2 (The Center for Islamic Propaganda).

Shorter Encyclopaedia of Islam. 1953. Leiden: E. J. Brill.

Siddiqi, Zeba. 1959. "Islamic Personality and Social System—Part 3: Family Life and Personal Relations." *Al-Ittihad* 12(2):14–18.

Silverman, Kaja. 1983. *The Subject of Semiotics.* New York: Oxford University Press.

Snouck Hurgronje, C. 1931. *Mekka in the Latter Part of 19th Century*, trans. by J. H. Monahan. London: Luzac.

Stern, G. H. 1939. *Marriage in Early Islam*. London: Royal Asiatic Society.

Surushian, Jamshid. 1352/1973. "A'in va Qanun-i Zanashu'i dar Iran-i Bastan" (Custom and law of marriage in ancient Iran). In *Majmu'ih-i Sukhanraniha-yi Duvvumin Kungirih-i Tahqiqat-i Irani* (A collection of lectures given at the Second Congress of Iranian Studies), ed. by H. Zarrinkub, 182–99. Mashhad: University of Mashhad Press.

Swanson, Mark N. 1984. "A Study of 20th Century Commentary of Surat al-Nur [Qur'an] 24:27–33." *The Muslim World* 74(3–4):187–203.

Sykes, E. C. 1910. *Persia and Its People*. London: Methuen.

Tabari, A., and N. Yeganeh. 1982. *In the Shadow of Islam*. London: Zed Press.

Tabataba'i, 'Allamih Sayyid Muhammad Husayn. 1338/1959. "Zan dar Islam," (Women in Islam). *Maktab-i Tashayyu'* 1 (May):7–30.

———. 1343/1964. "Mut'a ya Izdivaj-i Muvaqqat' (*Mut'a* or temporary marriage). *Maktab-i Tashayyu'* 6 (May):10–20.

———. 1977. *Shi'ite Islam*, trans. from Persian by Sayyid H. Nasr. Albany: State University of New York Press.

Tabataba'i, Allamih Sayyid Muhammad Husayn, et al. ca. 1985. *Izdivaj-i Muvaqqat dar Islam* (Temporary Marriage in Islam). Qom: Imam Sadiq Press.

Taj al-Saltanih. 1362/1983. *Khatirat-i Taj al-Saltanih* (Memoirs of Taj al-Saltanih), ed. by M. Itihadiah and S. Sa'dvandiyan. Tehran: Nashr-i Tarikh-i Iran (Iranian History Press).

Taqavi-Rad, M. A. 1356/1977. *Siksuluzhi-i Islami: Masa'il-i Jinsi Javanan dar Islam* (Islamic sexology: Sexual problems of youth in Islam). Tehran: n.p.

Thaiss, G. 1978. "The Conceptualization of Social Change Through Metaphor." *Journal of Asian and African Studies* 13(1–2):1–10.

Turner, Victor. 1969. *The Ritual Process*, 94–130. Chicago: Aldine.

———. 1974. *Dramas, Fields, and Metaphors*. Ithaca, N.Y.: Cornell University Press.

Tusi, Shaikh Abu Ja'far Muhammad. 1343/1964. *An-Nahayih*, trans. from Arabic to Persian by Muhammad Taqi Danishpazhuh. Tehran: Tehran University Press.

Validi, M. S. 1365/1986. "Barrasi-i Ahkam-i Siqt-i Janin ya Siqt-i Haml" (An examination of precepts regarding abortion). *Faslnamih-i Haqq* 5(March – April):870–90.

Vieille, Paul. 1978. "Iranian Women in the Politics of Family Alliance and in Sexual Politics." In *Women in the Muslim World*, ed. by Lois Beck and Nikki Keddie, 451–72. Cambridge, Mass.: Harvard University Press.

Waines, David. 1982. "Through a Veil Darkly: The Study of Women in Muslim Societies." *Comparative Studies of Society and History* 24(4):642–59.

Wehr, Hans. 1976. *Arabic English Dictionary: A Dictionary of Modern Written Arabic*, ed. and trans. by J. Milton Cowan. 3rd ed. Ithaca, N.Y.: Spoken Language Services, Inc.

Willes, Charles J. 1866. *Persia as It Is.* London: Low, Marston, Searle and Rivington.

Wilson, Arnold. 1941. *Southwest Persia: A Political Officer's Diary, 1907–14.* London: Oxford University Press.

Wishard, J. G. 1908. *Twenty Years in Persia.* London: Fleming H. Revell.

Wolf, Eric R. 1951. "The Social Organization of Mecca and the Origins of Islam." *South Western Journal of Anthropology* 7(4):329–56.

Woman's Commission of the Iranian Student Association in the U.S. 1982. *Woman's Struggle in Iran.* N.p.: Woman's Commission, September 1982.

Yaftabadi, Yahya. 1353/1974. *Bargha'i az Zaman* (Leaves from history). Tehran: Shams Press.

Yaghma. See Pizhman Bakhtiari.

Youssef, Nadia H. 1978. "The Status and Fertility Patterns of Muslim Women." In *Women in the Muslim World.* ed. by Lois Beck and Nikki Keddie, 69–99. Cambridge, Mass.: Harvard University Press.

Yusif Makki, Sayyid Husayn. 1342/1963. *Mut'a dar Islam* (*Mut'a* in Islam), trans. from Arabic to Persian. Damascus: n.p.

"Zan dar Islam." (Women in Islam). 1356/1977. *Kaveh* (Munich) 66 (March):46–52.

Zan-i Ruz (Today's woman) (Tehran). Weekly magazine.

Zanjani, Husayn Haqqani. 1348/1969b. "Izdivaj-i Muvaqqat az Fahsha Jilugiri Mikunad" (Temporary marriage prevents prostitution). *Maktab-i Islam* 10(9):31–33.

———. 1348/1969a. "Izdivaj-i Muvaqqat" (Temporary marriage). *Maktab-i Islam* 10(7):13–15.

al-Zein, `Abdul Hamid. 1977. "Beyond Ideology and Theology: The Search for the Anthropology of Islam." *Annual Review of Anthropology,* 6:227–54. N.p.: Annual Reviews, Inc.

INDEX

LAW OF DESIRE

was composed in 10 on 12 Caledonia on a Merganthaler Linotron 202
by Partners Composition;
printed by sheet-fed offset on 50-pound acid free Glatfelter Natural Hi-Bulk;
Smyth-sewn and bound over binder's boards in Holliston Roxite C and
Notch-bound and bound with paperback covers,
with dust jackets and paper covers printed in 2 colors and laminated
by Braun-Brumfield. Jnc.;
designed by Sara L. Eddy.
and published by

SYRACUSE UNIVERSITY PRESS
SYRACUSE, NEW YORK 13244-5160